SWEET RIDE

A NOVEL BY

BRUCE CRAVEN

C

CODHILL PRESS
NEW YORK • NEW PALTZ

Codhill books are published by
David Appelbaum for Codhill Press

codhill.com

Published in the United States of America

ISBN 978-1-949933-07-9
Library of Congress Control Number: 2021934717

Designed by Mark Shaw
MarkShawStudio.com

THIS NOVEL IS DEDICATED TO
MICHAEL GODSEY, JR.
1964-2012

"Love is the only passion
which rewards itself
in a coin of its own manufacture."
Stendahl, *Love*

1. Dirty Martini

A LIMITED ARRANGEMENT

At the 5th Avenue entrance of Bergdorf-Goodman's, a slender woman in her late-twenties moves light on her scuffed green sneakers, trailing a zippered plastic black store bag with the signature interlocking O's of Goodman's. The store bag ruffles horizontal in the woman's eagerness to show a certain man how she spent his money. The slender woman skips across the sidewalk. She could have selected the Chanel—she is sure the credit card he handed her a few hours earlier would have been accepted—but the $3,000 price tag did seem extreme. This Ralph Lauren will do. She opens her hand and the receipt tumbles down to the cement; the city glitters in the fading sunlight.

The slender woman's jeans, Levi's, are crisp, slanted high on her hips, and flattering if you have the right figure. The slender woman has noticed the new Brazilian cut and is curious. She has seen women adjust their cuffs over their pointed boots. Their visible thongs remind the slender woman of a dancer's spangly T-back and that first summer in Manhattan when she took employment in Chelsea at "Billy's Topless" and worked for tips.

Anything to keep the wolf from her door and make Manhattan stay real, anything to keep the city from disappearing behind a bus window.

The slender woman meant to scan the jean displays more closely in Bergdorf's, but honestly, was in a bit of a rush and lightheaded from forgetting to grab more than a croissant that afternoon after her pedicure.

Today is May 4th. There is talk in the press over the impending Y2K millennial threat of massive system-crashing on all governmental, service, and manufacturing-driven data systems. The dot-com bubble is swollen. Insightful analysts suggest the bubble could pop, but cashing out now seems premature. The stock values of the dot-coms are rising at an astronomical pace, regardless of the radical or nonexistent business models of the surging technology-driven start-ups. Most of the new companies don't even have a balance sheet for an analyst to evaluate, let alone cash flow. Value is perceived. The theory is get enough eye-balls, and you'll get market share, revenue, profit.

The slender woman is used to working with perceived value. Her business model is simple. There are rules to follow. If she follows the rules, things work out okay. Tonight, like every night, she tells her client that they have a limited arrangement.

Above her jeans, the slender woman wears a boy's sports jersey tight around her shoulders and breasts, with a large leather bag tossed over her shoulder. The jersey tells you that if the woman were on a team, her number would be 13. The jersey cinches up her hips, sliding across the small of her back as her sneakers tap down the steps and her hand opens for a taxi. A yellow cab swerves. A burst of pigeons lift from a splatter on 5th Avenue. The slender woman brushes her brown hair from her face, leans into the taxi and reveals her destination to the driver. The taxi pulls through a yellow traffic light, heading toward the Upper East Side. Central Park flashes in the rearview mirror, livery cabs are parked at Grand Army Plaza, there is a second spray of pigeons cluttered on the strong gold head of William Tecumseh Sherman as he marches his steed after Liberty, with her angel wings and olive branch. There is one more pigeon in his open hand.

The taxi stops in front of a building. Brushed-steel doors part and the doorman says, "Good afternoon, Ms. Caprice." The young woman flashes a smile and half-curtsies. "Much obliged, Dominguez." She hands Dominguez the Bergdorf's bag, her thick fingers wrapping her hair in a pony tail. "You are the most gentlemanly doorman in all of New York." Dominguez blushes as the slender woman takes the hanger back. "Keep your pockets clean, Dominguez," she says as she bounces to the bronze palm-leaf on the elevator doors.

The slender woman watches the elevator numbers descend toward the ground floor. A man stands next to her. He has read the magazine articles on courtship and seduction and takes the tapping of her scuffed green sneaker against the carpet as a sign she is nervous, yet interested in talking to him. He is wrong. The slender woman doesn't notice him, except that he stands too close and is male.

The elevator door opens. The man motions for the slender young woman with the Bergdorf's bag to enter. The man has a romantic history that is not as pleasant and universally admirable as the history of love that inspires Dominguez, who will go home and dance tonight with his wife to the music of Juan Luis Guerra while their children sleep in the next room. This man has a history of failed relationships. He could have any name. His heart beats a notch. The young woman steps into the elevator. The man's eyes are a wet sponge. He tries to keep his spongy eyes off the young woman's body, but can't, even when she glances coldly in his direction. This failure is like all of his relationships, except this failure just took seconds, rather than months or years. This failure didn't leave a hurt woman in tears or destroy the faith of a marriage. Ms. Caprice notices the man has not yet stepped into the elevator. She smiles. The smile is similar to the smile she offered Dominguez, but different. The man finds the smile encouraging. He is wrong again. The elevator doors close with him on the outside, reaching for the elevator button, wondering why the attractive woman didn't hold the door for him. The elevator ascends.

The abandoned man whistles in the empty foyer. Tonight he will surf through the X-rated channels of his cable television, searching for a woman resembling the woman in the rising elevator.

Ms. Lilly Lejeune, aka Ms. Suzy Caprice, reaches into her leather bag and removes her make-up mirror, touches up her lips, puckers a red smooch on the back of her hand and pats the red kiss on her jeans until the red kiss fades into the indigo cotton. The Finnish elevator cubicle rises within the Manhattan high-rise. Lilly's thick fingers tap on her thighs. Her copper eyes watch herself in the elevator's gold-veined mirror paneling.

She woke up to a phone call from Mr. Yvan Tait and has been running late all day. Yvan Tait told Lilly about tonight's limited arrangement: Mr. Leonard Karlson. Gentleman or creep? Either way, she's ready to get to work. It's time to make money.

ENCOUNTERS

Later that same evening, George and Nicolette sit at a table inside the new space-age restaurant at the top of the Theme Building, originally dedicated by Sam Yorty, the mayor of the city of Los Angeles in August 1961, almost 40 years ago. One-hundred-thirty-five-foot parabolic arches support the circular building offering a 360-degree view. The new restaurant in the old building was designed by Ed Sotto and Ellen Guevara for Walt Disney Imagineering. The restaurant opened one year before George pulled out this barstool and sat down. He is dressed in his typical vintage, with more than a few upgraded items, courtesy of Nicolette's accounts at Neiman-Marcus (sport coat) and Barney's

(Hamilton wristwatch) as well as her credit card (striped suit shirt with French cuffs, lightly starched and fitted from Fred Segal). He wears Johnston & Murphy wing-tips; a wide 1940s silk tie he picked up at vintage shop Yellowstone on La Brea, loosely knotted; and a tan straw fedora found in Burbank at a store that specialized in costumes for film and theater. The straw fedora is a short-brimmed Rat Pack number that makes George want to snap his Zippo and twirl his cuff-links. A silver plane rises across his face in the restaurant observation glass. His cuff-links are made from typewriter keys, a birthday gift ordered by Nicolette from Paul Smith. George's pocket square is from The Good Will in Glendale. He bought it himself for $1.

Nicolette rubs George's neck and kisses his cheek, "My baby boy flying out into the world." The interior of the restaurant resembles the starship Enterprise if the starship were lit with blue and purple Lava Lamps. The waiters, bartenders, and assorted staff dress in monochromatic skin-tight mock-turtlenecks.

Airplanes rise and descend against the Pacific Ocean sunset.

George gazes out the window at the red sky. Dean Martin croons, "Money burns a hole in my pocket," on the sound system. George sips a Manhattan cocktail, chilled. His fiancée, the luscious, successful Nicolette Amberson, sips an appletini. Nicki is sixteen months from turning 40. George is 31. He twirls a ring on his finger, a simple band of gold with one diamond, the gift box for the ring empty, a flower of tangled ribbon beside his pack of Lucky Filters, his Zippo.

George is handsome, even verging on pretty.

Nicolette places her hand on George's thigh. "Do you like it?"

"Yes, I do."

"You do?"

"It's great." George gives the ring a twist.

"It tells other girls to stay away. You are private property."

"Thank you," says George.

Nicolette laughs, "Don't look scared, George. I'm just marking my territory." Her beautiful, long fingers go under his sport coat and tickle his ribcage, "I'm a lioness."

George takes a sip of bourbon and remembers a TV show with a female lion rubbing her jaw against a boulder somewhere in the foothills of Los Angeles. George lights a cigarette, "Consider me marked."

Tonight will be his first trip to the East Coast. Tonight will be his first trip to New York City. If everything goes as planned, he will have a meeting tomorrow with a man named Mick Tanner, an Australian, about a job arranged through good fortune by Nicolette. George will meet Mick, and Mick will tell George details about a screenplay he has hired George to write.

George is a screenwriter, but so is most of Los Angeles. Some of these people even make a living at it. George is not one of them. He has keys in his pocket to his friend Dave's apartment in a place Dave called the "Lower East Side," or LES. George has an airplane ticket and Mick's address in his Filofax. George doesn't have confidence in himself, but sipping the whiskey helps. Mick promised George and Nicki the completed script would get filmed. This is an impossible concept to George. He has been at industry parties with Nicki and met men and women who have seen their projects carried to completion, arriving on the screen after years of preparation, after ambitious battles for money, after bitter casting struggles and in-fighting between the members of the production team and talent, after pre-production crises of every kind: music rights, intrusive producers, controlling actors, incompetent directors, disasters on the set, legal problems in editing and post-production. George has met writers who have stood glowing in the theater as their names rise on the huge screen in front of the black shadow of the packed audience.

These writers seem different from him.

George smokes his cigarette, imagines his airplane, silver in the black night, hurtling across a map of the continental United States, careering along, a missile filled with hopes and dreams and George's last chance. Getting this job was a complete fluke and the fact that anyone thinks he has the ability to deliver on this task is unprecedented. George watches his reflection as Nicki kisses his neck, pressing against him with her round, natural breasts. This cigarette tastes good. He tries to imagine himself trundling toward New York City in the tube of pressurized air. Nicki picks up the tab, as usual, for his steak. It's been one year since Nicki accepted his proposal of marriage on Catalina Island.

"You don't like it?"

He looks at his cocktail. "It's fine. I'll probably have another one."

"No," Nicolette pinches him. "The ring, honey?"

"I like it. I said, I liked it." He twirls the gold ring. "I've just never worn a ring."

"If it makes you nervous, don't."

George takes her hand. "It looks real sharp… and it means a lot."

Nicki can forgive George for being a bit of a project. He is handsome and filled with potential. George has great abs, still, he should be buying property, sealing up projects, signing on the dotted line, not looking for a break. But Nicki works in entertainment law. She understands better than most that creative careers have ups and downs. She will be strong for George.

When Nicolette met Mick Tanner at the Pig & Whistle on Hollywood Boulevard, she knew it was George's big chance or the closest chance he was going to get without turning out a high-concept spec-script, which required a discipline George seemed to lack. Mick was looking for an unknown, someone to take a risk on in exchange for saving money on the first draft of a script he was setting up to produce. Mick lived in New York, and New York was Nicki's favorite city, after Paris, of course, and Los Angeles. Nicki could see herself walking hand in hand with George down 5th Avenue.

Nicolette never had it easy. Her mother, Jacquelyn, or Jackie, had once been a showgirl in Vegas, a showgirl in the glamorous Vegas that was now legend. She had met Nicki's father, Jasper (Jax) Conner at the tables. Jasper was from Louisville, Kentucky, and after a whirlwind courtship, Jackie accepted his proposal for marriage.

Jacquelyn would have been happy to follow Jasper to Louisville, but the lure of good contacts in commercial property opportunities in Southern California tugged at Jax like the Handicapper's Favorite, so after a brief ceremony in the Graceland Wedding Chapel in Las Vegas, Jacquelyn took a week to finish her work commitment and pack up her few belongings, then walked out of her apartment and caught a Trans-World Convair 880 from McCarran Field down to Los Angeles Municipal Airport. Leaning from the red woven pattern of her window seat, Jacquelyn twisted the gold band and princess-cut diamonds on the fourth finger of her left hand, squinting out the bright Plexiglass at the layered hills and the blue ocean. Jacquelyn watched as the bright square window of the TWA aircraft descended toward the construction of what looked like a giant pod on stilts in the center of the airport, never guessing that in almost 40 years, her daughter, born one year after the descent of this short flight from Las Vegas, would sit in a restaurant in that giant pod on stilts, blushing with excitement beside a fiancé, who has a gold ring with a diamond on his ring finger, pinched between the thumb and forefinger of his right hand.

Nicki met George at a traffic accident on La Brea by Pink's Hot Dogs.

George hit the brakes of his dented, rust-scabbed Datsun 280Z at the yellow light, while Nicki, driving behind him, stepped on the gas of her cherry-red Mercedes SL600 convertible, cursing the ball-less wimp in the crap car as she hit the brakes too late. Nicolette's car skidded and smashed into the tail of the Datsun. She saw sprites, sparks, and silver ellipses and only realized the level of her righteous anger later. Nicki's spiked heels clacked on the concrete and her blond hair bounced as she stamped toward the man unfolding from the rusted Datsun in a green cardigan and flared yellow golfing slacks and a pale blue Bing Crosby hat with a red hatband. Nicolette prepared for the sun-blasted face of the dazed geezer to swivel her way, snapping dentures or gumming air like an angry turtle. The man moved carefully, one hand on the small of his back, but she wasn't having any. This man was an idiot, braking at the last second. Fucking purchase an electric wheelchair if you can't drive! This geezer spent his days squinting down the shuffleboard court or picking lint from his toes in the Men's locker room at the YMCA, but that didn't mean the DMV should authorize for him to be behind the wheel.

"Listen," Nicolette said firmly, moving into lawyer mode. "The yellow light…" The geezer faced her, standing straight, his chest cutting through the white T-shirt under the loose LaCoste sweater. Nicolette stopped. The Geezer was handsome and young—younger than her. He smiled with embarrassment, took off his ridiculous Bing Crosby hat and ran his fingers back through his luxurious brown hair. His thick hair ruffled in the wind, which was whipped up by passing traffic on the hot boulevard. She had been right about one thing: his eyes were dazed, wide from shock. Nicki wondered how hard the impact had reverberated through his crap car. She hoped she hadn't hurt him. At her end of the collision, the impact was a bolt of heat running from her toes through her waist to her eyes. His lips were so soft she wanted to kiss him. "I mean," she explained, "a yellow light does say to proceed with caution. If you felt the situation demanded that you stop, well…" The handsome man held up his hand, laughed in a charming way and leaned against the bashed end of the 280Z.

"Give me a second."

He had to be gay. Then he glanced at Nicki's boobs, and his face went red.

"Is it your back?" She asked, forgetting to strengthen her case by returning to the flaws of his decision-making behind the wheel, forgetting to emphasize that he had caused the collision and would be held responsible. "Are you hurt?" She wanted to put her arms out and pull him against her. This was a complete stranger who was going to cost Nicolette a lot of money if she ended up paying for the damage, but she wanted to comfort him.

"Nicolette." She gave him a firm hand shake; his eyes were above her shoulders.

Nicolette tried hard not to look at George's chest in the T-shirt under his vintage cardigan, tried not to look at his handsome chest, his firm butt, his grown-up *Tiger Beat* cover-boy pearly white teeth, rock-star lips, and very dreamy eyes. Nicolette wanted to have sex with George on the sidewalk. She knew he had a nice cock.

Somewhere along their short drive down Beverly Boulevard to get a sandwich at King's Road to Nicki's stunning apartment, Nicki asked George about his work and his current level of achievement.

George looked out the window and said, "I've never made a red cent."

George watches his reflection at the northern stretch of LAX. Silver planes lift and descend in the ink sky weighted over the tarmac.

"About that loan," George hates himself.

Nicolette reaches into her purse and pulls out a sealed envelope in her firm's stationary. "Don't open it now, open it on the plane." She squeezes George's arm, "Trust me. It will hold you until you see Mick and work things out. We better run, baby."

Standing at the gate, watching the flight attendant collecting tickets at the entrance to the jet-way, George turns to Nicki. She could be a poster, a blonde in a one-piece bathing suit, a single bright citrus orange in her right hand, her long shapely legs and her pretty feet with painted gold toenails and gold-strapped heels. Nicki's yellow hair could be ironed to her shoulders, lips as red as an open pomegranate, her eyes sky blue. Even right now, Nicki could be a poster for California in her pink leather jacket that is zipped up over her chest like a female superhero, her black slacks and heels, her designer bag and her eyes glistening with tears.

She gives him a kiss. "Be good."

George pulls his boarding pass out of his shirt pocket, sport coat folded over his arm.

His next cigarette will be on the other side of the country in a new city. Nicki wipes a tear from her eye. George Nichols walks into the mouth of the jet-way.

ASSUMPTIONS

As George's airplane descends toward the running lights of Newark tarmac, the 59th Street skyline blurs from night to dawn. Morning will wash Central Park in shades of rose, but right now Lilly Lejeune stands in the purple shadows, her solitary silhouette poised in front of the stone and glass façade of Tiffany's. The red, polished half-moons of her thick fingers ring a bottle of Dom Perignon, and she has her pre-party jersey and jeans, rolled in the zippered Bergdorf-Goodman dress wrap, stuffed in her shoulder bag. Lilly watches her reflection smile. A silver locket gleams on her throat.

Lilly sips champagne from the bottle. There is the problem of Leonard Karlson to be solved. He will be angry, but Lilly hadn't welched on her end of the deal. Karlson made assumptions and you know what happens when you make assumptions. Karlson assumed Lilly could be purchased. That was foolish of Lenny, who was a businessman. Business was business. Lenny should know Lilly was worth more than what he planned on paying. No matter how much Lenny planned on paying Lilly, Lilly was worth more. She would have put up with him—that was their deal and she didn't welch—but he grabbed at her in a rude manner in public and had the breath of an animal that ate garbage.

The crenulated curtains of Tiffany's display windows are pulled shut for the evening. The jewels are covered in the black velvet calm of a state-of-the-art security system. Lilly runs her finger along the marbled cinnamon stone window frames, touches the cold glass and smoothes her dress, straightening any remaining creases from Lenny pawing at her in a room that hummed with a computer projector, flashing charts and graphs. Lenny obviously made more money than he needed, if such a thing was possible. Lilly removes a toothbrush from her bag, gargles with the champagne and spits it out. She brushes her teeth, making a face in the curtained windows of Tiffany's. She isn't in a bad mood at all. She just walked off with an exquisite dress and four hundred bucks cash for suffering through a dull business party and allowing a man to think if he spent four hundred more dollars at the end of the evening, he could fuck her.

A wheeled street-cleaning tank grinds down 5th Avenue, spitting fanned garbage in sheens of garbage mist.

Lilly walks down the avenue. Across from the neo-Italian renaissance towers of the Peninsula Hotel, a homeless man sleeps beside the Presbyterian Church.

A phone trills. Lilly digs into her bag and removes a cell phone as a yellow taxi drifts down the street. Lilly waves the taxi to her and places the phone at the gray sneakers of the homeless man, tucking a twenty-dollar bill in the pocket of his stained jacket that is patched with duct tape. The phone continues to trill.

The taxi pulls to a stop at the corner of Houston and Ludlow Street in front of Katz's Deli. Lilly hands the taxi driver a tip and shoulders her bag, carrying the bottle of champagne into a brightly lit shop behind the neon sign Hot Bagels.

Lilly walks back out the store, sipping a cup of coffee and holding a croissant. Behind her in the brightly lit Hot Bagels, two men at the counter pour paper cups of champagne from Lilly's bottle.

She will explain to Tait that this Karlson, this investment whizbo, will not be a happy or completely satisfied customer. Lilly will probably use the migraine excuse. She almost feels one coming on just thinking about the evening and the problem that walking out on Karlson will present for her, but now the morning is perfect and Lilly is warm from champagne. Her heels tap the sidewalk. Lilly spies a grimy white pit bull puppy rummaging in a ripped garbage bag. The puppy tugs at a meat-stained rag of butcher's paper. Lilly gives a whistle. The puppy lifts its black nose from the blood-red paper scrap, waddles over and takes a lick at Lilly's ankle. Lilly steps back and stares at the puppy before breaking off a piece of chocolate croissant. The dog sniffs the bread and chocolate in Lilly's hand, knocks the croissant piece to the sidewalk, nudges it with her nose and returns to the bloody butcher's paper, chewing, growling, tugging, the bloody paper held down by a paint can filled with solidified roof tar.

Lilly shakes her head at the puppy. "Poochie… Little Poochie… aren't you finicky!"

A heavy vehicle on Rivington, shiny black Humvee limousine, rolls past.

Lilly clicks on her heels toward the door of 101 Stanton, hearing the Humvee brake and shift into reverse, appearing to rumble at her. Lilly's apartment key slips between her fingers like a sliver of ice. It is Leonard Karlson's voice that makes her cringe as he yells out the Humvee window at her, "Suzy! You!" Lilly waves over her shoulder, not turning from trying to open the door. Karlson's heavy shoulder pushes open the back door of the Humvee. Lilly hears him slam the vehicle door. "You, bitch! Wait!"

Lilly breathes once, twice, calms herself and slips past the street door, pushing up against the locked inner door, her door-key clicking against the key slot.

"You fucking little bitch," Karlson says, "Hey!"

Lilly drops her key, picks it up. She turns as if just hearing his voice and smiles at the man crossing the street, his eyes puffy from liquor. He reaches the door to push it open before Lilly can unlock the second door. Lilly grabs a New York Bell phonebook off a stack left for renters and jams a wedge of phonebook pages at the base of the first door. Karlson pushes, but the phonebook splays, wedging the entry door stuck.

"You cunt," Karlson's arm slips through the half-open door, grasping at her. He pulls back and puts his shoulder into the door with a heavy thump. Lilly slips her key into the slot and unlatches the lock as Karlson smashes his elbow into the glass, shattering it. Lilly feels fragments of glass hit her naked legs. Lilly whirls, facing Karlson, her eyes bright in a fake smile. Karlson has removed one of his tasseled loafers and smacks the glass window out of the door, glass shards flying as Lilly shields her face. He kicks the door hard and it slides as Lilly blows him a kiss, "Wonderful, Len," Lilly steps behind the stairwell door pressing the door shut behind her as Karlson reaches for the spot where Lilly had been standing, her kiss floating in the air. Karlson brings the sole of his shoe against the door with a thudding kick. "Fucking cunt!"

Lilly jiggles the door from inside, making sure it is locked. She waves at him confident from experience, knowing the reinforced security glass will hold, and walks up the stairs.

Entering her third-floor apartment, Lilly is a willowy black shadow behind an opaque bookshelf filled with empty martini glasses. Her phone rings. Lilly's answering machine kicks in: "Chirp, chirp, this is the parakeet that won't leave. Lilly is very, very busy at the moment, please leave all the important info and I'll tell Lilly you phoned. Big kiss. Chirp, chirp." Lilly clicks the dead-bolt shut on her front door, let's out a deep sigh and finds herself smiling in the cracked mirror of her bureau. Her heart is racing.

Karlson's voice screams from the machine. "Open the fucking door, you whore!"

Lilly turns down the volume on the answering machine, reminding herself to tell Tait not to give her number and address directly to clients. Lilly reaches into her bag and removes an empty martini glass. She steps on a wooden chair, locates an empty spot on the upper part of the bookshelf filled with empty martini glasses. Lilly places the new martini glass on the bookshelf, steps down and smooths her cocktail dress. Lilly's apartment phone rings again. The phone machine continues to click as messages register. The message light reads "10." The room is quiet, except for the chirping of a parakeet that clings to a small swing in a bent brass cage. The message light on the answering machine clicks to "11." Lilly walks over to the dented birdcage on top of a stack of cinderblocks. The

15

parakeet taps its beak on a tiny bell, making it ring.

The birdcage door is closed. "Now how did that happen?" Lilly opens the cage door, telling the parakeet, "You're free to leave anytime, sailor." Lilly peeks between the lime curtains of her apartment.

Karlson stands on the street, punching numbers into a cell phone. Lilly yawns and pulls the curtains shut. The message light on her answering machine clicks to "12." Lilly draws a bath. The bathtub in her one-room rental has clawed iron feet. The bathtub is deep and long enough for Lilly to stretch out in, if she lets her ankles and pretty toes drip Kiehl's eucalyptus oil on the hardwood floor. The bathtub was the second reason Lilly approved of the apartment. The first reason was that her friend Verreaux—who introduced her to Yvan Tait, this evening's contact with Karlson—had interceded with the landlord of the building. A small discussion between Verreaux and the landlord allowed Lilly to avoid explaining her credit history in any specific detail. In fact, the landlord had been very reasonable about accepting Lilly's rent when it was late, which happened a little too much for everyone concerned. Lilly tests the hot water pouring into the tub. This has been a long night and Lilly is excited about the prospect of sleep. Lilly dials up the volume on the answering machine. Karlson's voice screams, "I know you're in there! Do you think I'm some kind of sucker that can be played?! I got Tait's number, you cunt! This isn't over, fucking slut!"

Lilly turns to the parakeet, "Slut? Me?"

"What did you do with that fucking cell phone I gave you?!" Karlson's voice fraps the answering machine speakers. "First you tell me you need fresh air… next I'm sitting with shit on my face, talking to a room of cowards who can't taste a good deal when it's staring them in the face, a bunch of assholes drinking my booze, eating my food, and I'm wondering why I date whores!"

Lilly tells the parakeet, "If I was a whore, Lenny wouldn't scream so much."

"Running off with an expensive dress?! Talking after-party?! You bitch!"

Lilly's manicured fingers turn the dial down and Karlson's voice fades, becoming a faint echo from behind the curtains down on Stanton Street. "No wonder you have trouble with women, Lenny," Lilly tells the machine. "You've got a gutter mouth." Lilly unzips her dress, shimming out, "Good girls don't like boys with a gutter mouth."

Lilly puts a CD into her boom box and touches repeat. Antonio Carlos Jobim's "Cor Covedo" fills the apartment. Lilly whispers along about quiet nights of quiet stars… and wraps herself in a white towel. She walks over to the scarred bureau and picks up a wedding anniversary photograph of her grandfather and grandmother, who are young and attractive and smiling into the camera in Baltimore in 1954, after her grandfather returned from fighting in Korea. Lilly's grandmother resembles Lilly, with Veronica Lake hair pulled down in a brown peek-a-boo and the same silver locket on her beautiful neck. Lilly places down the photograph, removes the necklace, straightening the chain with religious care on the ravaged bureau. She reaches into her bag, pulls out her wallet and four hundred-dollar bills. She opens a drawer of folded sweaters, slacks, T-shirts and removes a yellow Bustelo coffee can, taking out a white envelope filled with a wad of hundreds, assorted fifties, twenties. Lilly puts two of the hundred-dollar bills into the envelope and places the envelope back in the coffee can. She parts the curtain, peeking out. Karlson and the Humvee limousine are gone. She turns off the bath water, dabs at the water with her toe, shivers and steps up into the bathtub, sliding down into the hot water, closing her eyes. As she submerges her head in the hot water, she stretches her legs out of the tub, wiggling her toes, and comes back up gasping. She wipes her hair from her forehead, lifts a hand mirror hanging from a nail in the plastered wall beside a soap dish, and arches her eyebrow at her reflection in the glass. Dawn sunlight warms the lime curtains. Lilly's work is done. The money is in the coffee can.

CINCO DE MAYO

The taxi heads out of the Lincoln Tunnel, lifting George into Manhattan. He looks at the city, too tired to process the blur of cement and buildings, storefronts, cars and people.

He removes the envelope Nicolette handed him at LAX. Four hundred-dollar bills slip out crisp and clean.

Nicki mentioned a surprise? George removes a piece of copy paper from an office printer. George unfolds the white sheet and finds himself staring at what looks like an airline ticket, but not his airplane ticket. This is American, not United. The name of the passenger: Nicolette Amberson. The date of the flight is May 7th. At the bottom of the sheet, in Nicki's careful printing: "Surprise! I'll be in town right away. I wanted to treat you on your first weekend! Kisses, Nicki."

The taxi lets George out next to a Mexican restaurant called "El Sombrero." George crosses the street. Looking back, he sees "The Hat" painted in translation on the other wall of the restaurant. At the entrance to Dave's building, George notices the glass pane of the first door is broken and glass is scattered in the entryway. He hears a creaking noise, shades his eyes and looks up the face of the building. A small girl in a yellow party dress climbs into the second floor window.

Inside the third floor apartment, samba music plays very loud. Still, the young girl, Lupe, is careful not to make noise as she walks on her shiny black shoes into the kitchen with a water bottle from the birdcage in her small hand. A blue ice-mask on her face and a duvet kicked to her feet, Lilly sleeps on her back on the futon. Lilly wears a man's white tuxedo shirt. Lupe turns on the faucet. The faucet-water spits, gurgles. Lilly rolls over in her sleep and scrunches a pillow against her stomach. Lupe fills the water bottle and tiptoes back to the birdcage, hitching the bottle to the wire cage. She reaches into a bag of seed in a plastic container and scoops up fresh birdseed, funneling the seed into the plastic dish in the cage. The parakeet taps the bell one ring. Lupe whispers, "Shhh!" and glances at Lilly. The parakeet nips at the seed. Lupe walks over to Lilly's bureau and lifts up a black Givenchy vintage hat, with a white gauze scarf wrapped around the hat. Lupe places the hat on her head. Too big, the hat covers her eyes. Lupe giggles, looking at herself in the mirror. She places the hat back on the bureau, looks around the apartment and climbs back out the window. It is too bad Lilly has to work all night. It must be hard to take care of your pet when you are tired and can't stay awake in the day.

At the ground-floor door, George pulls two keys from his pocket. He tries the first key in the door. The key doesn't work. George tries the second key, and the street-level door opens. George schleps his heavy attaché and suitcase up the dirty stairway, with sweat breaking down his back and thighs, dripping on to his forehead and stinging his eyes. His legs itch under his slacks. George knows Dave's apartment is going to be a far cry from Nicolette's swanky palace, but it will at least have a sofa and TV and air-conditioner. Dave told him that much when he mailed George the keys. Firecrackers pop in exploding ricochet on the street. A car horn honks "La Cucaracha." George stops to catch his breath at apartment #3A. Bossa Nova music drifts out the door, and George can almost recognize the tune. Manhattan feels more like some city south of the border than the cold urban jungle of rich white people George expected.

He grabs the handles of his bags and heads up the next round of stairs, trying to ignore the searing pain in his lungs. Too many cigarettes. The toe of his wing-tip catches on a broken linoleum tile and he stumbles up the creaking U of stairs, dropping his attaché and almost falling and crashing against the arm-rail with his thigh cutting into his suitcase. He makes it to Dave's apartment door—#4A—and puts the key in the lock, hungry for the hum of cool air and any kind of bed to fall on for a few quiet hours before his meeting with Mick. The key wedges hard. No tumbling lock. George tries the other key. Nothing. No getting inside where the hum of air-conditioned air and maybe a mumbling TV will guide him to sleep. George jiggles both keys, lifts and shakes the door knob. He steps back and kicks the door hard. Nothing. George lights up, sits down. Cigarette smoke twists and disperses against the hall ceiling, spiraling like the Bossa Nova music drifting up from the apartment one floor down. A smattering of small feet and the young girl in the yellow dress runs down the steps and spins around the banister, followed by a younger boy in a tiny suit with a bow tie, carrying a teddy bear. The two children slide on their shoes, trying not to trip over the big man and his luggage. Lupe, hands on her hips, looks down at George.

"Hey," says George. "You're the girl from the fire escape."

"No, I'm not," she says. "What fire escape?"

"That fire escape," George points toward the front of the building. "I saw you… or maybe it was another 15-year-old girl in a yellow dress?"

"I'm only 10," says Lupe.

"Ah-ha," George's tired eyes ache. "Got you."

"You didn't get me," says Lupe. "I'm right here." She points to the floor and her patent-leather shoes. "I can run faster."

"I know it was you." George crosses his fingers. "It's our secret."

Lupe crosses her fingers.

"Are you a cat burglar or a diamond thief?"

"I'm from the building. I was feeding Amanda."

"Who's Amanda?" George rubs his cigarette out on the floor and cups the cigarette butt.

"Amanda's the bird."

George nods as if this makes sense.

"Lupe!" Enrique bobs up and down. "Mami y Papi…"

Lupe looks at the gold diamond ring on George's finger. Her eyes watch his eyes as if he just got in trouble. "Did your wife make you leave? Did she lock you out?"

"Wife?" George asks confused.

Lupe points to the ring.

"My girlfriend gave me this," George explains, "back in Los Angeles. I'm just visiting… new to town and all of that."

"Why don't you marry her? Are you a mujeriego? My mother says that is what my uncle is…"

"What," asks George, "is a mujer…? He waits.

"Mujeriego," repeats Lupe. "That means a man with too many girlfriends."

The young girl's steady gaze makes him nervous. He must be tired. "I am going to marry her," George says. He holds out his hand. "My name is George Nichols. I'll send you an invitation to the wedding."

"I'm Lupe and this is Enrique, but we call him Ricky." She shakes George's hand. "Why are you here?" She motions as if identifying the whole of New York City.

"I'm here for work. At least that's the idea. I'm here for a job."

"In the hallway?"

"Oh, yeah, I mean, no," George points to the door. "My friend lives here and he mailed me the key, but it won't work. It looks new, but it won't work."

"Dave lives here," says Lupe. "He showed me how to play guitar… I think your key needs polishing. My mother makes them polish new keys extra times." Lupe points behind the building. "Rivington has the hardware store where they fix keys."

More firecrackers pop on the street. Enrique tugs at Lupe's skirt. Lupe pulls out a red, green, and white lollipop from the pocket of her dress and hands it to George. "Happy Cinco de Mayo! We're going to a picnic-party, then another party at El Sombrero."

"Oh, yeah," says George, "something about the battle for a town called Puebla…"

Lupe gives him a look.

"Cinco de Mayo," says George. "You know, Los Angeles is the second-largest Mexican city in the world."

18

Lupe thinks this over. "Maybe not," Lupe says. She points down the stairs. "But we're late. You better fix your key or you'll get dirty... George." Lupe grabs her brother's small hand and races off, with Enrique stumbling to keep up with his sister.

George waves, puts the lollipop in his shirt-pocket, glances at his wristwatch and leans back against the wall, welcoming dead sleep.

MATCH ME, SAILOR

George fell fast asleep on the stained linoleum, with his head against the locked door and his arm around his attaché. A brown-and-white loafer taps his elbow. George startles awake and his wing-tip kicks a box of bootleg cassettes held by a Dominican vendor. The box of cassettes flips out of the man's hands and scatters with a clatter on the hallway floor. The vendor squats and picks up the cassettes, filing them back in the wood box. George rubs his eyes.

The vendor asks, "Merengue? Tu gusta merengue?" His brown-and-white loafers break into a soft, sliding dance, and his arms hold an invisible female dance partner.

"Merengue? Sounds like something for a lemon pie..."

"Tu mujer tiro afuera?" The vendor makes a throwing motion and points to George's luggage in explanation. "Woman throw you, eh?"

"No... my key won't work. Llave no bueno?" George turns the imaginary key, points the key at the lock. "No trabajar... won't work."

The vendor tries to figure out if George's woman changed the locks on the door because he wouldn't go to work. If so, the vendor feels no sympathy. This man looked like a kept man. Maybe he deserves to sleep in the hallway.

"Llave," George repeats. "Llave no esta bien."

Ah! The vendor realizes the man has a sticky key. "Si! Needs clean job," he says, nodding his head. He points back in the direction Lupe pointed, toward Rivington Street. "Enseguida fix it, eh?" The vendor shows George his wristwatch, explaining why he himself can't accompany George on his mission. "Quiero almuerzo. Lunche, comprende?" The word *lunche* snaps George out of his grogginess. He has a meeting with Mick! How long has he been sleeping? George looks at his wristwatch. "Oh, man..." He jumps up and his shoulder hits the tape box, knocking it out of the vendor's hands again—bootleg cassettes clatter across the hall. The vendor stares at George. Is this idiot drunk? George picks up a cassette, the soundtrack from the movie *Selena*. "How much? Que cuesta?" The vendor thinks it over. Before he can say five dollars, George puts a ten-dollar bill in his hand. "Thanks again. I'll see you around." George looks at the cassettes on the floor. "Sorry, mi amigo... sorry."

Yes, thinks the vendor, this is a spoiled man, but the vendor keeps the ten-dollar bill. The vendor just made a good return on the bootleg cassette.

George drags his suitcase, bumping down the stairwell, the accordioned attaché clenched in his opposite fist. He is late for the meeting on the other side of town. The tropical music still drifts from behind door #3A. George assumes someone must be behind the door, maybe cooking lunch or taking care of an infant. George knocks and knocks. He slaps his hand flat against the door. One, two, three! *Bam! Bam! Bam!*

"Hola?" He leans close to the door. "Buenos dias? Anyone in there? Hello?" George can't miss this meeting and doesn't want to lug his luggage across town, but that might be his only option. George has three hundred dollars and a key that doesn't open an apartment door in what appears to be a poor Latin neighborhood in a city he doesn't know at all—a big city where George is supposed to have a job, if he can make his meeting.

Lilly sleeps on the other side of the door, knees scrunched up under her tuxedo shirt, wearing a blue ice mask. A sledgehammer pounds the concrete on Stanton Street. The parakeet chirps and then hops in the dented cage, ignoring the open cage door. Then it taps at the small gold bell, ringing it like a tiny monk working in a cathedral of bent wire. The parakeet joins the sledgehammer in celebrating the day. *Jingle, jingle, tap, tap, boom, boom.*

George's hand continues banging the door: *Bam! Bam! Bam!*

Lilly's nose twitches. She nestles deeper into the pillow, folding the pillow-end against her ears. The parakeet flies out of the cage and lands on Lilly's shoulder and then pecks her once on the neck. Lilly swats at the bird, sending it fluttering back to the top of its cage.

The sledgehammer hits a buried pipe—a keening scream of metal pike on metal tube.

George picks up his heavy suitcase, and his shoulder aches. George takes the handle of the attaché. He better schlep it. George is at the stairs when the door of #3A opens and George feels a shiver from the air-conditioned air on the back of his neck.

"Hola?" he turns at the brink of the stairs, "Buenos dias?" George, hand on the banister, faces a woman in a blue mask, her copper brown eyes stare at him, past the security chain. Half asleep, she wears a tuxedo shirt. George imagines confetti falling from the ceiling and a gentle orchestra. Firecrackers rattle the street.

Lilly rubs her eyes, her hand across the blue ice-mask. She unsnaps the Velcro, twirls the mask on her finger, and offers him a sleepy smile.

Behind the door, hidden from George, Lilly leans on the handle of a sledgehammer. She has never had to hit anyone with the sledgehammer, but she will go right for the guy's balls or head if he tries to push his way into her apartment.

"Hola," George repeats. "Amiga, I quiero…"

"Do I look Puerto Rican?"

"I don't know."

"Do I look Dominican? Mexican?"

"Hmm," George says, "maybe a little Mexican?"

Lilly laughs. He is handsome, but helpless. She leans behind the door and pushes the handle of the sledgehammer against the wall. "I'm not, as far as I know, even a little Mexican."

George is exhausted. "I'm sorry…." He points to the door.

"Sorry that I'm not a little bit Mexican?"

"No, I mean, I'm sorry to bother you."

"Sorry doesn't feed the bulldog."

George looks at her.

"I don't really know what it means either," she explains, "but my grandmother used to say it to me all the time. Why the Spanish?"

"Everyone in this building has been talking Spanish."

"That'll happen around here, but English works fine with me."

"Good thing. I just used all my Spanish… unless you want me to order a beer?"

"I'm not much of a beer drinker, but I'll keep that in mind." Lilly looks him up and down. "Salesman, are we? Let me guess… encyclopedias?"

"No, I'm not selling anything."

"Good, because I'm not buying."

"What's with the mask?"

"I was predicting a hangover." She touches her forehead. "I think I was right!"

He taps out a cigarette and holds the pack toward the chained door. She considers. "You're not some kind of psycho, right?"

"I'm a friend of Dave's upstairs." He points up with his unlit cigarette. "You might know him? He's a drummer."

"I know him, blue bird tattoo on his neck. Give me a moment." She pushes the door shut, unlocks the chain, and re-opens the door. George taps the cigarette pack, holding it out. Lilly takes a cigarette. "Okay, match me, sailor."

George clicks his Zippo and holds the red flame to the crisp white cigarette. Lilly touches his hand to guide the lighter, inhaling as the cigarette crackles lit.

She eyes the gold diamond ring on George's finger. She is wearing nothing except her tuxedo shirt and is barefoot. "Friend of Dave's, huh?"

"I haven't seen him for a while, but we went to college together in California."

"A college boy…"

"Is that unusual?"

Lilly exhales a stream of smoke right past George's ear. "So, college boy… why all the commotion?"

"I heard the music and assumed you were awake… I should say, I assumed someone was awake."

"The music usually means I'm asleep." She nods at George's wrist. "That's a nice wristwatch."

"Thanks."

"Is that really the time?"

George nods. "That's why I was knocking on your door."

"Because of the time?"

"I have an important meeting."

"Me, too," she says almost to herself.

"I saw a young girl crawl in your window."

"Lupe. She feeds this bird that is under the misconception it lives with me as some kind of pet. Between you and me and the walls of this dump, I wish it would just fly away."

"That's very warm of you."

"I'm warm enough when the time is right. What's your gig? You said something about a meeting?"

George points upstairs with his key. "Dave mailed me the key to his place, but it won't work and I have a meeting across town."

"What brings you to this 'burg?" Lilly remembers the previous night and the money in the coffee can, plus the two hundred-dollar bills in her wallet and the new Ralph Lauren cocktail dress hanging in her closet. Lilly wonders if Verreaux has some work for her, but she will have to ring up Yvan Tait and clear the air about this business with Mr. Leonard Karlson. Okay, in the bright light of morning or noon, as the case may be, Lilly might have overreacted last night, but Karlson had been too grabsy. She would tell Tait to ring up Lenny and suggest a vague future date for a cocktail at Balthazar or Clementine. It would be a comfortable way for them to tidy up loose ends after last night's confusion.

"I sell parakeets," George says.

"You do not sell parakeets."

"You're smart for a girl that sleeps all day… and talks like she learned English watching old movies on TV."

"I enjoy old movies and I'm a nocturnal creature. You don't look real bright-eyed yourself, sailor…"

"I spent the night on a red-eye from California, and I'm late for a meeting with a guy I barely know about a job I really need. I was wondering if I could leave my bags in your apartment and pick them up later… like I said, my key won't work."

"Did you try polishing it?"

"Yes," says George, "I mean, no. That's my plan, but I dozed off in the hallway and now I'm late. I wouldn't have bothered you, but this is about something I don't have and could really use… money."

Lilly takes another drag of her cigarette, rubs it out on the wall and flicks it down the hall. "Sure, you can stash your bags. I know Dave. He's cool. Plays Zeppelin at dawn and pisses out the window. Very classy and quite a sweetheart. He put me on the list once at Irving Plaza for Belly, but I was otherwise engaged."

"Yes," says George, "that sounds like Dave. He used to piss out his dorm window in

21

college. Sorry about that."

"I didn't say you did it." Lilly shrugs, "Besides, I told you, sorry doesn't feed the bulldog. And anyway, this is kind of a pissing-out-the-window neighborhood… although I can't say I've tried it yet."

"That might be risky," George lifts his luggage and moves toward the door. Lilly raises her bare foot and pushes the luggage back at George. "Just leave 'em, sailor. I'll drag them in and you can drop by later." Lilly closes the door. George stands in the hallway, unsure of what to do. George hears the samba music click off.

The door opens. "You still here?" Lilly has Capri pants under her tuxedo shirt.

"Yeah. I…" George shrugs.

Lilly grabs the handle on the suitcase. "Give a skinny girl a hand."

George takes the suitcase from her and carries it inside the apartment.

"Here," she hands him an invitation to a club. "Since you're new in town and seem rather gentlemanly, my friend asked me to hand these out. She's having a party tonight at this night club another friend of mine manages."

"What time?" asks George, deciding he will take his attaché to the meeting with Mick. He steps back into the hallway.

"Night time," says Lilly. "That's why they call it a 'night club.'" Lilly waves good-bye, "but I'm late. I really must run."

"Okay."

Lilly presses the door shut.

George knocks.

Lilly opens the door, arches an eyebrow. "Yes?"

George holds out his hand. "Nice to meet you. I'm George Nichols."

"Lilly," she takes his hand. "Lilly Lejeune."

"Lejeune?" asks George. "Is that French?"

"Close," says Lilly. "Creole… from New Orleans."

"Creole? Doesn't that mean… black?"

Lilly looks down at herself. "Some people seem to think I am part Mexican… and from what I've heard of the Lejeunes, I might have just a touch of African blood too. The Lejeunes were landed gentry. I think the saying goes my ancestors in Louisiana slept on both sides of the sheets. You know… got snuggly with the help. But we can catch up on our family history later. I really must put myself together for my meeting."

COLD & SHARKY

George steps out of the elevator, pushes his wet hair back from his forehead. The room is empty, but the floors are dusty from particle-board powder and sawdust. A stylish loft is in the process of construction. There are new filing cabinets, a few boxed Gateway PCs on empty desks, and an open door reveals a small screening room, with twelve theater seats still wrapped in plastic and stacked sideways and a plaque on the wall that reads, "TNP Entertainment."

The freshly painted wall is decorated with framed posters of surfers. George feels like he climbed from the ocean himself, fully dressed. Water drips from his clothes onto the cement floor.

George hears the tap of boots on a metal staircase and 40-year-old Mick Tanner turns the corner, raising his hand in greeting. Mick is a short, compact man with a nose battered from Aussie Rules football and a fat wallet from his career as a fashion photographer.

"How you going, George? Welcome to TNP."

"Hey, Mick," George feels good. Mick is that kind of guy.

"What'd you do, mate, swim over from L.A.?"

"I guess I should have bought the umbrella... back at the bagel shop."

Mick laughs, "Might have been worth the price."

When George first saw Mick in Hollywood at the Pig and Whistle, Mick was in deep conversation with Nicki. George was used to men hovering around Nicki, but George wasn't used to Nicki smiling, warm, enthralled. George had stopped into a dive-bar called Boardner's for a quick double-bourbon and could feel the alcohol stirring up insecurity when it should have been calming, soothing, numbing him. From that first moment, Mick was straight up. "Let me buy you a drink, George," he offered. "Your Nicki was just telling me about the screenplay. I like the focus on dolphins. Did you know dolphins have been used by the military to locate submerged explosive devices? They use a sonar breathing called 'echo'... 'locution' or 'location'? I've always been fascinated by the creatures. Honestly, I've been fascinated by the ocean, anything to do with the ocean."

"Me, too," said George, thinking about the glass of cold whiskey the bartender was pouring and wondering why he just said this untruth. The ocean scared the shit out of George. The script Mick referred to was the one spec-script George had completed and Nicki had unsuccessfully shopped to agents for representation. The script was about dolphins because George needed something for the autistic boy and the discredited scientist to bond over and dolphins were smart and could do interesting things for the autistic boy and the discredited scientist to watch and study. Dolphins gave the autistic boy and scientist the opportunity to bond. Plus, George saw a special on dolphins on PBS. He didn't know the word for the sonar breathing, but he knew dolphins were smart and entertaining. George ordered the VHS tape from the Public Broadcasting Station and watched the tape repeatedly, taking notes on dolphins. Mick was right. Dolphins were fascinating creatures, but so were great white sharks and moray eels and an endless list of creatures that lived in the blackness, squirming away while you sank in the brine, poisoned or bit in half, watching your leg float to the surface of the blue water. Fascinated by the ocean? George was full of shit. The ocean was a dark place of death... and embarrassment. The ocean was a place of robust sports and George was a wuss. Surfing? Forget surfing on a board, just body-surfing was enough, between the rip-tides and the crashing waves. George had tried surfing on a board once. It was like standing on a thin, brittle cliff, with your feet dancing on this huge balloon of cement-heavy water building up in a stadium to flip and crush you. You would drop off the cliff into the thin veil of water above the concrete sand floor of the ocean and the wave would slam you like a ceiling of stone. George was from California and knew people that fought for the privilege to surf, people who sat on their boards and gazed back at you on the sand with lazy pride. As for body-surfing or boogie boarding, George decided long ago as a kid that the best part was when you were under the water, in the white-wash, suffocating and alone with no one watching you fail, thrashing your naked feet for the mucky bottom, propelling yourself in the push back for oxygen.

That night in Los Angeles at the Pig & Whistle Mick said, "Nicki here has been talking up your abilities, George. It would be great if you could spend some time in New York. I could get you money for the first draft and we could see where we go from there or you could stay here in L.A. and we could try working through fax and the telephone."

"It's not the same," said Nicolette.

"Do you use e-mail?" asked Mick.

"I use a typewriter," said George.

"Right," said Mick. "Good on you, George. We're slaves to all this technology, right? I guess if you can get your typewriter back to New York, we might have something."

"I don't know," said George.

Nicolette gave Mick her big eyes, nodding at George. Isn't George quirky? Isn't he a creative type? "George is always like this in the negotiation stage, but he might be able to shake free," she said. Mick watched her. "It will depend on how your offer compares to this TV pilot George has been developing, strictly on spec at the moment, but one never knows. It's a commitment. It's a bump in the road when it comes to you two guys, but…" Nicki showed Mick her smile.

"Yeah," said George. "I forgot about the pilot…"

George had never read a television script, much less developed a pilot.

"What's the pilot about?" asked Mick. "I'm new to all this. Do you get paid upfront for that… or on delivering a draft of the story?"

"Let's not worry about the pilot," said Nicolette. "George could do the first draft of your spec for around twenty." She sipped her gin and tonic. "I won't kid you, Mick. You could shop for someone cheaper and you can certainly find people with more of a developed track record, but with George you get experience with… well, ocean scripts."

Nicki, George and Mick all stood, drinks in their hands, considering. Nicki said, "Maybe you want to read George's current project? That might give you a sense of how perfect he is for this…"

George bit his lip, holding the stem of his cocktail glass like a sparkler. Nicki said, "Twenty thousand for the first draft and two rewrites."

Mick responded, "I can't go quite that high, but let's work out the details."

George wipes water from his face, glancing at the surfing posters. The one time he tried surfing was at Laguna Beach. The memory wasn't great. George was in high school on summer vacation. The leash from his ankle to the board wrapped around his neck, choking him in the black water. George crawled to the shore, dragging the surging, receding surfboard as it struck him in the thighs. When he got to the shore, gasping for oxygen, a young woman in a wetsuit with great legs and a Mohawk punched him in the face.

Surfing had concepts. George knew there was information, like lessons, insights, and tips surfers shared. George never got that far. He splashed in the water. When he paddled his board for a wave, George's kicking feet created the propulsion equivalent to his grandmother spitting at a cake of birthday candles.

George looks around the office at the surfing posters. "What's this story about… I understand there's an ocean theme…" George can barely listen to himself talk. An ocean theme?! *Moby Dick*? *Big Wednesday*? *Waterworld*? What was he talking about?

"Surfing," says Mick. "The investors design surfing gear and beach apparel, and they want to get into the film business… but it's got to be about surfing." Mick shrugs, "I don't argue with the money… just put in a lot of jokes and Sheilas. Make it move fast."

"Surfing…"

Mick says, "I bet you didn't think I was serious back in Los Angeles?"

"I thought you were serious."

"Let's meet Zeke."

Zeke?

And then George is holding a big glass jar filled with salt water and fine white sand. Zeke Wilson, a svelte, cut surfer, faces him in orange Tibetan monk's robes.

Zeke puts his hands together, "Selemat, sore, pak!"

George cradles the jar Zeke just handed him. "Hello, Zeke… howdy."

Zeke reaches out and clasps George's arm, pulling George into Zeke's chest, bumping shoulders. George has seen athletes do this greeting on television. George tries not to drop the large jar of ocean water and sand. The jar appears to be a gift.

Zeke's sincere eyes scan George, his eyes as gray-blue as snow in the shade, his head shaved. Zeke points at the jar of sand. "See it?"

George leans close to the jar, his face swimming back at him. "…What am I looking for?"

Zeke's hands go wide. He rubs his open palms across his shaved head. "Photons are both particle and wave. Like the flux of energy…" Zeke's palms are turned up in supplication.

George thinks of the Dalai Lama. The handsome surfer Dalai Lama presses the jar George holds close to George's nose. "There it is," Zeke says. "The essential stoke at its source."

"The essential stoke," George repeats. "It just looks like saltwater..."

"Just saltwater?" Zeke adjusts his robes and kneels on the naked concrete floor. He places his forehead on the dusty concrete floor. Zeke looks up at George, "Just saltwater? Everything is just saltwater—salt and water and sand. The great pyramids, the huge skyscrapers... the big jet planes that soar across our skies... rumbling trains and trucks and hungry machines that scrape our Mother Earth with their wheels and forked tongues... Our Mother Earth cries and moans and you know what those tears are made of?"

Mick nods at George and takes a drag on the cigarette.

"Saltwater?" George guesses.

"Fucking right on!" Zeke punches the air. "Saltwater! You've got it. Tears of pain and tears of joy... saltwater tears. If you don't embrace the woven cloth of the ocean wave, the fluid silk of the sky curtain, if you don't embrace the unification, George, you will have a troubled soul. You will not surf. Your center will slip, your voice will ring false... your deeds will come unglued. Your brethren will bail on you. You will drown with your eyes wide open."

Zeke stands, dusts off his knees and adjusts his orange robes. His piercing eyes turn to George. "Abandon emptiness, George. Stop clinging to the rocks on shore. Go free-fall, my brother. Ride our Mother Earth. Cut out distrust and the small mind. Cut away weakness and safety. Cut free of fear. Ride the sweet and powerful wave of the universe's love-kiss! Let go, my bro, of the leash of cowardice...."

"Okay," says George. "I will."

"The equation goes thus," says Zeke. "Saltwater is essential stoke... and stoke plus motion equals waves and waves are...?" The blue-gray eyes watch George.

"Cool?"

"Yeah, okay," Zeke rubs his head as if speaking with a child. "Waves are cool. But one step further. Join me. Waves are...?"

"A curtain?" asks George. "You said something about a curtain."

"Waves are the life force. Waves are our fate. Our life chances come in waves, bro. You ride each chance, each wave or you don't ride it. No wave is the same and we can't predict, but we can ride what we are given. Are you with me?"

George imagines his new job where he is typing a surfing romance set in Australia. This job is a different wave.

Zeke motions out the window at New York City, rooftops strung with wire, fencing, spires of cement and brick. Zeke taps the jar of saltwater and sand. "This is the key to your new church. This is your key into the green room."

"What is... the green room?"

Zeke laughs, tears in his eyes. He crouches as if surfing. "The green room... the green room is LIFE!" Zeke gives George a long look. He walks around George as if evaluating a used car for sale. Zeke sighs, slaps George on the shoulder, turns to Mick, "We'll be fine."

"What exactly is the green room... besides, I mean... is it a place?" asks George, who decides to ground this conversation in something coherent and walk away with a few notes that make sense and might help with the project.

"The tube," says Zeke, motioning his hand in imitation of either A) a curling wave or B) a woman's round ass. "You'll know when you're inside," says Zeke.

"Great," Mick rubs his cigarette out on the bottom of his boot and tosses it into an empty wastebasket. "George, I've got to run. I'll leave you with Zeke." Mick and Zeke hug. Mick adds, "George, let's meet up tonight... have a drink and celebrate."

"Okay, I have an invite to a club... from a girl..."

Mick gives him a look and grins, "You work fast."

"It's not like that."

25

Mick laughs and nods toward Zeke. "Do you need a pen and paper?"

"I'm fine," says George, "but can I speak with you for a second?"

"Sure," says Mick, leading George toward the elevator. "What's up?"

"I don't know how to say this," George says, "I mean, is Zeke okay?"

"Okay? Zeke is a legend." Mick presses the button on the elevator and then puts his hand on George's shoulder. "Just use the resource, George, and keep me on schedule on the first draft. When do you think you can finish it?"

"Finish it… the first draft?"

"Zeke should help you figure out the surfing part, but I'm interested in the romance angle. Do you have a title?"

"No," George says. "Is this like *Point Break* or *Beach Blanket Bingo*?"

"I'll leave it to you. Give me a bell and we'll figure out tonight at that club."

"What time?"

Mick shrugs, "Night time." Mick steps inside the elevator, and George returns to Zeke. He takes a seat on a chair and watches as Zeke mimes rubbing wax onto his surfboard. Zeke's blue-gray eyes focus on the horizon. "First we wax, then we shred."

George watches Zeke's lean sculpted arm. His strong hand clenches the imaginary pad of surf wax. Zeke's chin points at the dark ocean.

"I'm twenty seven and I've spent my whole life in saltwater. In the water, get it? In the life-force. My only chat room is green and fast, dude, and the only chatting I do is the *tap, tap, tap* of my tail fin on the blue skin of Mother Ocean." Zeke watches the imaginary crests of the coming set. His voice gets hard. "Philosophy class is finito. Let's talk killer technique. First you need to learn how to paddle."

Zeke motions for George, still damp in his slacks and shirt with his wing-tips smudged with muddy white gunk, to join Zeke on the floor. George presses chest-first onto an imaginary surfboard.

"Follow me." Zeke arches his back, scanning the black sea. Zeke goes, "Paddle!" and he starts paddling. George follows, wiggling on his belly on the concrete. George looks up at the ceiling. Zeke grabs his board, "Roll!" and rolls onto his back then around onto his stomach. George rolls too, clenching his imaginary board. "Remember," Zeke's voice is intense, "take a big breath before you go under. Get your head up, and paddle. Here comes Mother Ocean…"

"Mother Ocean," says George.

"She's our bitch." Zeke paddles on the cement in the empty studio loft. "Wait for her to spread it and show us the pink, then climb up and knock the back off her. Ride her hard, leave the bitch wet and begging, bro. I don't care what she brings. Tap that ass! Tap it!"

Mother Earth? George wonders, *"is Mother Earth also the life-force? And that part about the curtain?"* George sits up and reaches in his pocket for his ball-point pen. "Excuse me—"

"Dude, focus!" Zeke's eyes are fierce. He grabs George by the arm and slams him hard to the concrete floor. "We're in the shit," Zeke whispers. "Pull it together."

George pretends to paddle on his imaginary board. Waves crash over them as Zeke yells, "Duck!" and "Paddle!" and "Roll!"

Zeke wipes his hand over his shaved head, speaking in voice-over from helicopter height, the ocean roiling black and green, crests of waves rippling. "It's a monster winter swell. Hard and spooky. Conditions are perfect, but the water is cold and sharky.…"

"Okay." George slaps his hands against the bare cold floor, water squeegees from his wet slacks, splunges from his wet socks and shoes. Zeke eyes the incoming swell.

Zeke paddles hard, "We make a mistake now and we're planted."

Planted? George thinks about grabbing his pen, but needs to stay on his board.

"Big wave riders die 'cause their lungs pop. The wave pushes them down too far and they can't make it to the surface." Zeke's board rises, lifting him and George as if they are on top of a giant elevator, a carpet rolling with unimaginable force, the concrete floor fluid, the woven curtain a liquid storm under the petals of their surfboards. Zeke looks down at George, small and insignificant. "Up the crest!" Zeke yells, "Paddle, you motherfucker!"

George paddles on the cement as if his life depends on it.

Sidled together, they float with the deep ocean lifting. The floor is breaking at the edges and a spray of sea gulls go across the black ocean. George and Zeke wait for the next set. Zeke grabs the sides of his board. "Do you know how to die, George?"

George rides up the side of the wave as if he is riding up the side of a huge building of blue glass. *No,* George thinks, *I don't want to die.*

Reading George's mind, Zeke says, "I'm not saying want to, George, but each man has to be prepared to face death."

Zeke stands on his board, the huge wave lifting him toward the red sun in the gray sky. "You better learn," Zeke says, so quiet George isn't sure he hears the words. George grabs the side of his board and moves in to a squat, crouched low, water dripping as his damp wing-tips squeak. "We all face it...."

Zeke's knees bending, with his arms out for balance, he says, "Ride, George, ride the bitch! Ride her sweet cunt!" Zeke shouts as the water roars around them and George takes his board into the skating edge of the big wave. George isn't afraid. The ride is perfect. The wave curling around him is shuttling him beside Zeke as they rip down the blue façade of skyscraper glass. A white trail from their fins slices like a strand of black birds in a groove against sunlit glass on a perfect morning. Names. George can't recognize the names that screech in front of his eyes, fill his world with heat and force. "Yeah, motherfucker!" Zeke's finger trails the glass wave, "Bring it, bitch!" With the low howl of the wave and Zeke's fired voice, "Bring it!" George balances on his surfboard and carves in a rhythm of edges. He has a settling focus of gentle adjustments and is skimming down a waterfall of glass panels and blue fast. Water and sky and foam fill the edges as he squints. "LOVE!" Zeke screams. "FUCKING LOVE! FUCKING SWEET FUCKING LIFE!" Zeke leaps off his board, rolling onto his back in his orange robes. His open hands slap the hard cement. Zeke sinks into the muddy white wash. Zeke bursts up through the water, gasping, standing next to George, alone in the quiet TNP loft. Zeke tugs at his leash, bouncing on his toes in the waist-water, the surfboard sliding toward Zeke and George in the surge of now shoulder-deep roil and chop. Zeke rubs his hand over his head, shakes his eyes clear. Wipes his face with the back of his hand. "That's how you surf. Just like that. Ain't nothing to it, brother."

WILD CHILD

George stands on the sidewalk in front of Dave's building, with a polished key in his pocket. He is sweaty from cleaning Dave's place, mopping, dusting, scrubbing. He holds a bouquet of twelve red roses. George opens the white card.

> Dear George,
> I hope you arrived safely. Mick signed the contract without any questions. I'll forward you a copy. You'll receive an advance from Mick. I imagine you're hard at work in your pied-a-terre. Congratulations!
> Love,
> Nicolette
>
> P.S. I made a decision about the wedding!
> P.P.S. I can't wait to see you, my sweet!!!
> xoxoxoxoxoxoxoxoxoxoxoxoxoxoxoxoxoxo

27

George places the card on the desk and sits down. Nicki made a decision about the wedding. Good thing. They should move forward. No use waiting around and delaying. It was time for George to stop wasting his life. George looks at the white page in the typewriter. He types, "Boy Meets Girl… Surfing." He pulls out the page and places it on the desk. He types, "The waves were gone now. He sat on his surfboard and watched the beautiful girl in the green dress standing on the sand. Yes, he would love her forever. The boy on the surfboard could be named Colin or Andrew, maybe Russ or Stiv?"

What had Nicolette decided?

The girl on the beach could be named Kate or Abigail or Skye? How do people meet surfing? George thinks of the time the surfer girl punched him in the face…

Why did Nicki have to rush this whole thing? George was only in New York for half a day and he was being nipped at his heels by Los Angeles, the city where he failed over and over, but, George reminded himself, he did ask Nicki to marry him. It was his idea.

A bottle-rocket shoots up the fire escape and sticks in the metal stairs, throwing sparks against the window. The sparks die out. George looks back at his typewriter. He looks at the empty martini glass. The martini glass had just been filled with cold bourbon, but the bourbon was gone. A knock on the window makes George jump. It's the little girl, Lupe, waving at him through the just-cleaned glass. Lupe has a parakeet on her wrist.

"Hi," Lupe says as George pulls up the window frame, shards of ancient paint falling on the scarred wood floor. "Did you fix your key?"

"Works like a charm. Are you lighting firecrackers?"

"No, my father won't let me." Lupe nods toward the parakeet. "They scared Amanda. I was feeding her. The firecracker could have hit us… but I'm okay."

"Happy Cinco de Mayo," George says. "Again, I mean."

"Lilly said I should let you get your suitcase." She looks around. "It's cleaner."

"Yeah," George says. "Dave's kind of messy."

Lupe nods. "So is Lilly's room…," Lupe looks embarrassed, "but it's not nice for me to say."

The bureau in Lilly's apartment reminded George of a piece of furniture thrown into the cement trench of the Los Angeles River. It looked like it had been used for target practice by kids throwing rocks, while the sun and the rain warped the wood. George picked up a photo of a young couple from the 1950s. They could be Lilly's grandparents. The mirror on the bureau was intact. Taped to the mirror was a photograph of Audrey Hepburn in a black cocktail dress, with a cigarette holder, tiara, and fetching smile.

"It's nice of you to take care of Lilly's bird." George picks up his suitcase.

"Lilly is my friend," says Lupe. "I have to go back to the party."

"Right," says George. "Thanks for helping me."

Lupe smiles. "What is your favorite kind of ice cream?"

George laughs, "I don't know, strawberry?"

"Mine is pineapple… but I like coconut too." Smiling, Lupe climbs out of the window with the bird on her wrist and waves.

Or bourbon, thinks George, waving to the little girl. I wonder if they make bourbon ice cream?

George stands on the corner of Sixth Street and Avenue A, showered and wearing clothes from his suitcase. George pulls out his Luckys. The box is empty. George scrunches the reinforced square and tosses it into the orange wire New York City trash can. The cigarette pack is just big enough to spill out on the street like most of the paper through the wire-weave of the waste receptacle.

"You want a real smoke?" asks a balding guy with a gray braid. "Not that corporate shit."

George looks at two men behind a card table filled with used books for sale. "Sure." He wants a smoke, but he's not sure if he wants one from this relic from Haight-Ashbury. The man pulls out the Drum and rolls the cigarette and rolls another, holding out his hand.

"Take 'em both."

George lights one with his Zippo, the rich shag hits his lungs. "Where can I get a drink?"

"Where can't you?" asks the balding guy with the gray braid. "This is the East Village. This is Vegas without the gambling. This is Bangok, man... this is Saigon in 1968."

George thinks of his father. Yeah, Saigon in 1968, except this old hippy didn't take a piece of shrapnel in his lung and bleed out.

The man with the Drum pack goes to the other man, "Giuliani wants to stop methadone? Can you fucking believe that?"

George walks up the block, sees a varnished wood sign with a green serpent crawling around a black diamond and the words "The Diamond Pub." The door is open and a neon beer sign glows in each window. There are red leatherette barstools, a pool table, jukebox, and shadows of a few bodies hunched over mugs of beer smoking cigarettes. George figures this is as good a place as any to kill time before meeting Mick at that club the girl downstairs recommended. Mick knew the place when they talked in more detail on the phone. He said something to George about getting there, but not too early. George waves his hand to the long-haired bartender and points at the bottle of Jim Beam behind the bar. "On ice!" George yells above the screeching juke box. The bar is loud and filled with smoke. It gets louder and smokier by the time George orders his third bourbon. He sees a girl with green hair point at the bartender and laugh, yelling to him, "Concentrate, Scout... concentrate!" She stands and pats her jeans at the pubic bone, wiggles her hips, giggles and falls deep into her cigarette. She starts coughing, guzzles her cocktail and then kisses a woman beside her, squeezing the women's breasts. The bar cheers and then the jukebox screams out a song George doesn't know.

Two muscle men in purple stretch-knit shirts and black dusters flip through clipboards and survey the people. At dramatic moments, the muscled guards remove the braided rope, unclasp the brass hook and allow the significant or the long-suffering to enter the nightclub. The security have ear-pieces and mumble into microphones. Black velvet curtains block the front of the club. A sign in black light reads "Haute Densite." George joins the crowd, checking his wristwatch as if he's in a hurry and people are waiting for him, both true.

One hour later, George stands by himself. George is alone, except for the bouncers in black and purple. George's bourbon high has dimmed to a grinding ache in the front of his skull. George wonders what solution could leverage him into being inside the night club instead of here outside on the street. The night club doors open and George gets a blast of the shattered rhythm of the inside: voices and laughter spilling out with music. George continues to stand near the two muscle men who think about Creatine, whey and egg whites, and dream of the next tuna wrap, packet of almonds, and pump session, maxing out in front of the mirrors, flooding their muscles with high reps at low weight.

George nods at one of the doormen. Pick me...

A sharp whistle snaps George to attention. It's Mick on the other side of the braided rope.

"What are you doing out here, mate?" The two bouncers look at Mick and look at George as if he just appeared from a cloud of smoke. They unhook the braided cord's brass-plated hook from the stand and motion for George to step forward. "C'mon," Mick slaps George on the back. "I've got this pretty waitress Eve waiting. She might join our venture, handle some of the office production. You been writing?"

"Yeah," George lies. His head hurts. This day has not ended for two days. He follows Mick down the hall, entering the crowded lounge area where there are purple banquettes, a long mirror behind the bar and a floor-to-ceiling painting of a Maasai warrior, gripping a spear. The carpet is blood red. An opaque partition of beveled glass reminds George of the glittering martini glasses stacked on Lilly's bookshelf.

A glass of fire passes in front of George in the hands of a man wearing a suit made out of shimmering white material. The man hands the red glass to a girl George has seen on a magazine cover.

Mick introduces George to Eve, who sits on a circular lounge pod upholstered in wine-colored leather. Her purple dress is crushed velvet and her hair is tossed around her shoulders. Mick looks at George, "This Eve is something. She might be the gem in the crown. She said she's on board with TNP." Eve's legs are crossed. She watches the room with amused calm. Eve's cigarette hovers above a blue ashtray on an ebony table that has legs that are carved like hooves. Mick takes one of Eve's cigarettes. "I told you about George... he just flew in today."

"Oh, sure," says Eve, "The surf writer."

Mick heads to the bar to buy a round of drinks.

George watches Eve smile at Mick as he turns and slides into the crowd. "Long day?" she asks George, still watching Mick.

"I don't have to say anything intelligent, do I?"

"I doubt it," Eve looks around the club. "Just arrived?"

"This morning... but it feels like this morning was two weeks ago."

Mick sets the cocktails on the ebony table, "Eve has experience in... is it theater production? In Montana?"

"Missouri," says Eve. "I majored in theater."

Mick leans back, sips his pint of beer. "Then it's settled. Hey! There's Lilly."

George tries to turn casually, but his bourbon splashes on his wrist. He raises the glass and takes a strong sip of cold liquor. Lilly shines in a white cocktail dress rippling with sequins. She points a black cigarette holder at the faces of the men that surround her and pencils them in. Her eyelashes are heavy with mascara and her eyelids are lined with rhinestones. A man offers Lilly a cigarette. George remembers the photo of Audrey Hepburn in a black cocktail dress, the photo taped onto Lilly's bureau. Lilly is a reflection in white, with a sequined clutch that has a silver clasp tucked under her arm. Mick and George watch her place the white cigarette in the long black stem and smile as the man lights her cigarette. The silver locket on Lilly's neck, her shoulders sculpted, her white dress clinging. Lilly reminds George of a shimmering goddess. Lilly touches one of the men. He leans close to her. She turns to Mick, holds her hand up in a half wave. "Be there in one minute," she says across the noise and people before leaning back to address the circle of men.

"Do you know her?" George asks Mick.

"Know her? You could say that. I'm the lucky man that discovered her down South in Alabama. Lilly was a wild child. Still is."

"Discovered her?"

"I was clipping away on editorial work, top-end material, on location in what the locals call the 'Redneck Riviera.' It was couture gear, all willowy crap no one could wear in the heat without sweating through it like tissue. My assistant was winding film when he made a sound in his throat." Mick laughs. "I thought he'd lost control of his bladder or was choking on a lozenge, but it was just Lilly he saw walking down the beach. He said, 'There's a lovely one.' I thought I better have a look, professional responsibility and all. Lilly was on the sand, walking toward us. I was working with the Pentax 6X7, instead of the Hasselblad 120. My assistant was loading the second camera. He was in a foul mood since we had the scrim on the sand and couldn't roll it. Two of his tall boys were trying to hold this 20X20-foot backdrop. I switched lenses and looked out near the water and focused on this young woman, late teens, in a bandana top and cut-off jeans. Lilly was licking an ice-cream cone, one of those ice creams with the swirly vanilla inside the hard chocolate. The ice cream dripped on her wrist as she walked and I snapped a few shots out of curiosity.

Lilly licked the ice cream. I got the snaps. The air was thick that day, high humidity. Our models were losing their patience and here walks this girl who just shimmered, licking the ice cream off her wrist, with a bandanna tied across her breasts and her sandals in one hand." Mick stops. "She was breathtaking."

Eve crushes her cigarette, "How Beverly Hillbillies."

"I actually was convinced she was with one of the agencies. I knew right away I wanted to shoot her. My assistant walked over to introduce himself. You never know when a skinny local girl might break in big."

Lilly makes her way through the crowd.

"She's only skinny in the right places," Eve says. "It's not fair."

Mick says, "She's got nothing on you, Eve."

Eve blushes. "My dad back in Kansas City would call her a 'looker,'"

"Us Aussies are vulnerable to beach girls."

"Men are just vulnerable," says Eve.

"Touché," says Mick. "My assistant brought Lilly over that day and she sat in the shade and watched us finish the shoot. I developed the shots back in New York and could tell she had something, but for all I knew, the girl was living in a trailer park in Baton Rouge or Memphis. I didn't know my assistant had slipped her a card. Six months later Lilly drops by my loft on a go-see."

Lilly continues to sidle toward them through the crowded nightclub. She pauses under the grip of a man. Her eyes flash down to his hand on her shoulder. She smiles politely and wiggles free, poking her burning cigarette in the long holder toward the man's hand in mock threat, smiling. Mick says, "I set her up with some contacts. Worked to get her going in the business, but Lilly didn't last. Hit a few road blocks… and created a few."

"Like what?" asks George, watching Lilly slide between two women, who hold black purses on gold chains, in black pants and white blouses. The women with flipped U's of over-bleached hair and red mouths sip from matching glasses of chartreuse. One of the women, the shorter one, tugs at the blouse of the taller woman. Lilly's eyes register a tall handsome man, with a narrow waist and a wide chest under his white open-collar shirt. He leans and kisses Lilly on each cheek. The taller of the two women grabs the handsome man, but his eyes are on Lilly. The man watches Lilly as he escorts the two women with dead hair and green cocktails to meet someone. Their gestures emphasize that they must meet now. Lilly watches the handsome man follow the two women into the crowd. The handsome man smiles at her and shrugs.

"Her hands didn't help," says Mick.

George's eyes go right to Lilly's mitts, manicured and clutching her sequined clutch with the silver clasp. Not freakish, but thick—her one visible imperfection.

Eve says, "She is quite beautiful, but I see what you mean."

"Fashion isn't the most-forgiving business," goes Mick. "Still, Lilly could have worked more. She has the personality, but Lilly doesn't have the discipline of the best girls. When she first walked into my loft, I felt here was a girl that would do what it took to make it, but I was wrong. What is it you Americans say? You can bring a horse somewhere?"

"To water," says Eve. "You can bring a horse to water…"

"But you can't make her drink," says Lilly, running a finger across Mick's neck. "Hey, Mickey…" Lilly skooches her sheathed butt onto George's purple leather lounge pod, scrunching him to the edge of the fat crouton. George has to keep his shoes anchored to the floor to keep from sliding off the leather lounge pod and falling on the floor. George balances against Lilly who tosses everyone a big smile. "What's up with the horses? You been hitting the OTB again, Mr. Tanner?"

Mick and George look at Lilly.

"Off Track Betting," Eve says. "The lady would like to know if you're playing the ponies, Mickey?"

31

Mick smiles, "Hello, Lilly, it's great to see you." George's jet lag gone, he sips his icy glass of bourbon. Lilly's sheathed white dress presses against his arm, and George smells a fragrance he remembers from a long time ago.

Lilly holds her hand out to Eve, "Lilly Lejeune, pleased to meet you." The women shake hands. "You must be a friend of Mick's?"

"Yes," says Eve. "I guess I must be."

"I know Mick's type," Lilly says.

Eve waits for Lilly to continue. "All I mean," Lilly explains, "is that Mick has exceptional taste. I hope I didn't over reach… you know, speak out of line?"

"Put your foot in your mouth?" asks Eve.

"Right," says Lilly and smiles. "Exactly."

"No problem," says Eve. "Compliment accepted."

"Eve and I are just getting acquainted," Mick says. "I invited her to join my company. We're going to pull together a feature film, and I want someone to manage the office… George here is writing the script."

"A surf story," George adds. "That was the meeting I was rushing off to this morning."

"A surf story?" says Lilly, without missing a beat. "All I know is that it better have teeny-boppers and hot-rods!"

Mick looks at George. "Teeny-boppers and hot-rods? What do you say, George?"

"Sounds good to me," adds Eve.

"Why not…," says George. *Vroom, vroom!*" He raises his glass. "It's really…" George has no idea what to add.

Mick clinks his glass against George's glass. "I can't wait to read it, George."

"George looks so handsome when he's writing," Lilly touches George on the arm. "Doesn't he, Eve?"

"Yes," Eve says, "If tonight is any indication… he must look very handsome."

Lilly pecks George's cheek with a kiss. "My upstairs writer…"

Mick looks at George. George shrugs at Mick. "I guess I'm the writer that lives upstairs…"

The handsome man walks up to the four of them. He places his hand on Lilly's bare shoulder. "Excuse me," he says. Lilly's hand touches his, their fingers fold together.

The man disengages and nods to a man in traditional Saudi white robes and the red and white shemagh headwear. The man walks over to the Saudi with the same hand extended in greeting.

George watches the handsome man. George doesn't enjoy envy, but envy enjoys George. Envy finds George in coffee shops, behind the wheel at stoplights or even here in a nightclub in Manhattan. Envy holds up the mirror, and George tries not to look at himself. "Who needs a drink?" George asks, "This round's on me."

HAMMOCK & UNICORN

It might be his fourth bourbon since entering the nightclub; George isn't sure. All he knows is he is calmly sitting on a purple-leather pod and is drunk. The handsome man Lilly introduced as Salvatore Kline sits close to a man Lilly described as a Saudi executive from the National Commercial Bank. This man wears a blue suit. The Saudi sits alongside the man in the white robe and shemagh. The Saudi and his Saudi friend both live in Riyadh, which Salvatore refers to as *the Kingdom*. George decides the city of Riyadh must be in Saudi Arabia, but he has never thought that much about the Middle East. Salvatore drinks mineral water. The Saudi banker in the suit drinks Johnny Walker Black, putting the blended whiskey down. He calls it "Saudi Coca Cola" and laughs. Warmly he takes George by the hand and offers to let George stay with him and his family in *the Kingdom*. Lilly smokes her cigarette in the long black cigarette holder. "Don't you just love it?"

she asks George, while Salvatore and the Saudis discuss currency risk and the stability concerns of investing in the Middle East. "It was my grandmother's. I call her Lilly the First. Women used to use these to keep the smoke from their faces. You know cigarette smoke isn't good for a girl's complexion."

George knocks out another cigarette from his pack.

"I hate to be bossy, but you smoke too much," Lilly says and then exhales a perfect smoke O.

"You smoke," George takes a sip of bourbon. The room sways.

"I smoke for atmosphere or when I feel very, very sad. You smoke like a man about to go to the electric chair."

George nods, "I'll take the guillotine, thanks."

"When I was a small girl," Lilly says, "I knew a man in Squirrel Junction with a hole in his throat... from cancer. You should protect your boyish good looks. They might be your best asset."

"What's that supposed to mean? My best asset?" George can't help it and rolls his eyes, "And where is Squirrel Junction?"

"Wow, Georgie... you're an easy target, but I guess you must be pretty tired." Lilly considers, "Squirrel Junction was a special name I had for my hometown." Lilly looks at George, "Are you tired?"

"Maybe," George sips his drink.

"Tired and sensitive," says Lilly, "but that's no excuse to smoke like a chimney."

"I like smoking."

"You're hiding," says Lilly. "Or afraid of something..."

"Okay, doctor. Thanks."

"Obsessive," says Lilly. George says nothing. Lilly says, "You don't think it's obsessive to light cigarettes off the tip of lit cigarettes, trying to find a third hand to pick up your drink? I tell you, George, you will hurt your handsome looks, Mr. Scaredy Cat."

"Didn't I meet you in the hallway this morning?" George asks. "Are you always this interested in other people's behavior?"

"If they're lucky," Lilly waves to a busboy, collecting empty glasses. "Why the electric chair, George... why the guillotine? I would think writing surfing movies would be loads of fun."

"Maybe if I knew how to surf... it would be loads of fun. Maybe if I knew what I was doing..."

"I can teach you to surf," says Lilly, "but we'll need a surfboard... and some waves."

"I'll see if I can set that up."

"Is it because you're handsome? Is that why you're afraid to fail?"

"Who said I was afraid to fail?"

"Sometimes handsome men get spoiled."

"Yeah, that's me. Spoiled."

"Have you suffered trials and tribulations, George?" Lilly smoothes her dress, cutting her eyes at him. "Have you fought long odds?"

"I'll have to answer that question after I get some sleep."

"No one should be scared of a challenge."

"You might have a point."

"I usually do," says Lilly. "At least, that's the idea."

"I mean, about smoking."

"Coffin nails," Lilly blows another perfect smoke ring toward Salvatore and his Saudi guests.

"Smoking is good," George holds his hand open around his cigarette. The smoke looks like a white cobra. "When I'm smoking... I'm smoking." The cobra spins, dissolves.

"You mean you're not doing anything else?"

"Meaning, I'm not thinking about what I'm not doing."

"Sounds scaredy cat to me."

He's had enough. "What are you afraid of?" asks George. Lilly adjusts on the pod of purple and sips her cocktail, a dirty martini. George saw the bartender drop in a spoon of olive water from the jar into the shaker, spilling out chilled gin into the frosted glass with an olive.

"Do all writers complain so much? I know a painter and he never complains. Of course, he owns a beach house in East Hampton and seems to have much too much money. You don't have much too much money, do you, George?"

"Not much too much," says George, "but more than I did yesterday."

"Good show," Lilly says brightly. "I imagine you are very talented, George... very talented indeed... a mighty river of talent."

"That's optimistic of you, but thanks... and just to make a point," George says, "I'm not complaining. You were critiquing me for smoking, and I was defending myself."

"You do sound defensive."

"Not defensive, *defending*. But since you're asking, I don't think it's easy to be a writer... at least, not in the movie business in L.A."

"For you." Lilly waves at a rugged man in a black suit with an open red shirt and shaved, oiled chest.

"Yes, for me," says George. "Since we are talking about me, I'll be specific and say it's not easy for me."

"See?" says Lilly, "you do fight long odds. You aren't a real scaredy cat."

George motions to the silver locket balanced on Lilly's chest, her breasts plumped up in the white sheath of her white dress. "That's beautiful," George tries not to stare at Lilly's décolletage. George looks into Lilly's eyes. "It's vintage?"

"Lilly the First gave it to me." Lilly scans the room. "What a fabulous night."

"Are you close with your grandparents?" George's cigarette tastes great. Another nail in the coffin, a hole in the throat, black-webbed lungs, whatever; you die when the time arrives. Cigarettes didn't kill his father. Shrapnel killed his father.

"Why do you ask?"

George looks at Lilly. His father on the hood of the Jeep in Vietnam, typewriter in his lap, dog tags on his chest, Audrey Hepburn and her tiara and cigarette holder, a strand of pearls where Lilly's locket catches the kaleidoscopic light from the distant dance floor. George forgets what they were talking about. No woman would have called George's father a "scaredy cat."

"Why do you ask about my grandparents? Is this small-talk?"

"Sorry."

"I thought I told you..." Lilly says, "Don't say, 'Sorry.'"

"I know... sorry doesn't feed the bulldog. I started thinking of something else." George begins to mention his father, but stops himself.

"It doesn't matter," Lilly takes a drag and flashes a glance at Salvatore. "Same old song and dance."

"Tell me," says George. "I'm tired and kind of drunk, but... I'm interested."

"Okay, my Grandpa Vida passed away. Grandma Vida's name was Lillian. She told me my grandfather was going to engrave the locket for her when they got married, but he never did. He told her he could never find the perfect words. Lillian the First gave the locket to me, then she moved back home to New Orleans." Lilly touches the locket. "But I'm a Chatty Cathy. Let's talk about your surfing picture. I'm actually very excited, and I absolutely insist that you have teeny-boppers and hot-rods."

"What's with the teeny-boppers?"

"Teeny-boppers make surf movies perky."

"Perky?" asks George. He keeps his eyes above her breasts, imagining the zipper of her gown slipping down across her naked back.

"So what happens?"

34

"What?" asks George. He is drunk. No question about it now. Different people stand in different positions at the bar. George takes a sip of bourbon.

"The screenplay," Lilly says. "Your project with Mr. Mick Tanner."

"I have no idea," says George. His eye twitches. He read in a magazine that eye-twitches were caused by a deficiency of zinc.

Lilly taps her foot.

"And where is your grandmother? Lillian the First?"

"New Orleans, my very tired sailor…"

George rubs out the butt of his cigarette, offering Lilly a fresh smoke. She shakes her head no. George clicks his Zippo open questioningly. Lilly shrugs, lifts the pack and takes one, placing the cigarette into her holder. "We're going to have headaches," she looks over at Salvatore. George clicks the Zippo, holding the flame for Lilly. Her breasts swell as she leans over. She adjusts the heel on her left foot, holds her cigarette into the tiny flame and inhales.

"And what's the rest of the story?"

Lilly looks at him.

"Your grandmother…"

"The rest of the story," says Lilly, "is that my grandmother is very ill. No health insurance. I save half of everything I earn. It's not much, but I'm putting away money, keeping it in a coffee can." Lilly glances at Salvatore Kline.

"How long have you known him?"

"One week," Lilly stage whispers, "*We're* in the middle of a passionate affair."

"Is this your only passionate affair?"

"Not every affair is passionate."

"Future plans?"

"Marriage, I guess… if he asks me, that is." She waves to a bald fat man in a black caftan. The bald fat man holds up an imaginary camera and snaps an imaginary photo of Lilly. Lilly vamps, takes a drag from her long cigarette holder and arches her back and smiles. Lilly's gaze shoots right back to Salvatore Kline.

"Sal," she says, "is very sensitive. His family owns half of West Palm Beach. He is what girls in this city call a 'great catch.'"

"Sounds like love."

"It might be."

"Or a treasure hunt?"

"Are you calling me a gold digger?" Lilly's hand goes up to the locket, her fingernails tap it. She puts her hand in her lap and holds out the cigarette holder with the other. George realizes Lilly is self-conscious of her hands.

"I'm not calling you anything except 'lucky.' Most people don't fall in love with rich people they just met last week."

"It might surprise you that I'm quite picky." She taps the gold, diamond ring on George's hand with the cigarette holder. "I assume a handsome fellow like you has a gal?"

"Yes," says George.

"And the gal has a name?"

"Nicolette Amberson."

"And?" Lilly continues. "Vital statistics? Is she attractive?" Lilly takes George's hand, looking closely at the gold diamond ring. "I hate to assume, but I conclude the two of you are serious, since you wear what looks like a wedding ring on your ring finger?"

"Nicki called it an 'engagement ring.' It was my going-away gift. I think the idea is to ward off evil temptation. Nicki will be in town tomorrow." Responding to Lilly's questioning look, "Nicki is an entertainment lawyer. She's flying into town to meet a client and…"

"A business trip?" Lilly looks at Salvatore chatting with a slinky blonde. "How romantic… a business trip."

"And to visit her fiancée."

35

The slinky blonde whispers into Salvatore's ear.

"Did you say to visit her finances?"

"Her fiancée," George points to himself.

"Wow," Lilly's eyes brighten. "This Nicolette must be beautiful. Is she rich?"

"Nicki is beautiful… and committed to her work. Her career."

"And?"

"Okay," George admits, "she has money, but she earned it. Nothing was given to Nicki."

"Except your love?"

George sips his drink.

"Or did she earn that too?"

"Has Salvatore earned yours?"

"Don't change the subject, George. You said this Nicolette was an entertainment lawyer… and successful. I wonder, and I'm just guessing here… but could she be a wee bit older than you?"

George thwacks the pack of cigarettes with his forefinger.

Lilly claps, "Bingo! And I imagine this Nicolette pays for the occasional bill and buys you presents?" Lilly rubs George's sportcoat. "Like this jacket on your muscular arms?"

"Lucky guess."

"How did you meet the gorgeous Nicki?"

"At a traffic accident," George says. "I ran into the back of her car."

"On purpose?"

"It was an accident."

"An accident…" says Lilly. "How romantic. When's the big day?"

George shrugs, "It's still in the planning stages."

"Hmm," Lilly considers, "a big event, huh?"

"She's a big-event girl… with a fiancée who, until today, didn't have enough money in his pocket to buy a pizza, forget a wedding."

"I thought you were implying love wasn't about money. For a nice, committed guy, you don't sound very passionate."

"You've got it mixed up," says George. "You're the passionate one. I'm the one who's not afraid of commitment."

"At least we each are good at something," says Lilly. "But I'll take passion over commitment every time." Lilly flicks a glance toward Salvatore. "How about you, George? Are you happy with commitment over passion?"

"I didn't know it was a mutually exclusive arrangement."

"We each can't be good at everything." She leans forward. Her bare knees touch his slacks. "Which is it… commitment or passion?"

"I'll tell you when I make up my mind."

"I'm curious why people get married. I mean, I understand when someone gets a green card or trades up on a rich husband. Otherwise, I'm not sure I get it. I wonder if you see some kind of sign?"

"You mean a big light in the sky or a talking, burning bush in the desert that tells you what to do?" George adds, "It's from the Bible."

"I know that. I used to go to Sunday school myself. I'm not some kind of… heathen."

"My apologies. I've never read the Bible or been to any church… I think my step-dad is Lutheran, but my mom doesn't believe in it."

"What was that movie about L.A.? The one where Steve Martin makes friends with a billboard?"

"*L.A. Story.* It wasn't a billboard. It was a freeway traffic sign."

"What's a traffic sign?"

"It gives you updates on the status of the freeway, accidents, that kind of thing."

"I wonder what a freeway traffic sign would say about your convenient car accident…

the one where you ran into your soon-to-be wife?"

"That was a movie," says George.

"Lillian the First told me that one day I would see a sign, but I don't think she had a traffic sign in mind. I told her I wanted my sign to be a big diamond. She would laugh and tell me whatever my sign was… it would happen very fast and I had to be paying attention or I could miss it. My grandmother says everything important happens fast. When I was a girl, I didn't know what she meant then one day my life was just different. It happened," she snaps her fingers, "that fast. I had been an ugly duckling…" Lilly shrugs, "maybe Lillian will be right again. The question is do I get my big diamond?"

"Do you get to pick your sign?" George asks.

"That's a good question." Lilly thinks it over. "When I asked my grandmother, she just laughed, so I took that as a yes. She's very wise, very romantic… and maybe a touch loony, depending on the time of day and whether she's had a few sips of brandy. But if it's up to me, I want to wake up one morning and be in the middle of the world's biggest diamond, bigger than any diamond at Tiffany's." Lilly watches George. "Do I sound silly?"

"Yes… a touch loony too."

"What do you think the inside of a huge diamond would be like?"

"Claustrophobic. Glassy, suffocating."

"George, you really aren't very passionate. I don't mean a diamond you can't be inside… but one you can be inside. Use your imagination."

"Sure. Okay."

"Geez, what kind of writer are you? Anyway, I'm just saying that diamonds are so gorgeous from the outside, it would be beautiful to stand inside a diamond and watch the world go past… like standing in a beautiful room filled with light."

"Maybe you could have a hammock inside your diamond?"

"A hammock would be nice, but I think the important thing is that when I fall in love, I will be in a big diamond. That will be my sign, since we were talking about signs."

"We were…" George kills the warm coin of bourbon in his glass. "Maybe I am more cynical than I want to be… although I bet Salvatore could buy you a diamond big enough to hang that hammock in."

"Are you making fun of me?"

"No," says George. "I'm just wondering if you could ride around on a unicorn inside your diamond. That would be fun."

"You are making fun of me. How dare you! Well, tell me, since waking up in a big diamond clearly didn't happen to you… how did you know you were in love? Did you have a different kind of sign? Something from the universe that told you to become a fiancée? Was there a bit of magic, George? A special moment? Did the freeway sign tell you what to do?"

"Don't get me wrong, I would like to believe in signs," says George.

"I would like to believe in signs," mimics Lilly. "You get kind of snooty sounding when you're drunk."

"I'm not that drunk," says George, clearly and specifically aware he is currently very drunk. "I just don't think we all get signs when we fall in love, like waking up in a big diamond… but I guess it would make the whole thing easier." George flicks cigarette ash off the crease of his slacks. "With you it's either about green cards or it's about magic signs from the universe. One extreme to the other extreme…"

"Yes, I am a woman. Maybe that part confuses you?"

"It doesn't confuse me." Women have always confused him.

"This Nicolette… do you love her?"

"Sure." Nicolette believes in George. Nicolette is beautiful. He loves Nicolette and Nicolette loves him. "Sure, sure, I love her."

"*Sure?* What kind of word is that?"

"It means *yes. Sure* means *yes.*"

"Not where I come from, sailor. Where I come from, *sure* means *okay* and *okay* is very different from *yes.*"

"Sure, okay, yes. I love her. Now you're the one being cynical."

"I'm not cynical, just good at reading a snow job."

"I'm not giving you a snow job. I want to marry Nicolette and not because she's a great catch."

"Anyway," says Lilly, "Salvatore must know some important people in Hollywood. He seems to know important people everywhere. I'll ask him if he can arrange a few contacts and help you out."

"Thanks, but I can handle my career myself."

"Really?" asks Lilly.

"Really," says George.

"You can?" Lilly says. "No help needed?"

"No. None. Thanks."

"You don't need any help at all?"

"None," repeats George.

"Except from… what's her name again?"

"You know her name. Nicolette."

"Yes, Nicolette can help, can't she? But I guess you're in love with her, so it's different. People in love can help each other, right? That's not cynical. That's just love."

"You're spinning a web."

"I'm not spinning a web. I'm just talking, thinking about Salvatore and about Nicolette and about you and about me helping you with your career in surf films and all of that stuff friends think about…"

George laughs, "We're friends?"

"I think so. Do you want to be friends?"

"Sure," says George. "I mean, okay. I mean, yes."

"But not friends like you and Nicolette," says Lilly. "She can help you, but I'm not allowed to help you, correct?"

"Nicki can do a few things you're not allowed to do."

Lilly's eyes light up, "Really? I guess she is one lucky girl."

"I'm lucky. Nicolette has helped me out, but I don't ask for her help."

"You just accept help? But if Salvatore were to offer to pay a few of my bills… you imply that is inappropriate. You think I'm taking advantage?"

"I guess I better get to leaving," George says. "You're staying?"

"It's early for us night birds."

"I need to start thinking up funny, romantic stuff to write… about surfing."

"Be careful. Romance can be dangerous."

"It's a story. I'm making it up. How dangerous is that?"

"Romance is always dangerous. Be careful or you might wake up inside of a big diamond."

"Thanks, I'll be careful."

Lilly air-kisses George on each cheek. "Bye, sailor."

"Have fun with your passionate affair," George inches from her perfumed neck, but wants to reach his arms around her waist.

"Get yourself some sleep for that pretty lawyer gal. We wouldn't want her to get angry and sue you for everything you own."

"Like what… my typewriter?"

"If you're carrying it around, it must be important to you." Lilly's rhinestone tiara sparkles, "Ciao. Sleep well, George."

The taxi ride back to the Lower East Side is a soup of stop lights. George walks out of Hot Bagels, unwrapping a garlic bagel from wax paper and smearing tuna salad on his finger as he weaves down Ludlow Street. Max Fish is still crowded at three in the morning, with shadows packed beneath Day-Glo paintings, voices spilling as the glass doors open and a couple stumbling out hold each other tight. A puppy barks at George and runs around George's feet, tripping him up.

George doesn't remember falling.

FLEAS & BLOOD

Hungover, exhausted and half awake, George looks at the telephone in Dave's apartment, trying to decide whether to ring Nicki's new cell phone. His knees are scraped, and his slacks are ripped from the fall on the cement. New York has a three-hour time difference with California. Nicki had probably finished up her Pilates class and was on her way to the airport, maybe even on the plane. George hadn't looked closely at the ticket. He jumps when the door of the apartment goes *chock, chock.* George stares at the door. He holds an empty can of tuna in his hand. He drops the can in the trash. Another *chock, chock* on the door. A small white puppy rattles a ceramic bowl at George's feet, licking up all the tuna. The puppy barks at George. George's head hurts. He looks at the puppy. The puppy is the size of a very big boot. What was George thinking? George vaguely remembers sitting on the curb at the corner of Ludlow and Stanton, trying to recite John Donne's *"The Flea"* as the puppy licked tuna off his fingers. The puppy barked and looked very hungry and cute and George saw blood on the knees of his slacks. The knocking gets louder. Maybe it's the little Mexican girl… could Nicki be surprising him already? George opens the door.

Lilly Lejeune is still dressed in her white gown and has the rhinestone tiara in her hair. Her eyes are a bit glazed from the long evening. She raises a brown bag of groceries, with her cigarette holder clenched in her teeth. "Can I come in, sailor?"

George looks down the hallway.

"Don't worry, it's just me, little Lilly Lejeune, all alone." Lilly steps into the apartment before George answers. She hands George the sack and surveys the room. "I decided we must absolutely celebrate the beginning of your new project." Lilly pulls a bottle of bubbly and a carton of orange juice from the grocery sack. "I love mimosas. Do you love mimosas too, George?"

"Sure."

"Sure?" Lilly gives him a look.

"Yes, I mean, yes. That sounds great. I was thinking how dull it felt being sober."

"Can you rustle up some ice cubes?"

George walks into the kitchen, pulls out a fresh tray and knocks them into a bowl.

Lilly walks around the apartment. "The place is cleaner than I remember? Did Dave fix it up for you?"

"No, I worked on it yesterday. It was in bad shape."

"I remember," Lilly says in response to George's look. "I popped up here on the rare moment, when Dave had friends over and it was too noisy to sleep."

"Uh huh," says George. Lilly would be Dave's style.

"Is this your animal?" Lilly looks down at the puppy sniffing Lilly's white heels.

"I guess so."

"This is a pit bull. Don't these dogs grow into big monsters that kill people?"

The puppy stares up at them. The act of sitting, a balancing act of incomprehensible delicacy, is a challenge that overwhelms the puppy, who keeps its eyes locked on George and Lilly. Ears flopping, the puppy rolls on its side, with its paws scrabbling for the floor.

"I think she wants to kill my shoe," says George, "but I stopped her."

"What's its name?"

"I don't know. I found her on the street, I guess. Last night is kind of hazy."

"What you choose to take care of is your own business, George, but I think this animal is spoiled. I tried to feed it a chocolate croissant on the street yesterday and the animal refused my offer." Lilly rubs the dog's head. "Maybe the little monster is on a diet?"

"She ate a whole can of tuna in three seconds. Maybe she doesn't like chocolate?"

"How can anyone not like chocolate?"

"She's a dog. I think dogs die if they eat chocolate."

"Do you know," Lilly asks, "how bothersome it is to have to take care of a creature all the time? I have a parakeet that simply will not escape from its cage."

Lilly unwraps foil from the cork of the champagne. She pops the cork and champagne foams, running down the bottle. George locates two glasses in the kitchen, mixes the champagne and orange juice together, clinks glasses and sips. "Hmm," says Lilly. "Too bad we don't have a yacht. It would be nice to be out on a big boat today."

George picks up the puppy, and rubs her head. The puppy nips at George's fingers. "No!" George points at the dog. "That is no!" He puts the puppy on the ground and watches it waddle toward his wing-tip near the unmade bed. "I think I better find her owner," George says. "Or get some chew toys… or at least some cheaper shoes."

"She needs a bath," Lilly says. "She probably has fleas."

George pulls the puppy away from the shoe and lifts her, running a finger over the puppy's fur. George extracts a flea and pinches it between his fingers.

"Yuck," says Lilly. "You better buy it a flea collar."

The flea bisects between George's fingernails. "Mark but this flea, and mark in this, how little that which thou deniest me is; it sucked me first, and now sucks thee…" George flicks the terminated flea out the window. "And in this flea our two bloods mingled be…"

"Maybe I'm just tired," says Lilly, "but what are you talking about?"

"It's from a poem called "The Flea," which was written a long time ago in England. It's about a man who wants to sleep with a woman. She resists him and he argues that she might as well give herself to him because their blood has already mingled in the flea."

"That's really disgusting," says Lilly. "Why does she resist him?"

"I never thought about that," says George. "Maybe he isn't a great catch?"

Lilly punches his arm. "You're too busy being smart. Shut up and drink your mimosa."

George sips the champagne and orange juice.

"You look like you could use a little hair-of-the-dog," Lilly says. "And not the kind filled with fleas."

"If she didn't resist him," George points out, "he wouldn't have written the poem…"

"Of course not. He would have been too busy making love to her." Lilly sips her mimosa. "It's a good thing what's-her-name isn't here. You probably wouldn't get anything done."

"Because I'd be making love?"

"Exactly," says Lilly. "You are sharp, George. What's-her-name must be terribly impressed to date the sort of man who can recite poetry, even if it is about fleas and blood."

"I seem to please her."

"Bottoms up," says Lilly and clinks his glass. They each down their drinks. Lilly gets the champagne and orange juice and pours another round. "Isn't this a grand way to start your new project?" Lilly sees the bouquet of roses. "Looks like someone beat me to it. Are these from what's-her-name?"

"Her name is Nicolette. Yes. Nicki sent me the flowers."

"She must love you terribly… or are you just a terribly good lover?"

"Do I have to choose?"

"Do you always date older women, George?"

"It's not a pattern. Like I said, we met at a car accident."

"Did you smash into her on purpose? Oh, wait… you already told me…"

"I was trying not to run a red light."

"Too bad," says Lilly. "Smashing into her on purpose is more romantic."

"Sorry to let you down."

"I wonder if she likes you because you're not threatening?"

"Who says I'm not threatening?"

"Is it possible this woman has taught you special skills in the art of the boudoir… skills that only a woman of experience might know?"

"I'm thirty-one. It's just an eight-year difference."

"Okay," Lilly holds up her hands. "Eight years seems like a lot, but I guess I'm used to the more traditional arrangement… older man, younger gal. Do you think this Nicolette would be jealous that I'm alone here… alone in your room with you?"

"No," says George, thinking, *Yes.* "Why would she be?"

"No reason."

"Do you flirt with every stranger that knocks on your door?"

"Just the nice men with *snazzy* engagement rings on their fingers," says Lilly. "A girl in the big city doesn't see that very often… a handsome man wearing a *snazzy* ring to ward off evil women. I doubt it works, quite the opposite… besides, who says I'm flirting?"

George walks into the kitchen and splashes water on his face and brushes his teeth. He smoothes water in his hair and checks his face in the cracked shard of mirror over the sink.

Lilly's image sways in the glass shard. "Women like the challenge. A man with an engagement ring must be flirted with… it's a test."

"It's not a test. It's safe."

"A-plus. You are bright." Lilly sips her mimosa. "I like you, George. I don't know quite why I like you so much, but I do."

"Thanks. That's nice to know."

"Is she the jealous type?" asks Lilly. "For some reason I imagine this Nicolette to be the jealous type."

"I imagine she gets jealous," George says, "but not about me if I can help it."

"Well, you better get to work on your project or I'm just going to get quite drunk." Lilly walks to the desk with the typewriter. "I bet important things happen here," she picks up the page on the desk and reads, "Boy meets girl… surfing." Her eyes scan the page in the typewriter. She reads, "The waves were gone now. He sat on his surfboard and watched the beautiful girl in the green dress standing on the sand. Yes, he would love her forever." Lilly sits on the edge of the desk, ponders the sentences. "I guess you got some work done already?"

"Very preliminary."

"It is a beautiful typewriter," she says. "Do writers still use typewriters?"

George shrugs. "I do, but I'm not sure if I count."

"Don't be silly, of course you count."

He lights a cigarette. His first smoke of the day. His second cocktail. He still has one can of tuna left. "Are you hungry?"

"Not really. Why do you use a typewriter? Are you trying to be cool?"

George points to the photograph of his father on the hood of the Army Jeep. "The typewriter was my dad's." Lilly looks close at the photograph and sees the hard face of a man with a cigarette, dog tags and fatigue pants. He is shirtless in the jungle, sitting on the hood of a U.S. Army Jeep, with the typewriter on his lap. "I barely knew him," George adds. "I was a little kid. All that came back from Vietnam were his dog tags and this typewriter. He was killed in a city called Quảng Trị."

"I see where you get your good looks," Lilly says, adding, "I'm sorry, George. I really am. I know what it's like to lose a Dad. Only mine just ran away."

"It's tough, no matter what the reason."

41

"Your father looks like an interesting man."

"What are you doing here, Lilly?"

"Salvatore was ready for bed. I wasn't."

"What about your passionate affair?"

"I said, Passionate. I didn't say, Predictable."

The phone rings, and it's a shattering rotary-dial rattle. George would let the answering machine pick it up, except there is no answering machine. "It's probably for Dave." George is thinking it's Nicki.

"Unless it's an emergency." Lilly points to the phone, "No answering machine."

"Yes."

"What if it's your girlfriend?"

"It's not."

"Good thing," says Lilly. "That is, if she's the jealous type."

"You act as if we have something to hide?"

The phone rings.

"Is she staying here with you?" Lilly makes a delicate attempt to sit in a chair. She hovers in a half-squat, with the tiara in her hair. "Dave's place is very romantic. Rustic yet charming…" She straightens and touches the chair with her heel. Flakes of green paint flutter to the wood floor. Lilly presses one of the dowels in the chair and the chair collapses into a pile of wood. "Did you say what's-her-name was an adventurous gal?"

"No, I didn't," George picks up the ringing phone.

SAY CIAO FOR ME

Nicolette sits in first class. Nicolette has just finished a delicious sliced pear. Nicolette twirls an empty champagne flute, gazing out the window at the sinkhole of the Grand Canyon. Only first class can accommodate her long, shapely legs. Nicki spends a few moments crossing one leg over the other, then reversing the process. She has recently made a Power Yoga class part of her regime and is convinced the workout has increased her muscle tone, without turning her into some kind of hulky thing. It's not just her imagination; she can feel the endorphins in her tuned body. Her glutes are getting more firm. Her "tread-and-shred" instructor works their class hard. Nicolette's feet are wrapped in synthetic ermine-soft slippers she purchased during a flight to Austin, Texas, for the South-by-Southwest film festival. Her client was a screenwriter who had recently sold a hardboiled script about two Irish brothers, one a cop, the other a career criminal. The brothers' paths crossed, as you might imagine, and the dialogue was great, but the third act required fixing. Nicolette had contributed to some sessions with the writer and a producer. Nicki had been on the phone with the writer as she raced in her luxury sedan to long-term parking at LAX. Nicki was secretly delighted that after talking most of a quiet afternoon in her office with the screenwriter, she found out that the Irish brothers were in the third draft of fighting for the heart of a confident female lawyer who dressed similar to the way she dressed the afternoon she first met the screenwriter. The writer tended a bar in an Irish pub on Sunset Boulevard and word was out that every actor in town with any heat was interested in the part of the criminal or possibly the cop, depending on how the screenwriter managed the cop's character arc and the final ten pages of the story.

Nicki pulls the Airfone out of the seat back and inserts her credit card.

Lilly leans over the collapsed pieces of the broken chair: the sheath of her white dress tight, her pale, shell-white slip visible under the dress in the sunlight through the windows above Stanton Street. Lilly attempts to fit a dowel back into one of the holes in the frame,

42

the muscles of her arm taut. Lilly's back is beautiful in the morning light. George can't take his eyes off her as she bends and tries to fix the chair.

"Hello," George says into the phone. "Hi honey," Nicki replies.

Lilly looks back over her shoulder, twisting at the waist, her eyes on George. "What?"

George shushes Lilly with a cutting motion across his neck. Lilly bats her eyelashes. "I'm fixing your chair for what's-her-name," she whispers louder than her normal voice.

George mouths, "Nick-O-Let!" and presses his finger to his lips.

"George are you there?" says Nicki, distractedly wondering if the screenwriter she was *not* engaged to marry, the screenwriter with a career and a go-script attached to a production company with a first-look arrangement at a major studio was the kind of guy, in a perfect world, Nicolette could love? He seemed self-involved, but he did pay attention to Nicki and it was no coincidence he rewrote his female lawyer into the script after he met her. "Hello?" Nicolette repeats. "George, is that you?"

"Nicki," says George. "Where are you?"

"Guess?"

"You sound like you're on Jupiter."

"It looks like Jupiter out the window, but I think it's Arizona, or Utah."

"Oh," responds George. Lilly sits on the edge of George's bed, her ankles together as she looks into her mimosa. She takes a sip and pouts at the glass. "You're in the air?" George asks. Lilly walks over with the champagne bottle and tilts champagne into George's glass.

"What?" George asks the phone.

Lilly makes a face at George, sticking out her tongue. George tries not to laugh.

Nicki's voice is garbled, "Did… you… like… the… flowers?"

Lilly takes the tiara out, allowing her dark hair to fall to her shoulders. Lilly rubs the flat of her hand along her hair, smoothing it across her shoulders. She pulls a cigarette out of her clutch and fits the cigarette into her cigarette holder. George pulls his Zippo from his slacks.

"They're beautiful," George says into the phone, "and thanks for working out the deal with Mick. It looks like I'm ready to get to work."

"You know," says Nicolette, "I expected a phone call or some attempt from my fiancée to ask me about the details of my arrival. Maybe a note sent by carrier pigeon?"

"I'm sorry. I had problems with the apartment key."

"But it worked," says Nicki. "You are inside the apartment and all is well?"

"Sure," says George. "I mean, yeah, but Dave left the place a wreck, so I needed to clean it before I went out. I'm sorry."

"Went out where? George, did I hear another voice?"

"No," says George, looking at Lilly. "It's just me here…" Lilly's eyes go wide and she makes a *tsk, tsk,* crossing her forefingers. "No one but me," he repeats. "I went out with Mick to celebrate. He gave me some money upfront too." He just wants to keep talking. The world is calm when George talks.

"People do get paid in this business," Nicolette says. "I see it all the time, George. It does happen, you know."

"Right," says George. "So when do you get into town? Are you coming straight here to Dave's? I should have called. I'm sorry."

"You already apologized, honey. Not twice."

"Okay."

Lilly mouths, "Sorry doesn't feed the bulldog."

"I've got myself a room at the Plaza," says Nicolette. "The client offered, and I wanted to respect your work. My friend Carol from law school is having a cocktail party tonight. I thought you could come up and meet me before the party. It would be nice to walk around at sunset and then we could take a quick visit to the hotel and freshen up and arrive at Carol's arm-in-arm, like two perfect people perfectly in love."

"Yes."

"Didn't you want to ask me something else?"

"Yes," says George. Lilly stretches back on the unmade bed, spreads out her arms and yawns. Her dark hair is spread around her shoulders.

"What?"

"Nothing," says George, shooting a glance between Lilly's thighs as Lilly stares up at the ceiling. Lilly shifts her legs, and the sunlight flips to shadow her thigh-high stockings, white dress and glowing skin. George's mind stalls.

"George?"

"What?"

"Are you okay, sweetheart? You sound strange. Are there other people there? Do you have another woman around?"

"No," he says. Lilly pulls herself up on her elbows and arches an eyebrow. "C'mon, Nicki… I told you there's no one else here. Stop it."

"You haven't changed, have you, darling? It's been so long since we've been together."

"It's been two days… almost two days. People don't change in two days."

"People change in a heartbeat, George. You know that. I changed when you ran into my car that day…"

"Tell me about the wedding idea."

"No," says Nicolette, "on second thought, I want to tell you in person. These air phones are expensive… although I'm sure I can write this one off. You know, we might be able to leverage this script with Mick into some extra attention, maybe find a way to shop your spec on the dolphin boy."

"He's not a dolphin boy," says George. Lilly straightens her skirt, walks back to the typewriter, rolls in a new piece of fresh white paper and types in a deliberate hunt-and-peck one-finger style, *"I am George. I am a mighty river of talent!"*

"Do you love me?" asks Nicki. George turns his back to Lilly. He really needs to concentrate for a moment on talking with Nicolette. Watching Lilly, George only concentrates on Lilly. George tells himself not to think of Lilly. Lilly is just a girl that lives downstairs while he writes his script and gets paid for a job, gets paid to write.

"Of course I do," he says. Lilly's ears perk. She looks over her shoulder at George and mouths the word *love?* George shakes his head no.

"Then say it," says Nicki.

"Oh, Nicki," he says. "I love you."

Lilly puts her hand to her mouth and turns her thumb at the floor.

"Oh, baby, I'm drinking champagne right now and maybe I'm feeling a bit tipsy, but I can't wait to see you."

"Me, too, baby," George says, mugging to Lilly. Lilly turns her thumb sideways.

"You can't wait to see me too?" Nicki asks.

"No, I'm a little tipsy, too, from champagne."

Long pause. Lilly grabs the side of her head in mock astonishment.

"You're drinking champagne by yourself?" asks Nicolette. "In the morning?"

"It's later here."

"I know what time it is. It's noon."

"I was just kidding. I'm drinking orange juice. Drinking orange juice and wishing you were here and we were drinking champagne together."

Lilly gives George a thumbs-up.

George watches Lilly smile. This is a slippery slope. He just lied to Nicki… a few times.

"Oh, that is sweet," says Nicolette. "I'll let you go, darling. I was about to insist that you meet me at the airport, but I'll just jump in a taxi, race to the hotel and freshen up. I'll ring you when I get settled."

"Absolutely," says George. "Perfect."

"Hmm," says Nicolette, "I hope you know I look good enough to eat."

"Yum," says George. Lilly watches him.

"Ciao, my darling," says Nicolette.

"Ciao," George says. He has never said, "Ciao." He hangs up the phone.

Lilly claps her hands and breaks into a giggle. "Basta, paparazzi! Basta!"

"What's so funny?"

"Oh, George," says Lilly. "Was that one of Dave's friends?"

"Very funny."

"Say *ciao* for me."

His face gets hot.

Lilly draws it out like a meow. *"CHI-A-OW..."* She claws at the air like a cat. *"CHI... AH... AOW!"*

"You're drunk."

"Yeah? So? It's noontime, sailor. In fact, it's still nighttime for me. I don't need an excuse. If I'm drunk, I'm drunk."

George puts on his wristwatch. He should get work done before Nicki calls him.

"How much time?" Lilly asks. "Before you turn into a pumpkin?"

Outside the windows, the day is white. George is on his third mimosa, and his headache is not a big deal. The sky is bright, and the tiny silver toy-like airplane is holding Nicki far away. Lilly sashays over and hooks him by the arm. "I'm going to take you to a movie."

"I have to work." He points at his typewriter.

"You need inspiration. I don't know much about you writers that live upstairs, but I do know you need inspiration. And that's why I'm here, right now." Lilly tugs on George's arm. "We're just going down one flight of stairs, silly. Don't worry. The moment you get inspired you can race back up the stairs two at a time and type until your fingers bleed." Lilly yawns.

"What's the movie?"

Lilly pours champagne in their glasses, adding a dash of orange juice.

"It's an oldie," says Lilly, "but you'll love it. *Breakfast at Tiffany's*. If you've already seen it... well, maybe you should get to work and type, but if you haven't, we can sip mimosas and just let the day slip away." George looks at Lilly's arm, her fingernails tap his forearm. Her sleepy, drunk eyes watch him.

"No," he lies. "I haven't seen it." Yeah, he's seen the movie. His feet were in cashmere socks kicked up on Nicki's coffee table as he sipped a Campari in the middle of the afternoon in Beverly Hills. "Holly," the gold-digger, and "Paul," the writer who lives upstairs, fall in love, but she pulls away from him for a rich man and then the rich man dumps her because of her connections with the mob and she throws the cat in the rain. Good story. It holds up since 1961, except for Mickey Rooney's lame schtick as the Japanese photographer. "Let me put on a real shirt," George motions to his white T-shirt.

"You look fine," Lilly opens the door. "You'll love the flick, sailor. It is quite unbelievable, but it is fabulous. Audrey Hepburn plays a girl who wants a rich husband, but falls for... do you know?" He shakes his head, caught in his lie, fib, or bending of the truth. Nicki will be in town this afternoon and his drunken interlude of watching a classic movie in a New York apartment will be nothing more than a story to remember after he is married.

"She falls for a guy with nothing but a typewriter... just like you... only I don't think he writes surfing pictures."

"Why is that so unbelievable?" George asks. "You don't think pretty women fall in love with poor writers?"

"I'm sure they can. Like what's-her-name... and by the looks of that gold ring on your finger, she fell hard. Women fall for men much worse than poor writers, but my personal experience is women who want rich men for husbands, find rich men for husbands."

"Like Salvatore Kline?"

"C'mon," she says, "grab your mimosa and we'll go down to my place. I rented the video from Kim's Video on St. Mark's Place, and I just keep forgetting to return it. I must owe those nice video clerks hundreds of dollars."

"I've had enough champagne."

"One more won't hurt you," Lilly puts the glass in his hand. George thinks there is a reason one more could hurt him, Lilly's arm wraps around his waist. "For good luck," she says.

"What's lucky about it?"

"This," she leans in against George, with the mint paste on his teeth and warm champagne on her lips, and kisses George soft. Her lips are a light dry glance as she slips away. "C'mon, sailor… let's go downstairs."

ALMOST A SYNDROME

George hasn't been in New York City for much longer than twenty-four hours and this is, counting his first desperate knock the previous morning, his third trip to Lilly's apartment. Lilly opens her front door, nodding for him to enter. Lilly Lejeune kissed George upstairs and her kiss reminds George how and why the bourbon at the nightclub tasted like iced tea. Lilly's lips touched George's lips and her nose tickled his nose. Nicolette traveling in the sky, cocooned above the flatlands of America. Nicolette with her marriage news, her tongue in his mouth at the Encounters restaurant at LAX, breasts smashed against him, her tongue and body filling him with dizzy scents and stirrings and alarms that were a low buzzing compared to the clang that happened when Lilly opened her apartment door and faced him in her white tuxedo shirt and her blue ice-box hangover mask.

"You better not be here," she yells into the apartment, adding to George, "That damn bird doesn't know how lucky it is. I wish I had wings and could just fly away any day of the week."

Lilly clicks over on her heels to the parakeet cage shining in a block of sunlight beside the open window. "You still here?" Lilly rattles the birdcage louder. "Hey, you, I'm talking to you."

"Lupe calls her 'Amanda.'"

"Lupe's a cute girl." Lilly rattles the cage, "You just like hanging around because you're afraid. You're one big scaredy cat… and quite afraid of cats, I might add." Lilly turns to George, "Excuse me, George. I really must pee. I hope you won't take offense if I close the door to the loo?"

"Not at all," says George. "I would expect nothing else."

"No, I guess you wouldn't…" Lilly spins. "Unzip me, sailor." George stands next to the bookshelf of empty martini glasses. Lilly backs up to him, smiling over her shoulder. George reaches for the zipper, his fingers clumsy. The zipper is slick in his fingers.

"Damn…"

"You'll get it, sailor. Just slow down and do it right."

George gets the zipper-tip and pulls the zipper down. She reaches up to each shoulder, slips down the gown, pressing the white material to her breasts. Lilly kicks off her heels and skips toward the bathroom. "Make yourself comfortable." The door shuts. George can't help but hear the silky shuffle of Lilly slipping out of the dress, the slight porcelain tremble as Lilly lowers on the toilet seat. George imagines Lilly, elbows digging red smudges into her thighs at the white band of her stockings, her dark hair falling across her face as her naked feet tap on the bathroom tiles. George hears the toilet paper roll and rattle and then the toilet flush.

The bathroom door flips open wide. A toothbrush in her mouth and a bath towel wrapped around her, Lilly brushes her teeth. "Can you toss me those jeans… and that shirt?" Lilly points to a faded men's shirt with a stripe pattern, crumpled on a chair beside a pair of jeans.

Lilly spits out toothpaste in the tiny bathroom sink.

George stands by the open door, holding the jeans and the men's shirt. "These?"

"Thanks." Lilly walks over and rifles a pair of cotton panties and cotton tank top from her bureau. "Un momento, señor." Lilly pops into the bathroom, leaving a gap so the bathroom mirror is visible. George makes himself look away. "There's a coffee pot if you feel like making a cup of joe, sailor." George sees Lilly, towel wrapped around her unclothed body, looking at herself in the mirror. She smiles at him and pushes the bathroom door shut.

George finds the Mr. Coffee and pours water into the plastic reservoir, takes the plastic top off the yellow can of Bustelo coffee and locates a box of filters.

"What's with the martini glasses?"

Lilly's voice is muffled, "I collect them."

"Of course," says George, "*that* makes sense."

Lilly steps out of the bathroom and runs a brush through her hair. She looks at the martini glasses on the book shelf. "Each glass is from a night on the town. Each martini glass has a story. They're not all pretty stories… but some were pretty fun." She stretches and yawns, "I'm comfy. Let's pop in the flick."

"Remember, I've got work to do before… well, before I see Nicki."

"Right, this Nicolette… do you think she would mind terribly that we are watching a movie together alone in my apartment?"

"What would your boyfriend think?"

"Salvatore is not my boyfriend. Salvatore is my lover." Lilly sips her mimosa, picks out an ice cube and tosses it at the birdcage. "Chicken!"

"It's a parakeet."

"Funny," says Lilly. "Really, you are quick. That must be one of the things what's-her-name likes about you… your quickness in the wit department, not in the boudoir, of course."

"Of course," says George.

"Do you know what boudoir means?" Lilly asks. George says nothing and Lilly says, "A room for pouting…"

"Yes." He drains his mimosa. "Nicki trusts me…"

"That's what's important," Lilly says, "Salvatore trusts me too, although you and I probably shouldn't kiss again. If Sal knew I kissed you, he would have to challenge you to a duel… and the rich don't lose duels."

"What's he going to do, throw his bank account at me?"

"Sword play, sailor!" Lilly makes a parry-and-thrust motion toward his heart. "If Sal got jealous, he would skewer you like an olive in a martini."

"Why did you kiss me?"

"You do have pretty lips. I mean, handsome… besides," Lilly adds, "if something interests me, I do it." Lilly takes the pink video cassette off the TV and places the cassette into the slot of the VCR. "I know a little bit about commitment too, you know."

George laughs, "You call that commitment?"

"I commit to the moment. It's just not a long-term arrangement." Lilly rolls the TV/VCR unit toward the sofa. Lilly wipes her forehead as if completing a big task. "Long-term arrangements aren't for me." She taps a finger on George's T-shirted chest. "Long-term arrangements are not my deal, get it?"

"Who's asking? I'm just here for the drive-in."

"Play," Lilly presses play. "Showtime."

The block of sunlight has stretched from the dented birdcage on the cinderblocks to the purple love seat that faces the TV/VCR. Lilly is curled against George, whose arm is on

47

the ridge of the love seat. Lilly's eyes flutter, half asleep. The ice in her mimosa has melted. George sips coffee. Lilly is folded against him, hushed. She yawns, rubs her eyes and hits pause on the remote. "Do you like?"

"Yeah," George says. His typewriter is just up the steps. He will write today. A wedge of sun is framing the birdcage, lighting the edge of the book shelf of empty martini glasses. George points to the photo of Audrey Hepburn on the bureau. "You're a fan?"

"A psychiatrist told me it was—" Lilly stops herself, "I wasn't seeing him for treatment… we were in a nightclub. I know it would be very chic for me to have a shrink or whatever you call them now, but I met him in a club. It was over a glass of exquisite brandy, if I recall, and we were both smoking cigars in the smoking lounge…" Lilly falls from the firm lip of the sofa's edge, smacking the floor. Her mimosa is still in her hand. "I was saying?"

"About Audrey?"

"Yes!" Lilly gets back on the sofa and props a pillow behind her. "We were watching the movie, you know…" She points at the TV screen.

"You paused it. I asked about Audrey Hepburn."

"The psychiatrist told me it was practically a syndrome. He said half the girls in New York want to be Audrey." She reaches to the arm of the love seat for George's pack of cigarettes. "Which makes sense," Lilly continues, "I guess, although that information does cause one to feel rather, well, typical… like having a crush on the same boy as every other girl in school." Lilly lights the cigarette, giving George a long look, "She had difficulty with romance, with men… but she helped poor children… and she was a wild thing. She did what she wanted…"

"You mean, Audrey Hepburn, not," George points to the TV, "the character Holly Golightly."

"Same thing. You must learn one thing, sailor, you can't take the Audrey out of Holly. She had a very bad accident on a horse…"

"Audrey or Holly?"

Lilly waves off the question, "I think… you've had too much champagne…"

George picks up the framed photograph of Lilly's grandparents. "Is this?"

"Yes, Lillian the First. My grandmother and my grandfather."

"She looks like you…"

"Or I look like her."

"You haven't mentioned your parents?"

"No, I told you, you are quick, sailor. No wonder you're a writer…. She had a very difficult time having a child. I saw a special on television. Audrey, I mean, not my grandmother."

"Where is Tiffany's?"

"Midtown, just below Central Park on Fifth Avenue." The video begins playing again. Lilly presses "stop." "I guess we're talking." Lilly tucks a strand of hair behind her ear. "I always go alone… to Tiffany's."

"Not with Salvatore?"

"Holly goes with the poor writer, except they only have enough money to engrave a ring from a box of Cracker Jack. You understand, George? A plastic ring, they take the plastic ring to be engraved." She holds up the champagne bottle. "Want some?" George shakes his head no. Lilly pours the rest of the bottle into her glass. "To your project," she lifts up her glass and drains it, places it on the floor. Lilly looks at the glass for a few extra seconds.

"I wish I had thought of that… the plastic ring," says George. "It's my favorite part of the movie."

Lilly looks at George, her hazy eyes drifting from sleep and liquor, "I thought you hadn't seen the movie?"

"It sounds smart," George covers. "I hope I can come up with a few ideas like that."

"I don't know if engraving a surfboard would work, but I'm sure you are very talented,

George. I'm sure you are a mighty river of talent. Otherwise, you wouldn't be living upstairs." Lilly scrunches back on the sofa, placing her head on one of the needlepoint pillows. She waves the remote control, clicking the VHS tape to play. Holly Golightly stands in the middle of a cocktail party, smoking a cigarette from a long black cigarette holder. "I'm sure," Lilly says, eyes closed, "you are a mighty river of talent…"

I'M NOT SURE

Her lush blond hair is swirled on George's naked stomach as one of her fingers twists a strand. Her body rises gently with her breathing. George stares at the ceiling of the Plaza Hotel suite. It is a beautiful ceiling. Nicki runs her finger up and down George's ribs, burrowing up under his arm. "You okay?" she whispers.

Sure, thinks George. "Sure."

Nicolette reaches down and runs her finger along George's cock.

George rolls on his side, burying his head into the space between Nicki's breast and her arm. George kisses Nicki under her arm, tasting her salty taste.

"Hey," she says, "I'm talking to you." She taps his cock with her finger. "Hello?"

George falls asleep.

He opens his eyes. Minutes have passed. Holding a split of champagne, Nicolette is on the edge of the bed, wrapped in a white bathrobe. She pops the top, and champagne foams. Champagne. George doesn't want more champagne. "Let's celebrate," says Nicki.

Cigarette. George wants to light up. George takes the glass Nicki offers him. Her robe is loose around her naked body, and her hair swirls blond at her shoulders. George looks at Nicki and wonders how he could ever have moments of doubt. Nicki is incredible. George is stuck in a pattern of immaturity and insecurity that keeps George over-evaluating, re-deciding and hammering at the point of no point. He needs to just relax and do his work and spend time with the woman he loves.

"That was great," George nudges his elbow toward the tangle of unmade hotel bed.

"I'm always great. You weren't bad either in that department."

"Which department?"

"Oh, you know," says Nicki. She puts a finger on his lips and then moves the finger over to her loose bathrobe and taps her navel, letting her finger tickle down toward her crossed thighs. "It's just been feeling right, honey… and I like this too." Nicki reaches across and pats George's limp cock. "I can always use more of this… when it's ready." George is quiet. Nicki says, "More is a good thing. Remember, I'm only in town for a few days, so don't be shy."

"I won't."

"It will be great when we get married. You can write on your little typewriter or maybe upgrade and buy a laptop. You can become more brilliant and sell big projects and once you are tired of typing, you can do a few push-ups and sit-ups and wait for me to come home from the office."

"That sounds like our life now."

"But it will be different, honey. We will be married. We will be together forever."

George slides to the end of the bed, where his gray slacks lay crumpled from Nicki stripping them to his ankles. George pulls on his boxers and steps back into his slacks, cinching his belt and tugging a T-shirt over his head. He digs the Lucky pack from his jacket. "I need a smoke." He taps out the last cigarette, crushes the pack and tosses it into the wastebasket.

Nicolette sips her glass of champagne. George lights his cigarette. His head hurts, but he drinks the champagne, "Here's to us." George says, "Let's go outside… we can catch the sunset in Central Park."

"George," Nicki says. "You are a romantic." Her suitcase is open on the floor beside the closet. "Let me get ready... it will just take a moment."

"Throw on some jeans," George says. "Let's go." George knows what it means when Nicki says it will just take a moment.

"George," Nicki says. She walks into the bathroom and closes the door. George pours himself another glass of champagne, pulls on his shirt, sportcoat and adjusts his pocket square. His head is a dull throb the champagne might soothe or inflame. It occurs to George he never makes the decisions with Nicki. Not once. Not ever. Not unless you count the night he asked her to marry him. He loves Nicki, but why did he need to ask her to marry him?

Thirty-five minutes later, Nicolette steps from the bathroom, dressed in flared khakis, a dark fitted top and gold flats. Nicki is relaxed and sophisticated, her sunglasses pushed up in her hair. "Well, how do I look?" Nicki lifts a foot, showing off the shoe. "Ferragamo."

"Perfect," says George. "But you looked perfect before too."

"I know, baby, but I haven't been to New York in forever, and I feel an urge to be elegant. You understand women, don't you?" She tugs at his pocket square, tweaking it.

"Hey!" George re-plumps the square of silk.

He understands why Nicolette wants to dress for their sunset stroll. He is just wound up. The walls feel tight, even after making love, even after the champagne and a cigarette.

"Okay, lover," says Nicki. "I have a great idea for what we should do!"

Nicolette and George drift in a rowboat on the pond in Central Park, looking up at a young man and woman in scuffed jeans, with knapsacks at their feet, holding hands on Bow Bridge, gazing out at the water. The young man and woman come together in a kiss.

"Ready?"

"Nicki, this isn't a great time for surprises. I've got a job ahead of me... I don't have a clue how to do it... and the money for the wedding? I can't even think about the money..."

"You don't have to think of money. That's the great news. Kamstein jumped to another agency. Which means that guess who gets promoted?"

"Hey," says George. "Congratulations!"

"Which means?"

"Pay raise?"

Nicolette takes the paddle from George's hands and taps the grip against the thigh of his gray slacks. "And... ?"

More money. More prestige. More freedom. Less time. More power. Money. "More money?"

"Exactly, which means we can do what, George?"

"Get married?" Yes, now they can get married and nothing can stop them.

"My bright boy."

"That's great."

"We can go ahead with our plans. Everything we talked about. We can set up our lives exactly as we want our lives to be." Nicolette takes George's hands, the oar balanced across her flared slacks. "What is it? Are you scared? I know you are a few years younger..."

"It's not that, Nicki." George watches the ducks drift, making duck noises. What do you call a bunch of ducks hanging out? A string, a brood, a pod, a coven? George knows about a covey of quail, a pride of lions, a murder of crows. But what about ducks? A loud of ducks? An annoyance? An interruption? A portent?

"What is it?" Nicki lets George's hands slip to his knees. George reaches to his jacket where there should be a pack of smokes.

"George, we have fun together. That's what this is all about. Us... spending time together because it's what we both want... a future together."

"It doesn't feel right living off of you like some gigolo."

"You are a bit of a gigolo, sweetheart, but since when did the gigolo care about spending my money? Besides, you can always go back to school and get a degree in something, if the writing doesn't work out."

"It's going to work out," George looks at the couple kissing on the bridge.

"I know it's going to work out. I believe in you. I'm the one that brought Mick and you together on this project." George's face darkens. "I was just saying…"

"Saying what?" He stares off.

Nicki says nothing. Why is George acting like this? She flew all the way across the country with good news. They are in a rowboat in Central Park. George has money in his pocket and for the first time, a writing contract, even if it is for a project that sounds more like a commercial for sports clothing than an actual feature, but that's not Nicki's concern. George needs to get paid and get some work in the can. He needs to earn his next, real break. Maybe someday the two of them can find a project to produce together. It would be soo romantic if she just could show the world George's talent!

George looks at Nicki. George has no reason to be angry with her. "Thank you," he says. "You know I appreciate all your help." His voice doesn't even sound like his voice.

"I'm just saying… I'm on your side and I believe in you. We've been engaged for a long time. You asked me to marry you. I said, Yes. Do you want to stay engaged forever?"

"That could work."

Nicolette looks up at the couple on bridge. They have their hands down each other's jeans, grinding thigh on thigh. "When you asked me to marry you… I told you my love was real. Do you still want to marry me?"

"Sure," says George. "Yes."

"My love is real," Nicki says. The couple on the bridge don't care who sees them. Her T-shirt is lifted up as he kisses her breasts. "That's happiness, George," Nicki nods at the mauling couple as they grind and sway on the bridge above the black water spotted with lily pads and prowling ducks. "Two people who can't keep their hands off each other… like us today in the hotel."

"Right," says George, remembering how Nicki held his head as he licked and kissed her between her thighs, burying his tongue in her and letting her grind against him and find her rhythm. It was perfect, right? George could smell Nicki on his fingers. He liked her smell, but something was happening and George couldn't pretend it wasn't happening. George couldn't lie, but he tries. "You know I still want to marry you, Nicki…"

The annoyance of ducks watches Nicki and George in the rowboat, one duck dips down into the water and nibbles under its wing.

Nicki's eyes soften. She believes him.

George is a bad person. George doesn't want to marry Nicolette. He can't believe he asked her to marry him. George has changed. People change. "I mean, I'm not sure," George adds.

"What?!" The ducks explode off the water, with large circles expanding in ripples across the green pond. George has a brick in his stomach. George watches his beautiful fiancée, Nicolette Amberson. George can't keep saying yes when he means no. George wants to keep saying yes. Yes is a perfect word, but no is the word George needs to say to Nicki. No, I can't marry you.

"Listen," he begins, "it's not you. It's me."

"It's you what?" Her hands clench the handle of the rowboat paddle.

He could rewind this idyllic rowboat-in-the-water scene to the sleepy post-coital calm when George fell asleep against Nicki's breasts and the hum of the city down on the boulevards, but now George moves forward, "I feel like something isn't right. I don't know… I'm not sure."

"You're not sure? Remember when you asked me? Remember when I said yes?"

"I like things the way they are now," he listens to his voice. When did his voice get that

51

nervous liar's twitch? When did his voice turn into a can of worms?

Nicolette's voice is also different. She doesn't understand why George is saying what George is saying. Her old world required Nicki to come to terms with a younger boyfriend who had trouble making his way, but who loved her and wanted her by his side. This world has the same younger guy, but the guy she has introduced to her professional life, her family, her friends, her heart, this man is reneging on his contract. This new world mocks Nicolette because it steals back the happiness she enjoyed in the young couple on the bridge, the paddle in her hand as she and George drifted on the water. This new world mocks Nicolette because it steals back her happiness this afternoon in the hotel room and last night, packing her luggage for her journey to Manhattan to join her love in his struggle, the early morning drive through twinkling, quiet Los Angeles, the counter agent at the terminal. All of those moments are taken back, reversed, replaced, soiled with rot.

"The way things are is that we have the money and the opportunity to go ahead with our wedding, which is what I thought you wanted. Now, as in this moment in this boat, George, you change everything? Is that what you are doing… changing everything?"

Nicki's hands grip the paddle as it balances upon the side of the rowboat. George is aware the paddle could swing in any direction, for example, right at George's teeth, if Nicki completely loses her temper. George's hand hovers above the paddle. "Nicki," Nicki doesn't deserve this and George will also get hurt before this is finished. The paddle in the teeth would be easier than what they will have to work out. George is the loser, not Nicki. George is still the boy that never gets the perfect girl because even when she is right in front of him, he screws it up, isn't content—runs away. Nicki wants George forever, and George is throwing her away. "Nicki," he says. Nicki stares off at the empty bridge, where the young couple walk down the path with knapsacks over their shoulders. "Can you live with a man who never makes any money? A man with nothing but a typewriter… who is thirty-one years old and can't pay his rent?"

"You just made money," Nicolette points out. "We made it together as a team." Nicolette wants to scream. "This could be romantic… this could be very different right now, George." Nicolette tries to look some direction where her eyes won't sting, but the green park shimmers. "Yes, George, to answer your question, I can live with that man… if he loves me. That's why I said yes when you asked me to marry you. Don't think I never considered the challenges or what could be difficult. I did. But I still said yes."

"You're okay with it now, but that could change," says George. "I guess I'm thinking about the future, thinking more about it than I was and it makes me nervous."

"I can see that, but we're engaged and we have the money for the wedding now. I can't believe you have doubts…" Nicki rubs the sting of the tears. She doesn't want to cry, but it's too late. "Is it really just the money? You sound different to me."

"Money is a big thing," he says. "Maybe I'm realizing it now because of this advance from Mick, but I can't live off of you, Nicki." *Stay focused on the money issue. Money is real. Money is not personal. Money is important. Money must be discussed by adults.*

"You didn't have trouble letting me pay for your airplane ticket or lending you money I know you won't pay back."

"That's what I'm saying," he says, knowing it's not really what he is saying. What George is saying, without using the words is, "I don't love you."

George doesn't like what he is, the kind of man he has become, the kind of man that lets his girlfriend pay for everything and then shakes when some flighty, nightclubbing, failed model asks him to unzip her dress. Even if he did love Nicolette, he wouldn't know it right now. Nicki takes care of him. He doesn't take care of himself. He needs to make his own choices. He needs to understand what he wants. George needs to stand alone. If he doesn't love her, he can't marry her.

"You're right," he says, "I didn't have trouble letting you buy the airplane ticket for me to fly out here, and I didn't have trouble having you give me the four hundred dollars."

"Or just about anything else we spend my money on," she adds.

"That's what bothers me," George says. "But it's not you, Nicki, it's me. Something has changed."

Nicolette laughs a dry laugh. "Like I said, George, people can change in a heartbeat."

"Nicki…"

"Row me to the dock, George. I don't want to see you anymore. Not tonight, not ever."

"You're just mad."

Nicolette laughs, "You think so?"

CASH & CARRY

George looks down East 6th Street at the sign with the serpent and the black diamond. The Indian restaurants on East 6th are packed with couples sharing dinner, sipping glasses of wine, eating and talking and enjoying the evening. George knows he did the right thing earlier that day telling Nicki he wasn't ready to get married. George looks in the window of a restaurant called "Gandhi" and sees himself sitting across from Nicolette. They have discussed the difficulties of marriage and have resolved George's momentary doubt. They are together and understand the risks and challenges of a serious relationship. Nicki offers George a vegetable samosa. George offers Nicki the basmati rice. They are relaxed, allowing time to drift before George pays the bill and they stroll hand in hand through the East Village. George pulls away from the restaurant glass and walks to the sign with the green snake curling around the diamond.

The Diamond is crowded. George pushes to the bar, and the Smashing Pumpkins "1979" plays on the jukebox. The long-haired bartender, who calls himself "Scout," works the bar, popping bottles of beer, slamming liquor bottles into the well-racks and hitting the register keys. George orders a Manhattan.

"Right. Bourbon or blended?"

"Jim Beam," George says. Scout lifts the bottle and spins it in his hand, pouring whiskey into a metal shaker and nodding down the bar to a girl with long brown hair and sleepy eyes. "Annabelle, you cool?" The girl holds up her empty highball glass. "Don't hurt me, Scout. I've got to work tomorrow." Scout takes a bitters bottle and knocks some dashes into the shaker with the bourbon and sweet vermouth.

Scout leaves the shaker to chill and pours Annabelle a heavy V&T and slides the glass in front of her. Scout raps the bar with his knuckles. "On me."

Annabelle winks at Scout, "Thanks."

George and a girl with green hair share an ashtray. "Scout," the girl with green hair says, "crank that shit!" She takes a drag on her smoke, "Fucking Sabbath, dude…."

Scout says, "Turn it up, Cynthia, but not too loud. The upstairs is whining…" He nods to the foam sound insulation layering the ceiling. "If we get too loud, they pour water through the cracks in the floor." He shakes his head, "I guess it's better than having the cops roll to the door."

Cynthia gets off her seat, moving through people like a surgeon in a room of ghosts. She crouches at the jukebox and reaches behind it. The room blasts Black Sabbath's "War Pigs."

Scout turns from the register and slashes his hand in a downward motion. "Junkie," he says under his breath in the noisy room. Cynthia twists the dial behind the juke until Scout gives her the that's-cool signal. Scout pours the chilled bourbon into a frosted martini glass and then drops in a maraschino cherry. "There you go, bro."

George takes a sip. "Nice."

"Fucking A," Scout wipes the top of the bar with a damp rag stained in black streaks of cigarette ash. "The bitters is the killer."

George already feels better than he felt uptown. George sips, "Really good."

Two bodies move from the bar, holding red cans of Tecate. Lilly sits at a table with a handsome dark-skinned man with slicked black hair. The man kisses her cheek and smiles, walking away. Lilly watches him. She wears a green hooded cape, with the hood obscuring her face. A martini is against her lips as she sips. The Beastie Boys' "Girls" follows Black Sabbath. George maneuvers his glass of cold bourbon through the crowd and leans against the radiator behind Lilly's seat. Lilly taps a Camel Wide unlit against the stem of her martini.

"Hey…"

Lilly's eyes turn up. She has been crying. She dabs at the tears with a bar napkin. "You drop in to shoot some stick, sailor?"

"Not really, just needed some time to myself… with a hundred strangers."

"And too much cigarette smoke," Lilly gives a small laugh. "I know the feeling. Sometimes it's easiest to be alone in a crowded room."

George nods towards the handsome dark-skinned man at the bar, "He a friend of yours?"

Lilly smiles, "Oh, that's Ralph. He's from Texas and apparently some kind of new dot-com millionaire… or on his way to become one." Off George's look, Lilly goes, "Now, George, don't think I'm involved with every handsome man in New York City… some of them are just good friends. Ralph is a sweetheart, besides he's married to a beautiful woman… although she might not be happy he is in this bar almost every night… at least every night I'm here, I see him…"

"You come here often?"

"I have a ritual on certain nights. To get my courage up," Lilly lifts the martini and takes a sip. "One dirty martini before I see Verreaux."

"Is this one of those affairs that isn't passionate?"

"Take it easy, sailor. I'm feeling down. My grandmother isn't doing well. I just called her… in the hospital." Lilly looks up, "Did you like Breakfast at Tiffany's?"

"I left when you started snoring."

"I do many things after a late night, but I do not snore. And you didn't answer my question."

"I have a confession to make," George says. "I've seen the movie before."

"You have?" Lilly asks, intrigued. "Why did you say you hadn't?"

"I didn't want to spoil the party."

"That's sweet, a bit strange, but sweet. You can be sweet, can't you, George?"

He pulls out his Zippo.

Lilly holds up her cigarette. "If you're nice, maybe we can keep each other company. I'm having a blue night."

"Sure," says George, "I mean, yes. I'm not having the best night either." He lights her cigarette. "You've been crying."

"I've said it before and I'll say it again… you are very quick, sailor. You notice things."

"I am a writer, at least in theory."

"You will be in practice too. That's why you moved upstairs."

"Like in the movie," George says, "but Paul Varjack had a collection of short stories published. I haven't done anything… at all."

"You will. It's in the cards."

"Good to know. I didn't expect to see you in this watering hole."

She holds up her martini, "The water is good. Besides this watering hole is the bar of the moment. Everyone is famous or has famous parents, which I guess is the same thing."

George points to the girl with the green hair, Cynthia, nodding beside a tough-looking girl with tattoo sleeves. "Are they famous?"

"No, they're junkies… not that the two don't go together on occasion."

George looks around the pub splashed with red light, which comes from the carnival glow of the jukebox. People are in jeans and ragged shorts, T-shirts and wife-beaters.

"Famous people, huh? You wouldn't know it."

"That's kind of the idea…" Lilly sniffles and wipes her nose. "You hick."

"Me? A hick?" George looks down at his blue linen jacket with the plumped pocket-square and the crease in his gray slacks.

"Why don't you have that rich boyfriend buy the bar for you? It would cut down on your tab."

"I don't have a tab. I'm strictly cash and carry. One dirty martini, then off to work."

"Who's the lucky guy tonight?"

"Remember, be nice." Lilly takes another sip. "But you might have a point, sailor, champagne in the morning, gin at night… what kind of girl am I?"

"Well-oiled. Did you sleep all afternoon?"

"I tried to reach my grandmother Lilly the First at home… but her friend answered the phone and said my grandmother was at the hospital. I called and left a message, but I haven't spoken to her yet. I want to get her some money… I'm very worried…" Lilly looks at her martini glass and swirls her speared olive. "I used to come to this place before, you know, it was popular. The bartender makes an excellent dirty martini." Lilly cuts her eyes at George. "You do know how to make a dirty martini, don't you?"

"Not really."

"Just drop in a touch of juice from the olive jar… always use a glass shaker and stir very gently. You must be gentle. You don't want to bruise the gin." Lilly offers George the martini. "Here…"

George sips the cold martini. "Tastes like the ocean."

"Salty and cold, like the Gulf of Mexico."

"Or the Pacific."

"I wonder if they taste the same, oceans?"

"Probably not to an expert."

"Like a surfer?" Lilly asks. "Why aren't you back on Stanton Street working on your masterpiece?"

"I'm stuck at the beginning," says George. "Besides Nicolette came to town, remember?"

Lilly looks around, eyes lighting up. "The older woman. How exciting. Do I see her? Is she in the loo?"

"No, she's not in the loo and you can't see her… unless you can see all the way uptown. Things didn't go well. Maybe you were right. Maybe I am scared of commitment."

"Put your tail between your legs and ran like a man?" Lilly taps her glass against George's and drains her martini. "Then you must come with me. It will cheer us both up." Lilly slips the empty martini glass into her shoulder bag. "Shhh," she says to George, not attempting to be quiet. "Don't say a word. Scout gets touchy when you lift his precious martini glasses." Lilly moves to the door, waving at Scout across the noisy bar. Scout holds up his fingers in a peace sign. Lilly holds her hand in the call me sign, right thumb and pinkie extended. Scout flips Lilly the finger and grins. "C'mon," Lilly says to George. "Verreaux appreciates punctuality, especially when I am hired to deliver gifts."

"Deliver gifts?"

"Oops! I let the cat out of the bag and you know what that means?"

"The mice get scared?"

"That could be true," considers Lilly, "I hadn't thought about the poor mice, but either way… now you're my accomplice."

"Who is Verreaux, another boyfriend?"

"No, sweet darling hick, George… Verreaux is one of my employers. He is one of the concerned men who help me keep the wolf from the door. Mr. Salvatore Kline, who you met, is my lover… and, I guess, you can be my boyfriend." Lilly takes George's hand as they walk down Avenue A. "I haven't had a boyfriend in quite a long time. I'm not even sure I remember what a boyfriend is supposed to do?"

"Really?" George walks fast to keep up with Lilly.

"Really," says Lilly. "C'mon, baby, and I don't mean maybe."

VERREAUX

Verreaux's apartment is on Avenue C. George and Lilly walk down 3rd Street. The neighborhood is a mix of slum and garden. Dave told him the neighborhood had been called "Alphabet City," but more and more, it became known as a part of the East Village. George and Lilly see women sit in the pillows of streetlamp light, with their legs crossed on milk crates or folding chairs sipping cans of soda and nibbling from bags of chips. Children ride bicycles and swing at rubber balls with stick-ball bats. Men watch TV on card tables, sipping bottles of malt beverage or beer in paper sacks.

Lilly pulls George into the alcove of Verreaux's building and traces her finger down the call buttons. She notices George's gold engagement ring is gone. Lilly squeezes his hand. "Oh, my… a real crisis."

"Maybe I'm not so safe now?"

"Maybe not." She pulls the green hood of her cape down to her shoulders, revealing her tousled hair. "Do you think you're dangerous, sailor?"

"I don't know what I am right now."

"Maybe you're a heart-breaker?"

"Maybe." George moves to kiss Lilly, but two of her fingers rise up and touch his lips, pushing him back. "You can be my boyfriend, but I didn't say you could kiss me."

The intercom hisses, "What?"

Lilly pushes "talk." "Hello, darlings! It's little Red Riding Hood." Lilly crosses her fingers at George and whispers, "This part is tricky… they can be touchy upstairs." The door buzzes. Lilly pushes the door, holding it open for George. "Game on!" She motions for George to go first, but Lilly places her hand on his chest and runs her fingers up the label of his linen jacket. "By the way, sailor, I don't kiss boys just because they got in a fight with their sugar momma."

"I don't care who you kiss."

He steps into the doorway. She grabs the back of his jacket, balling up a fist of linen. "I thought I told you to be nice?"

"I was being nice," he says, his back still to Lilly. "I just tried to kiss you. Where I come from, that's nice." George can't believe he made the move and failed.

Lilly presses her lips to George's ear. The door buzzes. "One more thing… I make the decisions here." She turns him and leans up, and with her hands on his neck, gives George a slow kiss. "There. See? I make the decisions, sailor. Not you, but me!"

George thinks of Nicolette, uptown at a party, flirting with a man, crying with a friend in a room or alone. George doesn't feel guilty. He knows he should, but he follows Lilly three flights up and Lilly knocks on a door that opens, revealing a muscular man in a Versace shirt and leather pants. The man stares at George. "What's this guy?"

"He's okay. He's a good friend of mine. Actually," Lilly says, "he's my boyfriend." She hooks her arm around George's waist.

"Against the wall," says Versace, turning George hands-flat against the concrete wall with cop confidence. He pats George down.

"George meet Bader. He's in the security business." Lilly smiles at Bader, who reaches up George's thigh. George jumps. "Bader is thorough."

"Wait," Bader closes the door. Seconds pass. Lilly says, "Fun, huh?" The door re-opens and Bader motions the two of them inside an apartment glowing with purple light and walls covered with figurines and wood prints. The collection goes floor to ceiling in no apparent order, covering every inch of apartment space. The artwork is in a thick layer of dust. A large Balinese table made of dark teak fills the main room of the railroad apartment. The table looks like a giant scrolled tablet. The windows of the apartment are covered in heavy drapes of black material that needs dusting or washing or replacing. The table has stacks of unopened mail, boxes of ammunition, empty Chinese take-out cartons, a handgun, a vase of very dead flowers rotting at the stalks and a large scimitar with ornate carvings on the handle of the sword. The room smells like the inside of a cardboard box left in the rain. Lilly runs her finger on a dusty, wood figurine of the Bali earth-spirit, Bhuta. The figurine is a drum. Lilly removes what appears to be the earth spirit's extended penis and raps it against the figurine. "Yvan," Lilly suggests to the man standing in the center of the apartment, "I still think a maid would be a good idea."

The man wears a white suit with an interlocking Gucci pattern that looks vaguely familiar to George. Did George see this guy at the nightclub?

Yvan Tait says, "Yes, Lilly, I agree with you, however, I think we both know that Verreaux is a man of rituals and habits. He prefers that nothing be touched."

Tait looks at George. "I'm afraid this can't be your wealthy lover, Mr. Kline? Yet, you told Bader this was your boyfriend?"

"Yes, Yvan, it can be confusing. Please meet George Nichols from Los Angeles. George, this is Yvan. He owns one of the most chic galleries in SoHo. Yvan is also an amateur shutterbug... and one of my biggest fans."

Tait's eyes are on Lilly as he talks to George, "Lilly could make quite a bit of money if she would let me take a few photographs. She is well-known to certain people and considered..." Tait pauses, watching Lilly watch him, "a rare creature."

"How flattering," Lilly looks around the room.

"Some women have a special beauty men desire," Yvan continues, "Lilly has this quality. Lilly is a fantasy that won't go away."

George wants to smack Tait in his face.

"You understand, George," Tait's eyes remain on Lilly. "*Fetish* is a word that opens up so many possibilities... but one needs the right fetish model."

"Yvan—" Lilly waves him off, "enough about this subject. George isn't interested."

"I'm sure George is interested," Tait steps close to Lilly. "All men are interested."

"How nice for them," says Lilly, "aren't there magazines for that sort of thing?"

"There are magazines for everything, Lilly; however, this is not about magazines. This is about you. I have men on a list who have expressed interest."

"Yes," says Lilly, "any interest those gentlemen have in me is entirely their own problem."

"You are good with most customers, Lilly. Some of these customers would like a private memento for their private reflection."

"Yvan, you know I don't model anymore... and I particularly don't plan to work au naturel."

"That's a shame," says Tait. "Well, if anything encourages you to reconsider..."

Adrenaline slams the roots of George's eyes. He wants to punch out this jerk in the white suit.

Tait tells Lilly, "You should drop by the gallery. We have a very interesting show at the moment, a new series by Alexis Rockman."

"That sounds wonderful," Lilly smiles. "I know Alexis."

"We really need to spend more time together, Lilly. You always cheer me up... but a Leonard Karlson—"

Bader opens the door to the back room. "Okay, Mr. Tait," he motions for Yvan to enter the back room.

"Yes," says Lilly to Tait as he walks past her. "Lenny..."

Lilly and George wait to enter the back room. Lilly whispers to George, "Don't let Tait rattle you."

"What's going on here?" George asks.

"I run errands certain evenings for Verreaux. I deliver packages. And there's Tait too. We have an arrangement. These gentlemen help keep the wolf from my door."

"It must be one hungry wolf."

Bader returns and motions for them to enter the darkened bedroom. It takes a moment for George's eyes to adjust to the fluttering candles, a fireplace crackling in the May heat, air-conditioners humming behind the black curtains. A large man sits in a high-back chair carved from teak. The room has a church pew which faces the large man. The large man wears black silk pajamas and writes in what looks like a diary. "You're one hour late."

"My apologies." Lilly curtsies, turning on her bright smile. "George Nichols, meet my benefactor, Mr. Verreaux."

Verreaux says, "Lilly, what is the first rule of assisting me with deliveries?"

Lilly, reciting like a school girl, "If you feel the heat, I get burned."

"Exactly." Verreaux places the leather-bound book down and hefts himself to his feet. He is one of those very large men with a body that merges fat with muscle. He slumps to the padlocked ammunition box. George wonders if the man's heart will explode or if his knees will buckle or if he will lift the large box in some kind of feat of Herculean strength. Verreaux removes a key from a chain around his neck and unlocks the padlock, removing five gift-wrapped packages about seven-by-seven inches and hands the stack to Lilly, who secures the boxes in her leather shoulder bag. Verreaux hands Lilly a manila envelope, "List of addresses, taxi fare, individual envelopes for compensation due me." Verreaux says, with his silk black pajamas tight on his wide shoulders but ballooned at the heavy round weight of his stomach. "Remember the restrictions, Lilly."

"No guests during delivery. Yes, I know the rules. I just asked George to escort me over here… Avenue C, you know. I get spooked."

Verreaux's lips pull up in a chuckle. "I don't think you get spooked easy, Lee Ann, but okay."

"I hate to interrupt," Tait says. Verreaux looks at Tait.

"I arranged a very important evening for a man named Karlson. It appears Lilly made the evening less than memorable."

"Really," says Lilly, glancing at Verreaux, "can't we discuss this later, Yvan? Maybe you can put Leonard on your list for buying future mementos?"

"Charming, Lilly," Tait says, "sarcasm under pressure, admirable, but not a real solution. This debt has to be resolved. I made that arrangement as a favor to you as well as Karlson. This behavior will hurt my other business relationships."

"Oh, Yvan, don't be so dramatic. I promise to visit the gallery and we will talk. Leonard is a sweetheart. I'm sure he'll understand. I just had a terrible migraine. I find my migraines embarrassing for everyone involved, so I ran home."

Yvan nods, "I've heard about your migraines, Lilly. A few times."

THREE SHAKES

Lilly flags a taxi on Houston, with the bag of gifts slung over her shoulder and her hood and cape cloaking her. "Wait for me at the Diamond. I'll be back in three shakes of a lamb's tail."

It feels like a long time ago that George told Nicki he didn't want to get married. He should just walk back to Dave's apartment and sleep.

"Maybe four shakes," Lilly says with her hand on the taxi door.

"Make it two," says George, but he won't go back to Dave's right now. George is too awake; the East Village is busy with crowded restaurants and bars. The sidewalks are full of people. With one foot in the taxi, Lilly asks, "Are you okay?"

"Does Salvatore know about all this?" George points to the leather shoulder bag filled with the wrapped gifts. "The gifts... or whatever they are?"

"I don't think Salvatore would understand, but you understand, don't you, George?"

"Yeah, sure... yes, I understand. Just be careful."

"Careful?" Lilly laughs, "that's no fun. Three shakes, baby. See you at the Diamond. Ciao!"
Lilly closes the taxi door and watches George through the window as the taxi drives off.

George chain smokes as he leans against the locked gate pulled down at the Diamond, careful that his blue linen jacket isn't smudged with grime. George watches the quiet sidewalks. Lilly turns the corner and struts up to him, opening her empty bag. "All gone," Lilly loops her arm in George's arm. "That wasn't so bad, was it?"

"You're not a very fast lamb. Lucky for me that bartender tossed a few on the house."

"Scout is a good guy," says Lilly. "He knows how to keep the joint jumping." She looks at the metal grate of the locked Diamond. "Or maybe not?"

"It was dead," says George, "he shut early."

"Shut early?," says Lilly. "That doesn't sound like Scout. He is a full-shift kind of guy, holding down the fort until sunrise." Lilly pulls out her pack of Camel Wides, "But he's been acting brave. The singer in his band died. OD'd. Scout's best friend. Billy. Maybe it's getting to him."

"Oh well," Lilly takes George's arm. "We can both use a break from the hooch. Let's walk."
Lilly leads him down East 6th Street.

"Is this how you pay your bills? Keep that wolf away?"

"Don't worry about me. Let's enjoy the night. I love this time." Lilly looks up at the faint starlight in the black sky as a gray van rolls toward them. A man in a hooded sweatshirt jumps out of the side of the van and swings a net attached to a long handle, sweeping up a pigeon who is interrupted from nipping at a pool of vomit on the sidewalk. The rest of the pigeons scatter. The man grins at Lilly and George, his mouth black from missing teeth. He disappears into the van.

"Daddy used to call that poaching," says Lilly. "Just don't order anything called 'quail' or 'squab,' unless you know the chef."

"Good idea. How about some breakfast?"

"My treat," Lilly points toward a Polish diner, "I'm flush." Lilly pulls a white envelope out of her bag, removing a twenty dollar bill from a wad of cash. A homeless woman sleeps on a strip of cardboard stretched over a grate. Her body is curled beside an empty child's stroller packed with garbage bags stuffed with clothes. Lilly tucks the twenty in the pocket of the woman's coat. The woman opens her eyes, blinking. Lilly squeezes the toe of the woman's sneaker, "Check your pocket, honey." The woman stares at Lilly, still dreaming, eyes open. She reaches for the pocket and pulls out the twenty dollar bill. Lilly leans against George as they walk away, "That's rough duty, sailor. Real rough duty."

Lilly takes the last bite of her omelet. George takes his clean spoon and pushes some of the home fries on Lilly's plate toward her fork.

Lilly pushes the potatoes back with her finger.

"Who's Verreaux?"

"An old friend from New Orleans. I met him when I was staying with Lilly the First, years ago. Verreaux has always been stand-up. Keeps me in the chips."

"What's in those packages?" asks George. An exhausted waitress pours coffee as the window of the diner catches silver shards of taxi headlights. The taxis move as slivers of gray around the black buildings.

"Contraband, I suppose. I deliver the gifts to people around the city, sometimes at hotels in the bar or lobby, sometimes at apartments. Verreaux provides me with an envelope for each package. I return what the people put in the envelopes. The less I know, the better. Verreaux pays me." Lilly wipes her hands, "All clean. It certainly beats dinner with an aggressive gentleman caller."

"And Tait?"

"It appears I owe Yvan a marker."

"A marker? Are you some kind of escort?"

"Tait knows the game. He's just annoyed I didn't give more than was promised to some guy. I mean, rules are rules. There are limits to the arrangement."

"Karlson," says George. "Was he one of these arrangements?"

Lilly sips her coffee.

"What if someone knew what you were carrying in those gifts and jumped you?"

"It's safe. I take a taxi ride or three, say polite hellos to a few strangers. I'm like that parakeet. I can fly away whenever I want. Verreaux sometimes uses boys that run around on bicycles with beepers… can you imagine me riding around on a bicycle in this get-up? I would look like the Wicked Witch of the North." Lilly stares out the diner window at the quiet city. "You know all about the big, bad wolf, George. You have your sugar momma… or had. I have my arrangements too. Verreaux has done his part, kept up his end of the deal. Without him, I don't know where I'd be right now. I'm a bad waitress, George… and I was a failure in the fashion game." Lilly places her hand on George's. "It's easy money. Don't worry…"

"What if you get busted?"

"Everything interesting in life requires risk." She takes a bite of her home fries. "Not bad… sort of fortifying. Have you ever had a pirozhki? They are quite delicious." George shakes his head. "Do you think, speaking of risk, I should consider taking Tait up on his photography offer?"

"Are you kidding?"

"Just thinking…"

"Does escort mean you're a hooker?"

She gives him a look. "I'm paid to go to parties. I'm paid to make men look good and feel good, but I'm not paid to make them feel that good."

"And what happens if you actually like the man? What if you want something more than money?"

"For a hick, I would still think you were more savvy, George. Liking men when you're an escort doesn't happen. C'mon, let's go. I want to show you something…"

Lilly removes her wallet, reaching for money. Her driver's license hits the diner table. Lilly reaches for it, but George picks it up. "Nice photo. Looks like a magazine cover."

"Lucky day," she says. "Hand it over."

George reads, "Hair, brown… okay, although brown doesn't capture it…. Height, weight, okay… ," George holds up the license.

Lilly grabs for it.

"Name," reads George.

Lilly grabs the license, puts it in her wallet. "Find out anything new, gumshoe?"

"Lee Ann Boxner?"

"A name's just a name," Lilly says. "That's the one my mother gave me after my daddy ran off."

"I really can't see you as a Lee Ann."

Lilly takes him by the sleeve of his linen jacket. "Let's blow this pop stand."

The night sky hums, turning toward dawn. Lilly and George are perched high on the Williamsburg Bridge, sipping coffee and gazing at the silvering East River. Manhattan is rolled out in blocks of stacked windows and brick and steel, glowing roofs, charcoal bridges—one white helicopter pierces the haze at the perimeter of the Bronx. George takes another bite of the pirozhki. "These are really good."

"They sure are, but kind of heavy for a girl keeping an eye on her figure."

"I wouldn't worry about your figure. Whatever you're doing works."

"Did Scout slip something in your drink? Maybe it's what happened uptown with what's-her-name?"

He nods at the grid of streets. "Maybe it's just New York?"

"Or the whiskey…"

"I'm not usually up all night in L.A., but I feel great." He finishes the pirozhki, folds the white wrapping paper and places the wrapper in his jacket pocket.

"We better get you home," she says. "You need some rest so you can finish your masterpiece."

"Or start it."

Lilly removes the martini glass from her bag and holds it up so he can look through the glass at the distant Empire State Building.

"What's with stealing martini glasses?"

"I mark each night of work."

They sit on the bridge lattice, high above the city.

"My grandfather used to drink martinis," Lilly says. "My mother never approved of cocktails, but one night I ran through the kitchen and hit the table and broke his favorite martini glass. *Kerblammie!*" Lilly clicks her finger nail against the martini glass. *"Kapow!"*

"You've got extras now. In case anyone gets thirsty."

"Grandpa Vida didn't care about the stupid glass, but my mother hit me with a magazine. She rolled the magazine up and hit me on the nose like I was a dog. My grandfather tried to stop her. He pulled me away, but my mother kept swinging at me…"

"I'm sorry."

"Don't be," Lilly looks at the traffic honking below them on the bridge, sunlight warming their faces. "I know it's a bit silly, sailor, but it helps when I put a glass on that shelf. My grandfather took me out for ice cream. Pistachio, I think it was… I don't really remember, but I did like pistachio. It sounded very adult to me and had those nuts."

"Pistachios?"

She laughs, "Yeah, those are the ones."

George lights her cigarette. Lilly takes a long drag, exhales. "Families will fuck you up." Lilly clicks the heels of her boots. "Pistachio ice cream always seemed like something you would serve in a silver bowl at an elegant dinner party. Most kids liked chocolate or strawberry, but I wanted to grow up and wear fancy clothes, order my shoes in the mail from Paris."

George points at Lilly's boots.

"I got these at a boutique on Spring Street. They're Italian. Growing up, my mom bought my shoes at Sears. You didn't find French or Italian shoes in Paineville."

"Paineville? Squirrel Junction?" George takes a hit from his cigarette. "You just make this stuff up, right?"

"I guess you could say I made up Squirrel Junction, but it was good make-believe. Squirrel Junction was filled with all the things Paineville didn't have. And Paineville didn't have much. Paineville…" Lilly swirls her cigarette and the white smoke sways against the backdrop of Manhattan. "Paineville was as real as it gets, sailor. Paineville was rough duty."

"It doesn't sound like a fun place, although I'm from Studio City… maybe not the greatest name, depending on your taste."

"Studio City sounds jazzy. Paineville was named after Thomas Paine. At Paineville High School, we were called the 'Pamphleteers.'"

"What's a Pamphleteer?"

"A guy in a funny hat with a feather pen," says Lilly. "It rhymed with cheer."

"Were you a cheerleader?"

"No, I wasn't popular enough to be a cheerleader. Cheerleaders didn't have horrible acne. Cheerleaders had pretty clothes. I practiced with the baton because I thought I might be a baton girl, but my mother closed the cage on her batony little bird. Didn't want me to fly away off the football field, I guess."

"Your mom doesn't sound like a great parent."

"She used to hide the shampoo and hair conditioner from me when she said I was ungrateful. She hit me once in junior high because a friend let me try on lipstick."

"What did your friends say?"

"My mother didn't let me have friends. She didn't let people come over to our house. No," Lilly makes a smile, "I can't say I had much of a social life."

"You're making up for it now." George tries to smile, but can't, stuck with the sad image of a young Lee Ann Boxner, throwing her baton, alone in the backyard of a grim house. "If the last forty-eight hours are an example, you're a social girl."

"I don't think you can really make up for things that are gone, but at least I can fly away, right? I could fly right off this bridge and no one could stop me."

"I'd try to stop you."

"You could try, sailor, but that doesn't mean you could do it." Lilly tosses the cigarette at the dawn-wrinkled East River.

George watches Lee Ann Boxner in her square of fenced yard. Lee Ann's feet are tucked beneath her skirt, sitting in the dirt. She taps her baton against her knees. George watches Lee Ann's mother roll up a magazine and smack Lee Ann on the nose in front of her grandfather. "Being a Pamphleteer doesn't sound like much fun."

"I listened to records and watched TV. I was a loner. I still am... in some ways." Lilly looks at George and forces a smile, "It's getting time to send in the clowns, as my grandmother would say."

"Tell me about modeling."

"You are a Chatty Cathy. How did you know about that? Oh, Mick, of course. I bet he told you that silly story about me walking on the beach in Alabama? I'm better known in some circles for licking ice cream off my arm than anything I did in the industry... which is probably a good thing."

"Was it?"

"Mick would be the one to know," Lilly says, "but all I did as a model was make people mad. C'mon, we'll talk as we move." Lilly climbs down the lattice, careful in her green cape and boots with her bag over her shoulder. "Modeling sounded exciting," she says as they walk back on the bridge toward Delancey Street, "at least until I did some of it."

"So you deliver contraband for Verreaux?"

"It's how I fill the coffee can."

"What?"

"Nothing," she takes his hand. "Just walk with me."

"Can Salvatore help you with your grandmother?"

"I might ask Sal, if I have to ask him, but it's different once you've slept with a man. I've done a few things I'm not proud of, but I've never slept with a man for his money."

George isn't sure he believes her.

"Technically," Lilly adds. "Never."

"Technically?"

"Do you sleep with what's-her-name for her money?"

"No."

"But it doesn't hurt that she has the money. You didn't throw her money out the window or burn the money or insist that she never spend the money on you, right?"

"I get your point. You're telling me you never accept money in exchange for sex?"

"I'm telling you a lot of things. I'm not even sure I know what they all are, sailor, just that I care about Salvatore and I care about Lillian the First and then there's this thing we all call 'money.'"

"Which you don't care about?"

"Not really... but I need it. We all need it."

"Why do you like Salvatore Kline?"

"He's calm and confident."

"That could be the money."

"Money's never bad, George, but I doubt you like what's-her-name just because she has some bonus spending cash? And Salvatore is a beautiful man, which is nice. He is just physically gorgeous." Lilly puts her arm on George's arm, "I can say that to you, sailor, because you are quite handsome yourself."

"Are you in love with Salvatore?" They walk into the Lower East Side's narrow grid of streets, past discount emporiums for household products, clothing, shoes, activated alarms, metal grates pulled shut.

"What happened with your fiancée?"

"Good question, but you didn't answer mine."

"You're right, and no one says I have to."

They walk up Essex. George says, "I think I don't want to get married." They cross Rivington. Lilly watches George. George says, "In fact, I know I don't want to get married. That's what happened with my fiancée."

"Maybe you should get married?" Lilly stops on the corner. "She sounds like a great catch."

"Maybe that's why I don't want to. It feels like I'm making a good deal on a car. It doesn't feel like love."

"What does love feel like for you?"

"It doesn't feel like a good deal on a car. At least I hope not."

"And it doesn't feel like being inside a big diamond," Lilly adds, "unless you have a hammock... and?"

"A unicorn," George says. "But I was just giving you a hard time. If you wake up in a big diamond and the world stands still... then good for you."

They walk up Ludlow to Stanton and take a left past the hat shop. "End of the road," says Lilly as George digs in his slacks for his key. Lilly squeezes his arm. "I hope that damn bird is gone." George follows Lilly to her door, puts his hand under her cloak and grabs her arm, turning her to face him.

Her eyes flash. "What do you think you're doing, mister?"

He should pull her close and kiss her.

"Are you an aggressive gentleman caller?" Lilly holds a half-smile, eyeing George. "Maybe you aren't the heart-breaker... maybe you're the heart-broken?"

George lets go of Lilly's arm. He wants to reach up and touch her hair, but places his hand in his pocket, jingling his door keys, the other useless hand is in the other pocket of his gray slacks. "Maybe it's something else?" They walk up the steps to Lilly's apartment door.

Lilly opens the door and looks back at George. "I warned you about that, sailor." The parakeet chirps. Lilly sighs, "Damn it..."

"Warned me about what?"

"About romance," Lilly leans against the door jamb, yawning, "I warned you romance is dangerous... and it doesn't pay the bills." Lilly reaches over and straightens George's shirt collar under his jacket. "You look nice and you still have a fiancée somewhere uptown. Go sleep. You have work in the morning."

"In the morning?" Morning light warms Lilly's windows. George leans against the door-jamb, tired, but wide awake.

"You know what I mean," Lilly says. She steps inside and closes the door.

George is alone in the hallway as the bolt on Lilly's front door locks. George schleps up one flight of stairs and unlocks his apartment door. He steps inside and trips on the white puppy. George stumbles forward, almost falling, feet tangled in the remains of some cloth. The puppy sits on the chewed corpse of George's houndstooth sport coat. George digs a can of dog food off the wire rack of canned and boxed goods he purchased downstairs at the bodega. George dumps the can into an enamel cereal bowl and places the bowl beside the hungry puppy. The puppy's tail wiggles as it tucks into breakfast. George cleans up the shit and piss. He washes his hands and looks at his typewriter and the stack of blank pages. George picks up the photograph of his father on the hood of a military jeep in Vietnam. His father might have chased women—George didn't know. His father might have stayed up all night, after drinking whiskey and talking to pretty girls that had no direction and were obviously trouble. George's father might have even broken engagements with pretty women that loved him. George didn't know much about his father, except that his father died young doing something he believed in—at least that's what George's mother had told George. According to George's mother and his grandparents, George's dad was a man that gave his life up for his profession as a journalist.

If a piece of shrapnel took out George right now, or tomorrow… or two weeks or three years from now, what would have been his purpose? What does he care about? George asks himself, *When is one time that you didn't quit? Name one time you stuck it out for something you believed in?*

OLD & ALONE

Day three in New York City: George is awake. George mops up another puddle of puppy urine, washes his hands and walks up Ludlow Street to Avenue A to the magazine shop, where he buys a copy of *Surfer*. He walks back to Stanton Street from Hot Bagels on Houston with a Gatorade, a pirozhki, the *New York Post, Surfer* and a black coffee, which stains the brown paper sack that holds everything.

It is late-afternoon. George has bed-head and red eyes. He wears a brown polo shirt, 501s and his tan Hush Puppies. Juggling his purchases, George turns the corner on Stanton and walks right into Salvatore Kline, who wears a crisp white shirt, untucked, and linen shorts and complex sandals that look European. Kline's muscular, tan arm cradle the pretty shoulders of Lilly, who is in a pale salmon sleeveless sweater and black Capris. Her big sunglasses reflect George's warped face and his scrawl of hair. "Hello, George. Beautiful afternoon, isn't it?"

George can't believe this is the same woman that stood with him in the hallway not so many hours ago. Lilly doesn't just look rested, Lilly appears to be returning from a spa. Lilly runs her fingers along Salvatore's neck, and Salvatore gives her a private smile. It is clear to George that this man and this woman have recently completed an incredible session of sexual athletics. "You are the surf writer?" Salvatore asks. George adjusts his grip on the brown sack.

Lilly tilts down her sunglasses and winks at George, "Just wake up, sailor?"

"Yes," says George. "I had a big night touring the neighborhood."

"That must have been interesting." she says. "A late-night tour?"

"Very late. And you?"

Lilly peers over her sunglasses into the paper sack, "Let me guess? Pirozhki?"

"Yes," says George. Salvatore watches, focused, attentive. "How'd you know?"

"I have a man on the inside," Lilly smiles.

"A good man?"

"The best," says Lilly. "How's the project?" Lilly taps the *Surfer*. "Research?"

George nods.

"Yes?" asks Salvatore. "Are you making progress?"

"Yes," George says. "I've been wrapping up some of the initial steps in my process."

George wonders why he chooses the word *wrapping* and not *initiating* or *beginning* or *considering*? *Wrapping* connotes finishing, and it should be clear, certainly to Lilly if not to Salvatore, that George was not only not finishing something, he hadn't started anything either. Of course, George reasoned, he could be in the middle of something, what with his hair sticking straight up. He could be in the middle of something more complicated than just waking up. But he wasn't. And as for mentioning the initial steps of his process, George could tell from Lilly's smile that she knew he was full of it, but she was entertained.

"Remember," says Lilly, "Hot-rods."

"And teeny-boppers," George adds.

Salvatore says, "We should catch a taxi, Lilly, or we will be late."

"Excellent," says George, for no reason.

"Enjoy your pirozhki," Lilly says. "And I'm glad that tour went well." She pats Salvatore on his butt. "Taxi it is, Mr. Kline."

The two lovers stroll toward Houston and the flash of yellow cabs. George crosses the street toward 101 Stanton where Lupe's brother, Ricky, sits on the curb, holding a headless teddy bear. Ricky wears a Hulk T-shirt, with the green superhero creature flexing his muscles. Lupe walks over and sits next to Ricky, sees George and waves. "Hey, mujeriego!"

"What are you guys doing?"

Lupe points to a Rottweiler leashed to a parking meter. "That dog ate Ricky's bear."

George pats Ricky on the shoulder. "Buck up. The bear will be all right. He looks real strong."

Ricky stares at George. The teddy bear in his arms doesn't have a head. Ricky is troubled by a world where adults can't tell the difference between a normal teddy bear and a teddy bear without a head. Ricky begins to cry. Lupe takes the remains of the bear and rests it on the curb. "The bear is gone, Enrique. Stop crying and act like a man."

Ricky sniffles, puffs out his chest. "I'm the Hulk."

George goes into the bodega and walks back out with three frozen-fruit ice cream bars. "Who likes peach?"

Ricky raises his hand.

"And pineapple?"

"I like pineapple," says Lupe.

"Lucky guess." George holds out the frozen fruit. "I'll try the coconut."

Ricky, Lupe and George sit on the curb, licking their treats. Lupe looks in George's paper bag. "What about that stuff? Will it get cold?"

George shrugs.

"Sometimes," Lupe says, "you're weird."

"Yes," says George. "Most adults are weird sometimes, aren't they?"

Lupe nods, "Yes… but you're more weird."

George nods. "You're probably right."

A yellow taxi stops at the corner of Stanton and Orchard beside a rack of hanging leather jackets on the sidewalk. The taxi door opens and George watches Nicki step out of the taxi, straighten her skirt, brush back her hair and look at her Palm Pilot, with the sunlight glinting off her oval, pink sunglasses.

George nudges Lupe with his elbow. Nicki hasn't recognized him, but struts down the block in his direction.

The men sitting at the card table in front of Arlene's Grocery watch Nicolette strut.

"That's my fiancée," George says to Lupe and Ricky.

"She gave you the gold ring?" Lupe looks on George's hand. No ring.

"And took it back." George explains, "I haven't been nice."

"You were bad," Ricky states. The headless teddy bear is in the orange N.Y.C. trash receptacle.

"Here we go," George says.

"She's beautiful," says Lupe, "but I think you like Lilly."

"Lilly has a boyfriend," George says. Nicki's pink, oval sunglasses flash along the addresses then turn toward the men at the card tables. Their heads dip away as Nicki struts past. Her pink, oval sunglasses target Lupe, Enrique… George.

Lupe says, "I still think you like Lilly better."

George laughs for the last time that day, "What do you know? You're not even eleven years old."

Nicki didn't wait for George to apologize or fix things. She threw the gold ring at him, told him to keep it and buy typewriter ribbons. Then she told him to forget that since he didn't even write. George was going to die old and alone in a one room apartment and would always regret losing Nicolette. Nicki stood in the hallway with tears in her eyes after her anger passed. She asked George if he had fucked some other girl. George said he hadn't. In the time he had been with Nicki, he had been loyal to her. It felt good to say this to Nicki, but George knew it wasn't completely true. If he was loyal, he would still want to marry her. His loyalty shifted when Lilly opened her apartment door in her tuxedo shirt and blue sleeping mask. George watched Nicki cross Stanton Street, heading for a taxi. The engagement was over.

THE BARGAIN DISTRICT

"Have you seen the Bargain District?" Lilly asks George, motioning toward Orchard Street halfway down the block from their apartment building. "T-shirts, socks, plastic toy motorcycles, battery-powered frogmen, you name it." She points to the northwest corner, where Nicki's taxi let her out in front of a rack of leather jackets. There are more leather jackets hanging from a line strung across the entrance. "Their specialty," Lilly says, "seems to be black jackets with padded shoulders to give you that special charm of a Russian gangster." Lilly leans against George, motioning back to Arlene's Grocery under their building, the inside of the bodega is gutted in a construction project that seems to have happened overnight to George. "Heard they're turning that into a club of some kind… Salvatore says this whole area is being bought up for clubs, restaurants. It will be snazzy, George… but Sal says it won't ever be the same."

George watches the streets shimmer in the heat. Awnings and buildings cast long shadows on the sidewalk. The shade is popular real estate. Locals linger and lean, watching the heat like fisherman watch a river.

"It's beautiful, isn't it?" Lilly asks.

George says, "It is. I'm glad to be standing here…"

"If we'd run into each other next year, sailor…" Lilly shrugs. "Everything changes."

George points to the locket on her neck above the spray of freckles. Lilly's summer dress reveals the frail bands of pink her cinnamon bra straps cut against her soft skin. Lilly leans to pull the heel of her white sock up in her green sneaker.

"You," George points to her locket, "ever take that off?"

"Rarely. You know, Lilly the First, and all that."

Lilly nods across the street to a small storefront with a rack of clothes on the sidewalk. Many of the stores have ancient signs with Polish or Russian surnames in script, although the proprietors seem to be either Asian or Latino. This store has a new neon sign in glowing script in the window: *Benigno's*. In the window a male mannequin wears a vintage suit from the 1970s. Next to him, a female mannequin is wearing an exotic dress from India. A tall Dominican man chews a toothpick, wearing a brown felt fedora. His blue slacks are creased, flared. He wears a purple vintage poly-blend polo shirt with a coronet over the right chest pocket. He stands next to a shorter Italian man in a peach suit with a yellow riding cap, brown boots, a red shirt and a gold necktie. The Italian man has a pencil-thin mustache and twirls a pocket watch. George looks up and down Orchard Street, wondering if he just walked on to the back lot at Universal. Extras, he thinks. Everyone in New York looks like an extra.

"I imagine it's similar to your typewriter," Lilly explains, long after George forgot the question. They stand on the east side corner of Orchard as a flat-bed truck rumbles past. Lilly touches the silver locket on her neck. "This," she says, reminding George of his question. George eyes the strap of cinnamon lingerie, the brassiere strap under Lilly's slippery dress of chiffon and shadow.

"You know," Lilly says, "like your typewriter—sentimental, but important." She pauses. "Although, you would look silly with a typewriter hanging around your neck."

Lilly's dress is a patchwork of burgundy squares that fade to rose at the waist. The heat reminds him of Mick's story of seeing Lilly on the beach, licking ice cream off her arm. George concentrates on not thinking about Lilly and how he would like to lift up the loose dress and watch her stand in her panties, her bare legs, her green sneakers, protected from public view by the racks of shirts and slacks on sidewalk display.

"Don't be sad," Lilly says to George as she waves to the tall Dominican man. "I didn't mean to make you sad by talking about your typewriter... and let's not even mention what's-her-name, otherwise we'll have to send in the clowns."

"As your grandmother would say."

"Exactly."

George watches Lilly shade her eyes, smiling at him. Funny how serious thoughts slip away when a beautiful girl catches sunlight on her dress.

"My typewriter doesn't make me sad."

"I didn't want to get you thinking your father and that city of Palm Tree."

"Quảng Trị," corrects George.

"Because," Lilly says, "if you're sad, you will write a sad surfing movie. I just know it, and I don't imagine they do well, sad surfing movies."

"I wouldn't think so, but you never know," says George. Sunlight flutters light in the gap between Lilly's slender thighs as she walks to the sidewalk.

"Particularly in Australia," she says over her shoulder.

"Right," George says. "They don't get sad in Australia?"

"Not if our friend Mick is an example of the men-folk." Lilly turns. "This is the start of your new future, George, and you must be happy today of all days. Whatever it takes."

"Why is my happiness so important?"

"Because," Lilly explains. "If you don't write this romantic surfing story... who will?"

"It could be a great loss."

"That's the spirit, sailor!" Lilly disappears into the racks of shirts and slacks.

"Bennie!" Lilly pops up on the stairs in front of the storefront and jumps into the arms of the tall Dominican. "Benigno!"

He holds her off the ground as Lilly snatches his fedora.

"Hey, give that back, chica." He puts her down. "You know Short Frank?" he nods to the man beside him.

"Sure I do." Lilly pops the hat on her head and spins, twirling her dress as it spins at her thighs. "How much for le chapeau?"

Bennie grabs the hat and makes a half-hearted slap in the direction of Lilly's butt as she skips away. "Ouch," she laughs. "Watch it, big fella!"

"The hat's not for sale." Bennie takes her hand and Lilly smiles at him. "Oye mami!" says Bennie, "Qué chula tu estés!"

George steps from the racks of clothes.

Bennie unfolds a turtleneck knit dress, with thin bands of black and white around each wrist and the waist. "This dress… baby?"

Lilly takes the dress, "Done deal, Bennie, if it fits." Lilly holds it up and looks down at the dress, "Nice… but we need to cheer George up today." She nods serious, "His woman stuck a dagger in his heart."

The two men look at George. Bennie says, "That shit is fucked up."

"It was my own fault, really," George says. Bennie and Short Frank shift on their chairs, not comfortable with the confessional tone.

"That," says Lilly, "is poppycock." Bennie and Short Frank sip green bottles of Presidente beer. "Poppy—," Lilly repeats. "It might not translate…"

"This chica," Bennie laughs, "is like a movie star every day, right?"

Short Frank nods, "I just listen." He adjusts his tie. "Pretty lady like her can use any words she wants."

"Anyway," Lilly says, "George's day today is going to be a great, great day. We're shopping, right, George?" Lilly turns her back before George gets to answer. Lilly drags a hanger with a pair of peg-leg men's slacks in black. "Here you go, George… Beatles pants." Thumbing the racks, she pulls down a black turtleneck, "Cashmere," she says to herself, running a finger along the back. "This isn't dead-stock, Benigno. This piece has a moth hole."

"They just did a bad job of storage," Bennie explains.

Lilly tosses the sweater to George, "You can wear a black T-shirt underneath…" Lilly points to the back of the store, where a full-length mirror is attached to the wall, particle board hangs from two pieces of pipe drilled into the wall and a six-foot rectangle of cloth hangs down flag-wide, forming a makeshift, half-private dressing space. "Try it on, sailor."

George pulls the slacks on over his boxers, clipping the inner waist clip and zipping it up. He tugs the sweater over his shoulders. Lilly's voice is behind the curtain. Lilly's reflection is in the mirror, unblocked from view, "Turn up the radio, Bennie." The radio goes into loud trumpets. Lilly tosses George a lime polyester jacket with a Western yoke and flapped front pockets. George catches the jacket. Lilly looks at him in his turtleneck and slacks, "George, you are a catch." She holds up a polyester suit from the 1970s, "What about this one, Shaft?"

George holds the door of the Mexican restaurant, El Sombrero, open for Lilly, the fluttering pure sheen of air-conditioned air slipping behind them as they step onto Ludlow Street, each holding a styrofoam cup with a lid and a plastic straw filled with tequila-fueled slushy. The cement heat claws up the bells of his 1970s polyester suit, boiling the soles of his Hush Puppies. His sunglasses are as rosy as the sting of the margarita in the illegal to-go cup that hits his tongue.

"Yum!" Lilly says with a big flash of her smile. She shades her eyes and points toward Houston Street. "Off we go, sailor."

"Where?" George feels the gentle buzz. The puppy will be okay. He will clean up the mess when he gets back and then take her for a walk. He can't say no to Lilly. Today is about George having a great day. Lilly said it herself and George isn't going to argue. George needs a great day. Lilly is right. This will help him with his project.

New York City shines beyond his rose-tinted shades.

"Tiffany's, of course," says Lilly. She struts up the street, hips swinging, snapping her fingers, perched on her platform heels.

Tiffany's? George looks down at the cuffs of his bells, bagging to the cement. He takes a margarita gurgle. "Tiffany's?" he asks out loud. Lilly spins, mid-strut, arms akimbo. "But first you're going to buy me a plastic ring, baby, like in the movie."

"From a Cracker Jack box?"

"I don't know how you're going to get my plastic ring, you cracker," Lilly says, "all I know is we're going to get it engraved at Tiffany's, so you better find me one…"

"Or what?"

Lilly peers over her sunglasses, "Don't test me, sailor."

"Hey," says George, the traffic on Houston Street pink from his sunglasses. "Remember, I'm the pimp…"

"I'm just saying… ," Lilly smiles, "you can slap me around, baby, and teach me who's my daddy… but don't test me 'cause this baby's got back." Lilly turns and struts up Ludlow, waving her hand at George.

"You look ridiculous," George yells, but he follows her. He's in a great mood, having a great day and slurping on his margarita dressed like… a white guy in a seventies pimp suit.

TIFFANY'S

The fountain near the bandshell in Central Park gurgles and splashes. The spouting water is cut by the laughter of children and the shelling honks of distant traffic. A Hasidic man and woman scrape past, roller blading down the concrete trail with their hands interlocked. A young boy with red hair stands next to his parents, digging in a box of Cracker Jack. His father reads a book of poetry. The mother listens to music on her Discman, watching her son eat the caramelized corn and peanut snack. Very close to the red-haired boy, a dark-complexioned young girl with long hair in ringlets tugs on the box of Cracker Jack in her twin-sister's hands. The two girls' parents sit on a blanket, the dad slices an apple with a curved pocket knife as the mother reads a fashion magazine. A line of children of various ages wait patiently for the man and woman in the odd clothes to give them a free box of caramelized corn. The man and woman could be a part of a group of musicians or members of a theater collective. The mother of the red-haired boy thinks the pair's clothes are a costume, while the mother of the girl with dark ringlets feels comfortable, because she spoke with the woman in the pantsuit who said they just needed to find a toy in each box and were happy to give the boxes of Cracker Jack to the children. Maybe they should wear plastic gloves, the mother thinks, but even the deli workers were lazy about wearing gloves and the kids were the real germ-carriers. One afternoon at the daycare center could give you all the colds and viruses you would ever need. One mother, her blond hair braided in cornrows, asks the woman in the 1970s pantsuit, big sunglasses and white Kangol, where she got the cool outfit. The woman with cornrows writes down the address as the Lower East Side. "Go, Jordan," she tells her tiny blond daughter in the all-pink combo (pink scallop T-shirt, pink stretch ballerina tights, pink ballerina skirt and pink sandals). The woman tells the woman in the Kangol hat, "Jordan calls those her fancy clothes. She wears them all the time."

The woman in the wild pantsuit and white hat hands Jordan a box of Cracker Jack, "I like your fancy clothes."

The child in pink grasps the box of caramel corn and peanuts, "Yes," she says, as if the word *yes* explains a complex world that demands one outfit forever, every day.

George and Lilly are surrounded by children, holding boxes of Cracker Jack.

"No ring?" Lilly asks.

"Lots of fake tattoos and plastic monkeys…"

"I guess we'll just have to go to Tiffany's and see if we can pony up for a sterling silver telephone dialer."

George looks at her.

"It's from the movie, sailor. Keep up with me…."

Lilly, with George following, pushes through the doors and enters the grand cathedral of jewelry retail. Glass cabinets shine under a vaulted ceiling. Bells ring, signaling a new purchase. Lilly takes George by the hand. They walk up to a counter. An elegant sales clerk stands behind the glass. He is handsome, in his mid-50s, African American and dressed like Cary Grant in a sharp gray suit, a white shirt and black silk tie. George and Lilly stand before him in their 1970s gaudy, Polyester outfits.

"But what," Lilly whispers, "are we engraving?"

George reaches to the locket on Lilly's neck. "This," he says. George unclasps and removes the locket. His eyes on Lilly, she nods okay, whispering, "Do it, sailor."

"Can I help you with something?" the man asks. "My name is Sherwood…" as if just noticing their clothes, he pauses, "and you?"

"Yo," says Lilly.

George raises his fist in unity for Black Power.

"Yes," says Sherwood, "may I help you, Mr… Dolomite?" His gaze moves from George to Lilly, "You must be 'Foxy' or could it be 'Coffy'?"

Lilly puts her hand on her hip, "Now… Sherwood, brown sugar ain't the only kind for a sweet tooth, baby…"

"Yes," says Sherwood. "You're right, I'm sure, but brown sugar, white sugar… it's all too sweet for my taste."

Lilly snaps her fingers, "Gotcha! Maybe you're after my man?" She points to George. "Us gals on the street call him 'Killer'… 'Killer George.'"

"Hello, Sherwood," says George. "This is Lilly. You can ignore her."

"Sherwood," says Lilly, "that's a very stylish suit."

"Thank you," says Sherwood. "You both look rather stylish yourselves."

"Yes," says George. "That's kind of you."

"Not at all, Killer," says Sherwood. "Or should I say, Killer George?"

"George is just fine."

Lilly puts her finger to her lips, "George is wanted in several states."

"We were wondering," asks George, "I know this is unusual, but we were wondering if we could have this locket engraved?"

Sherwood considers the locket, "Very beautiful… a family heirloom or stolen goods?"

"The family heirloom," says Lilly. "Everything else burned when the Yankees came through Georgia."

"Yes," says Sherwood, looking at Lilly.

"I'm shifting roles," says Lilly. "Are you with me?"

"You are very talented," says Sherwood.

Lilly nudges George, "Tough crowd… maybe we need to buy something, darling. Like a big rock."

"Young lovers," Sherwood continues, "much like yourselves, brought a plastic ring into Tiffany's once…"

"Like in the movie?" asks Lilly.

"Exactly," says Sherwood, "only neither of them much resembled Audrey Hepburn."

"No one really does," Lilly says brightly.

"They were two gentlemen," says Sherwood. "One was black and one was white…" He places the locket on the glass counter. "They had traveled to New York together and one of the things on their list was to see Tiffany's."

"It is a grand place," Lilly adds.

"What happened?" George politely asks, "with the ring?"

"They had it engraved," says Sherwood. "Then after a few years, the white gentleman moved away, back home to Georgia actually…"

"Oh," says Lilly. "I'm sorry."

"And the black gentleman stayed in town…" Sherwood spreads his hands and bows his head. "He found a good job."

"And the ring?" asks Lilly.

"I imagine it's buried in a box somewhere," Sherwood says, "in a suburb in Atlanta." Sherwood appraises the locket.

"Of course," says Lilly, "we would have preferred plastic, however, it was utterly impossible to find a plastic ring. We purchased twenty five boxes of Cracker Jack… and not one plastic ring."

"I understand the difficulty," Sherwood places the locket on the glass counter, adjusting the silver chain as if for display.

"You see," George says, "it's embarrassing, but this is all we have at the moment. We planned on plastic, but we have this… silver."

"We did," says Lilly. "We must have fed Cracker Jack to half the children in Central Park." Sherwood turns the locket in his fingers, "This is a beautiful piece."

"In all seriousness… my grandmother gave it to me," says Lilly.

"Don't turn serious on me," says Sherwood, "I see enough of that every day. Engraving won't be a problem. What would you like it to say?"

Lilly and George look at each other.

"Happy Hanukkah?" says Lilly. "Merry Easter? Bon Voyage? Rock on?"

George takes a pen from the counter and pulls the Cracker Jack receipt from his pocket, writing on it. He hands the note to Sherwood.

"Very tasteful," Sherwood reads, "To my darling granddaughter, Lilly, with love from Lillian the First."

Lilly kisses George on the cheek. "See, George, you really can write."

George places a dollop of sauerkraut on his hot dog. "This is New York City… right here, standing in the middle of the city eating hot dogs outside of Tiffany's."

"It is perfect, isn't it, Killer," Lilly holds a garnished hot dog wrapped in foil. "This whole day is really New York, isn't it? The thrift store and margaritas to-go and Central Park and Tiffany's? We even found something perfect to have engraved… and now lunch," says Lilly, handing the vendor a ten-dollar bill. Lilly takes a bite of her hot dog and tries to keep the garnish from spilling. "We have to do something I haven't done before, you know, like in the movie. They take turns doing things the other person hasn't done before… of course," Lilly says, "there isn't much I haven't done before…"

George and Lilly walk south on 5th Avenue.

"I think that was Audrey's line," says George.

"Well, it's a good line," says Lilly, "and I've got the martini glasses to prove it."

The day is warm and it crosses George's mind he could run into Nicolette. The Plaza Hotel is only a few blocks north and Nicki still had that business meeting. Running into Nicki would not be George's favorite thing. It would be hard on Nicki and would give the wrong impression, since George is walking with a woman… an attractive woman, and they are dressed up sharing some odd special moment of fun.

Lilly tosses the foil from her hot dog into a trash bin and wipes her hands with the napkin. They stand on the corner of 5th Avenue and 42nd Street.

George says, "I know what we're going to do… and I bet you haven't done it before."

"I've been to the library," says Lilly, pointing to the grand New York Public Library, "believe it or not, I used to go there and read books by myself when I first moved to the city, so you're going to have to think of something else. In the movie, they go to the library…"

"And check out his book," says George, "but since I don't have a book to check out, that would just be painful."

They walk a few blocks south and George says, "I have a better idea."

"Let's hear it. You're killing me."

"That's why they call me 'Killer George.'"

The Chrysler Building shines in the sky. George points to the Empire State Building.

"Have you ever been up there?"

Lilly stops, claps her hands and looks up at the building as if for the first time. "Oh, George," she laughs. "I haven't. I really never have. What a wonderful idea!"

The Empire State Building blocks the sky.

"I love tall buildings." Lilly says, taking George's hand, "I once took a shower on a cloud." George looks at Lilly. "Well, it felt like I was on a cloud," Lilly explains as they wait for a break in the traffic. "It was an apartment building around here… the shower glass was built into the wall of the fifty-seventh floor. It was amazing."

"Sounds like delivering those gifts has some perks."

"If I ever had a real job… I wouldn't mind working in a tall building."

"Going to work on a cloud?"

"You got it, sailor." She takes him by the hand as they cross the street against the light, cars honking, weaving around them in slow motion. George and Lilly enter the Art Deco foyer, pausing to read the history of the Empire State Building on a plaque and following the signs to the ticket counter and the elevator queues.

"This is amazing," says Lilly, "and we're not even at the top yet."

George buys them each a ticket and guides Lilly to the entry line. They ride up one elevator and follow the arrows to the high-speed elevator. In a box of people, they rise to the top of the building, following the crowd into a gift shop stacked with the curios of New York: taxi cab designs and Empire State Building logos on coffee cups, key chains, coasters, T-shirts of the New York Police Department and Fire Department of New York.

"You can taste the air," says Lilly, breathing in the thin, cold bursts deeply as the doors open onto the observation platform.

"It sure is different from down there in the oven," says George as they step out and walk to the edge of the platform, looking at the island of Manhattan and the neighboring boroughs.

"Hey," says Lilly. "There's the Lower East Side… and the bridges… can you name them, sailor?"

George points, "Is that the Williamsburg?"

"Good job," says Lilly, "you were on that one… and that's the Manhattan and that really beautiful one is the Brooklyn Bridge."

George looks out at the twin black towers of the Word Trade Center at the south edge along the Hudson River. Helicopters whirl below, the wind ripples Lilly's hair as she presses her hand to the white Kangol cap. Her other hand lets go of his and grabs the metal bars that extend up from the wall to prevent suicides. "Look at all those windows, George. All those lives wrapped up behind tiny squares of glass. It's hard to believe, isn't it? Each window holds a complete story… I feel strangely happy," she says, "unusually happy. What a place. We're on top of the world."

George nods south to the World Trade Center. "Those people might be the ones on top of the world."

Lilly considers, "We'll try that building some other day, okay?"

"Fine by me," says George. "I like the view from here."

Lilly takes his hand again and walks George around the platform, facing Central Park and the reservoir of blue water. Lilly points out Harlem and the Bronx. George asks, "What's that bridge?"

"The George Nichols Bridge," says Lilly. "Oh, no, wait… they renamed it after that other George that cut down the cherry tree." She squeezes his arm.

George shivers.

They walk around the platform, looking off toward Queens, the East River, Brooklyn and the rooftops of the East Village. Lilly presses against George, who puts his arm around her shoulders as she holds onto her white cap and the city shines. "Sailor," Lilly says, "I just remembered something."

"What?"

"I had forgotten exactly what a boyfriend does… but this is it." Lilly pulls his arm around her and it's her turn to shiver. "This…"

"This?"

"This is exactly what a boyfriend does…" Lilly says almost to herself.

Wrapped in his arms, Lilly nudges George over to one of the Beaux Arts telescopes on the platform, and peers in the eyepiece. "I think I can see Lupe crawling in my window."

He looks in the telescope, "It's just black. It needs a coin or a token."

She looks back in the telescope eyepiece. "You're a writer?" She gives him a sideways glance. "Use your imagination."

He looks into the dark eyepiece. "Hey, it is Lupe. She's wearing a yellow dress and she's got a cup of birdseed for your hungry parakeet."

George turns from the telescope, with Lilly pressed close. Does Lilly want George to kiss her? George tells himself Lilly might push him away, but he will kiss her on this platform above the city. He'll try again, right now. George doesn't listen. George doesn't try.

Lilly smiles, "C'mon, sailor, let's bail this pop-stand."

Lilly and George dressed in their 1970s get-ups, gaze at their reflections in the window of an expensive vintage store on Ludlow, one block east from Benigno's and across the street from Red Devil tattoo and Max Fish. Lilly points at her reflection in the glass and George's focus shifts to the beautiful long surfboard behind the glass, propped up beside a Playboy pinball machine with Hugh Hefner surrounded by Bunnies. George says, "We could get a tattoo. Maybe a retro thing with a hula girl?"

Lilly says, "I've got a different idea."

George looks in at the surfboard. "What am I supposed to do with that?"

"Surf. It's called a *surfboard.*"

"Surf? This is New York City."

"Yeah," says Lilly. "So?"

"What do you want me to do?" asks George. "We need waves. We can't ride off a building. We need an ocean, Lilly."

"It's my turn to pick something… and I just picked surfing."

"Surfing," George repeats, looking through the glass.

"Besides," she adds, "we're not having sex. I have a lover. You're a boyfriend. We must keep those two things separate." She hugs him. "We really must."

"Why?"

Lilly looks at George; her eyes have the same look George saw in her eyes on the Empire State Building. "It's better this way. You have work." She touches the display window. "But I promised you would have a great day—"

"It's already been a great day."

"Not quite. We're close to great… but we're still at *sure,* sailor. I want to get to *yes.*"

The surfboard leans against the pinball machine.

"Will you surf with me, George, no matter what it takes? Today? Tonight?" She squeezes herself against his thick polyester flared, wide-lapel suit. "Have I mentioned," she continues, "how good you look, you pimp motherfucker?"

"I do look fine," George watches their reflections. "But I've got you, babe."

"I'm your bitch today, Killer. And now I'm going to be your surfing bitch."

George runs his fingers along her ear. "Let's shred."

Lilly adjusts her white Kangol hat and smiles at George's reflection. "Confidence looks good on you, Killer."

SURFING

The boardwalk at Long Beach has a decayed elegance. It's a walk from the subway, carrying the long board between them, but the night is warm and people are out strolling, jogging and riding bikes over the boardwalk that stretches along the line of houses, where the cement meets the sand. The dim glow of Manhattan is in the black sky on the horizon. George carries the skeg end of the surfboard, with a lit cigarette in his teeth. Lilly holds the nose of the board and their towels, a blanket and a bottle of wine with a canvas bag over her shoulder. He can't believe he's doing this, but then, looking at Lilly walking in front of him in her cut-off Levi's and loose T-shirt and a hooded sweatshirt wrapped around her waist, George knows Lilly in a bikini will be worth it.

"Okay, Moondoggy," she glances back over her shoulder, "Time for you to do your homework."

They place the surfboard on the sand.

She touches his hand, "Don't be afraid, sailor."

George takes the last drag of his smoke, rubs it out in the sand and sticks the cigarette butt in his pocket. "Those aren't even waves," he says. He tries to remember what Zeke told him in Mick's office, but all George can see is Keanu Reeves yelling at Patrick Swayze in the rain in *Point Break*. They aren't waves, but that doesn't mean he won't be cold and look like an idiot.

"Ready, Killer?"

Lilly unknots her sweatshirt and shucks her T-shirt, stepping out of her cut-offs. Her bikini is canary yellow with string ties on the hips. Lilly picks up the skeg of the board and drags it toward the surf. The ocean appears speckled as gentle waves roll toward the sand. George did enough body surfing as a kid at Huntington and Newport in California to know that the waves are barely big enough. Lilly looks back at George, "C'mon, sailor, don't be afraid…"

Lilly presses forward into the ocean. She dives under the water and comes up spitting, gasping, and breathing deep. Lilly pulls herself up, straddling the long surfboard. George wades forward, dips down and swims to where Lilly floats. "Watch me," she presses her body flat on the board and paddles toward the incoming waves, ducking as one rolls over her, holding the sides of the board. Lilly turns the board and faces George, blinking as she wipes the wet dark hair from across her eyes.

A small wave builds behind her and she glances once at George as the wave reaches her. It is more of a curb of rolling black water. Lilly presses down on the board and paddles. The wave gently lifts the board. Lilly grasps the board and jumps up into a semi-crouch, wobbling back and forth, holding her hands out for a few seconds. Yelping, she falls off the surfboard and splashes into the black water.

Lilly resurfaces, sputtering.

George bobs in the water, dog paddling. "Hey, you're not bad!"

"I learned in Florida, sailor… here, I'll give you a lesson. The long board is easy." Lilly shows George how to sit on the board and how to push up when the wave catches the board. "Watch me, these waves are kind of puny… but here—" Lilly paddles as the rolling crest of a wave builds behind her, catching the board. Lilly jumps up again in a crouch and turns sideways. Her moonlit body is poised; her hands are out for balance. Lilly rides the wave, shaky, but upright. She raises her fist under the purple sky, splashes under water and rises up squirting water through her teeth. "Sailor," she says, "you look hot! And now it's your turn to ride!"

She pushes the surfboard to George and hangs onto the side of the board. He grabs the opposite side of the board and they face each other. Their feet tap under the water as they kick. "Are you having fun?" she asks. "You know… researching stuff… with the crazy girl downstairs… oh, here comes a wave!"

George climbs on the board and thinks of Zeke's lesson, flat on the cement in Mick's office. George imagines he is Zeke ready to ride a fifty-foot monster wave.

He paddles too fast and the wave breaks into a rail of foam, shooting him forward in the churn. George gets off the board and presses back into the ocean, getting on the board and paddling toward Lilly who is bobbing in the dark water. "C'mon, George," she stretches on her back, her white body floating with the swells, "Look at all the stars."

George says, "Here comes one." He turns, waits, paddles, feels the swell rise against the board as he crouches and skates along the surface. George can't believe he is up on the surfboard, and before he knows it, he's not on the surfboard, but under the water, with the board trailing ahead toward the shore.

"We could use a leash," says Lilly, swimming toward shore. "I'll get it."

Toweled off and back in their clothes, George and Lilly are curled up on a blanket. Lilly is in her hooded sweatshirt, with legs tucked beneath her. The hood is over her towel-dried hair. George is in a thermal shirt, khakis and a gray crewneck sweatshirt. George picks up the bottle of wine.

"Sure," Lilly holds up her plastic cup. George fills it. An oyster tin is on the sand. Lilly picks out a smoked oyster and places it on a cracker, offering the oyster and cracker to him. She sips wine and then places a smoked oyster on a cracker and eats it. "Yummy."

Lilly looks down the boardwalk at the bright windows in a row of apartments. "It's strange thinking about all those lives wrapped up behind windows…" She snuggles against George. "Just like on the Empire State Building… those windows remind me of gifts from Verreaux, little boxes filled with mystery."

"Working for that guy is dangerous."

"Everything is dangerous, Killer. You should know that." Lilly stretches back on the blanket, her plastic glass of wine balanced on her stomach. "Everything good is dangerous… otherwise, it's just a cage and you might as well throw away the key."

"There are different kinds of dangerous."

Lilly leans against George's chest, her hair scented with saltwater, her bare legs traced with sand. "Which kind of dangerous is this, Killer?" She looks up at him. "If this is romance, we're both in big trouble."

George leans awkwardly toward her, then Lilly's eyelashes flutter and they kiss. Her eyes are closed as George pulls back to look at her in the moonlight.

"Watch out," Lilly whispers. Her eyes open, watching him.

"I wish I could."

"That's what they all say." She slips her hands to his shoulders and pulls him against her, kissing him, her lips soft. "This one is my treat, sailor."

He pulls her tight against his chest.

She smiles up at him, "You are a killer, aren't you?" She kisses George on the neck, her fingers running through his hair. "We better go home…"

"One more kiss. I'm your boyfriend. I demand it."

"Oh, really?"

They kiss again. Lilly puts one of George's hands under her sweatshirt and presses his hand against her breast. "Confident and forceful…" Lilly whispers, adjusting her hips. George's knee presses between her thighs. "How can a girlfriend resist?"

"Don't."

"It must be the surfing."

George reaches for the top button of Lilly's cut-offs.

Lilly is beneath him and the blanket is between her and the sand as she shimmies out of her cut-offs, still in her damp bikini. He rolls up the hooded sweatshirt and kisses her breasts.

The ocean slaps the sand. Lilly reaches for George's zipper. Her eyes flash as her hand goes around his cock. "That," she says, "explains it."

"What?"

"That pretty lawyer gal… I knew she had a reason to buy you that diamond." Her kisses turn very soft and industrious. "I think we might be a nice fit…"

"I don't have a condom."

Lilly scoots up her hips and slides down the bottom of her damp bikini, "But I do." She looks off at the boardwalk. "We must be discreet… we don't want to end up on *Page Six* for canoodling…" Lilly reaches into her bag, digs in her small purse and pulls out a condom. "Here," she hands the condom to George, "a sailor like you must know how to use these."

When George sinks inside of Lilly, she gasps and buries her head against his neck. Lilly rocks with him as the blanket is pulled around them and sand spills on her stomach. George thinks about Nicolette, but Nicolette doesn't matter. What matters is Lilly's pale face in the night and her moan as she feels him deep inside her.

Lilly pulls back, breathing in short gasps. "Having fun?"

"Yes," George slips his hands under her and lifts himself deeper into her.

"Is this," Lilly rakes his back with her fingernails, "a great day?"

"Yes," George says. "This is a great, great day."

She whispers, "I'm glad about your key…" Her hair is swept back in the sand. Eyes closed, she moves against him. "C'mon, Killer… fuck me!" George tries not to look at how beautiful Lilly is in the moonlight, tries to keep himself off of the edge, where the waves are lapping. With her fingers on his neck, she whispers, "Let yourself go, sailor…" George is gone. There is an explosion of bright windows behind his eyes. "Sailor," she whispers. "Sailor…"

George doesn't know if he is asleep, but he opens his eyes when Lilly says, "Wow." Her sweatshirt and blanket are pulled against her. Her cut-off jeans are on and buttoned as she holds two unlit cigarettes in her mouth, snapping George's Zippo. She hands him a cigarette.

George exhales a ring of smoke toward the black sky.

"Hey," Lilly exhales a thin stream of white smoke, smiles at George, inhales and puffs out a perfect smoke ring. It trails George's ring into the blackness. Their cigarette rings are marbled, drifting into confetti. Sand spills from George as he shifts Lilly against his chest, holding her chilled, warm body. Their hearts are pounding.

"Yeah," he says, and closes his eyes.

NOTHING BUT MONDAYS

Spangles of sun and grime smears, dust flecks float in a spiral, a bouquet of tulips dropped into an empty coffee can. This was Lilly's gift to console him before they began their adventure to the Bargain District. The white pit bull puppy sleeps curled on Lilly's jeans. Her yellow bikini is draped to dry on the back of the wood chair. Lilly is next to George in bed. Their bodies aren't touching, but both are naked in the hot apartment. George faces the dawn light of the windows over Stanton Street. Dave's air-conditioner unit is on the floor with a scorched, blackened plug. Gently sweating in the heat, George dozes off again then awakes to the creak of the mattress. In the window reflection the pale shadow of Lilly slips upright, moving quietly. The puppy whimpers. George listens as Lilly slips into her clothes. George waits for her breath against his neck, the press of her breasts against his warm body, but instead hears the rustle of Lilly putting on her T-shirt, her sneakers slipped onto her feet. George watches the spangled grime of the window above Stanton Street and Lilly's reflection lifting the bikini off the chair. She tiptoes to the front door.

George holds still while Lilly opens the front door, steps into the hallway and shuts the door. George can smell her perfume on his body. Her scent is in the sheets, on the pillow.

They woke up once in the early dawn and made love again. Lilly's moans rose and she was on top of George, running her fingernails down his chest, her brown hair swaying as her head ducked and she ground her pubic bone against his, riding him hard. Her eyes went wide, she kissed him deeply again and bounced up and down on him, a rapid thrust as her breath escalated and she bent down and bit his chest, punched his chest with her fists, kissing his neck and talking to herself. George's hands were on her hips, their bodies limned with sweat. Lilly cried out and fell against George. He kissed her neck, tasted the salt of the ocean, beach sand on the bed sheet. He held her hand against his chest next to the red mark of her teeth. Lilly kissed George's fingers.

"They all taste the same?" Lilly had whispered.

"Oceans?" whispered George. "Or women?"

Lilly whispers, "Women."

"You know they don't."

Lilly sighed. "You're quick...."

And George had slept until Lilly slipped away, and now he stares at the smudged window white with morning. Lilly gone.

George rolls onto his back, stares at the high ceiling above him. The ceiling needs a coat of paint. The room feels like a corner. Lilly is gone and it is difficult to be sure she was in the room at all. Why didn't she say good-bye? The surfboard leans against the wall. George pulls on a pair of Levi's, brushes his teeth, splashes faucet water on his hair and combs it back. He soaps his hands and washes his pits, toweling off. He could use a shave, but needs food, a cup of coffee. The typewriter sits on the desk beside the photograph of George's father and the jar of ocean water. George just had sex with the gold-digger. George pulls on a white T-shirt and walks to the window. Late last night, he had cleaned up after the puppy and carried it down the steps to the sidewalk with Lilly, walking the puppy over to Allen Street to run around on the cement and pee. He had carried the puppy back and he and Lilly had slept until making love again.

George looks out of the window at the restaurant El Sombrero, with "The Hat" painted on the side of the building. George first smiled seeing the translation, now George watches Lilly Lejeune cross Stanton Street, dressed in black Capri pants and a white blouse tied at the waist. She has her big sunglasses on and her hair pulled back under an aqua scarf. Lilly's leather bag and another carry-all are over her shoulder. She looks like she might be off for a weekend get-away. Not the kind of guy who follows women, George decides a man will do anything. It's not stalking, he tells himself, pulling on his sneakers and checking the puppy's water dish. He'll talk to Lilly. He just wants to know where she's going. He's not being creepy. He wants to know if she's okay.

George pulls the door shut and remembers his wallet when he crosses Stanton. He finds fifteen bucks in his pocket. Lilly walks across Ludlow at Houston, heading to Avenue A. She sips a coffee she must have bought at Hot Bagels. George tries to do two very different things at the same time: 1) run up Ludlow, trailing Lilly and 2) stay out of her sight and not appear to be tailing her. George doesn't want Lilly to turn and see him, half-running, his eyes insecure, following her. What is she carrying in the bag? As George turns the corner onto Houston, Lilly is crossing the street, hailing a taxi. Her sunglasses flash his way. George stops, hands in pockets, and cuts into a walk toward Avenue A, but she just stares forward and the taxi heads west on Houston.

George hails a taxi and persuades the cab-driver to hustle west on Houston for his tip.

Lilly's cab stops at the corner of Spring and Thompson, across from a small park where children splash in an elevated swimming pool and men slap hand-balls off a cement wall and a basketball arcs, rattling the perforated metal backboard. Lilly pauses in front of an ornate marble doorway. She reaches to a buzzer and waits to be allowed to enter. The gallery doesn't appear large from the front, but windows reveal thick curtains pulled open, with paintings visible inside the bright gallery. George sees a small brass sign, "Tait

Gallery." He pays his cab driver. The gallery is empty. Through the windows of the gallery, George watches Lilly walk straight past the paintings on the walls, nodding to a woman who points Lilly down a hallway. George looks around the neighborhood, remembering only a few days earlier when he lugged his attaché and jar of sea water up from Mick's office in Tribeca. People sit at an Italian restaurant next to the Tait Gallery. A pizza joint is across from the park with orange plastic tables and people eating pizza slices off paper plates. George crosses Spring Street toward the pizza joint.

He orders a slice of pepperoni and a Coke and carries the greasy brown sack over to the park. He is dizzy from hunger and can't quite remember when he ate a real meal. There was the tin of oysters and crackers and wine at the beach, pirozhki, the hot dog near Central Park, some Cracker Jack and a bagel with tuna fish when he was pretending to work on his surfing film. The neighborhood is bustling. It's another warm day, with a bit of breeze. George spent an incredible night with an incredible girl; his engagement is over. George surfed last night and Lilly kissed him on the LIRR, heading back to Manhattan. Lilly had walked with George to take the puppy down the street to pee. Lilly had walked back up to Dave's apartment with George, not saying a word, just slipping out of her damp clothes and curling in his arms. "What are you going to do now, George Nichols? I'm spoken for, you know…"

Moonlight filled the apartment. Lilly and George lay together on the bed, while the puppy snored on Lilly's cut-offs. "I'm going steady," Lilly said to George.

George had tucked a strand of Lilly's brown hair behind her ear.

She pressed against him, "You know you are a good catch too, sailor…."

George responded, "Let's not talk about it."

"Is it okay if we don't?"

"Completely okay," said George. And it was true, with Lilly pressed against him in the moonlight, George didn't care if she was going to fly away like some wild thing. He would knock out a draft for Mick. He would prove to himself he could earn a paycheck… and whatever happened next would just happen. Maybe he would write a spec-script, based on real research, something commercial that would leverage his career and get people to pay attention, to pay him money, to produce his project.

The train ride with Lilly back to Manhattan passed in a slow jazz of grainy snapshots of empty subway platforms, people frozen, heads bent in reflection or sleep. Lilly's image rippled in the opening and closing subway doors. She looked like a pale shadow as she stepped from the mattress and slipped into her shorts and shirt, closing the apartment door with a hush.

The pizza finished, George doesn't have a reason to be sitting on this park bench. He can't be suspicious of Lilly. She is spoken for. She told George that from the beginning. It must be that Lilly didn't say good-bye and that she has plans she didn't want to share.

Children yell on the jungle gym, hand balls hit the wall, basketballs clatter on rims, cars honk and George drops his third cigarette butt on the cement, tosses his greasy brown pizza sack in the trash, walks back to his bench and finds a gentleman in a black cowboy hat with a white ponytail and a black handle-bar mustache sitting on the bench. The white-haired man clips his fingernails with a tiny pair of nail scissors. He wears a black suit, a dark blue shirt open at the neck and black cowboy boots. He has a silver ring in his left ear lobe and his neck is weathered. His nails are clean, hands smooth. He looks close at each cuticle and then notices George in front of him. "Something," he asks, "I should know?" His voice is raspy, but strong. His chin is square and cheekbones sharp. He reminds George of the actor Jack Palance… with a white ponytail.

George wants to sit and watch the Tait Gallery door. "No," he says to Jack Palance. "Nothing." George walks across the street to the gallery and presses the buzzer, waits and walks inside the gallery, standing in a room filled with paintings reminiscent of naturalist panoramas of Darwinian rainforest ecosystems. There is a layered presentation from the bottom of the riverbed to the top of the interwoven trees, insects, reptiles, fish, birds and creatures of the earth. George looks closely at the paintings and sees that they are not realistic representations of natural life-forms, but a tortured jungle carnival of mating and death, reminding George of the Masterpiece game he used to play as a young boy and the card for the painting by Hieronymus Bosch.

A woman approaches him, "Can I help you?"

"Just looking," he says, moving close to read the caption. "Is there a price list?"

The woman hands George a brochure. George nods in thoughtful silence, as if on the verge of spending thousands of dollars. George should just walk back to Dave's apartment and get to work. George should call Nicki and see how her meeting went and tell her he's been thinking about her. George shouldn't do what George is about to do right now. "Do you," he asks the woman, "have a restroom?"

The woman points down the hallway.

George locates the small restroom. He will head back to the apartment and start writing his surf story for Mick. George will get to work. It is time for bold steps, time to prove himself.

Walking out of the bathroom after wiping his hands with the softest hand towel he has ever touched, George sees a crack of light further down the hall, a white door ajar. "Studio" is painted in black letters on the white door. George walks to the white door, even though he is on his way home and should walk in the opposite direction. George walks to the white door and stands beside it. A camera behind the white door goes *click, click.* A voice gives a direction. A second voice answers the direction. George pushes open the white door as careful as Lilly pulled the front door of his apartment shut when she left this morning. George sees a polished wood floor and a white paper backdrop scrolled down from a fixture hanging from the ceiling. Yvan Tait, with his back to George, snaps photos of a naked woman with her eyes closed. She is in black heels beside a mannequin wearing a black cocktail dress. The naked woman holds a chain attached to the collar of a large expensive-looking dog. The naked woman wears a strand of white pearls around her waist and white gloves. She holds a long black cigarette holder and her hair is coiffed, pinned up under a wide black hat that George remembers from photos of Audrey Hepburn.

Two men sit on chairs to the side, watching. George recognizes one of the men as Verreaux. The naked woman is Lilly. Eyes still closed, she moves the cigarette holder, rubbing it back and forth over her naked stomach as the camera flashes white. Tait says something and Lilly moves the cigarette holder between her thighs. George walks back up the hallway. He doesn't need to see more of Tait's arrangement.

Lilly is not doing anything wrong. George passes the dioramas of the copulating insects and warring avian creatures. Plenty of women pose naked for cameras in more graphic, gratuitous and demeaning poses, drinking, snorting or shooting up the paychecks with some even buying property and making a sustainable living taking care of their families. Lilly is not doing anything wrong, except George remembers the look in Tait's eyes. Lilly could have told George. He would have talked her out of it. Money is just money. George doesn't care. It's Lilly's decision. Maybe money is her justification for another chance to put a martini glass on her shelf.

George walks up to the white-haired man in the black cowboy hat.

"You still here?" Jack Palance asks, not looking up, finishing his cuticle work.

"Anyone ever tell you that you look like—"

"I get it all the time."

"Jack Palance?"

"Like I said," he holds out his hand, "name's King Hailey."

"George Nichols, nice to meet you."

"Likewise," says King Hailey.

"I was going to ask you for a favor. I want to buy some time from you."

"Time?" asks Hailey. "That's something I have too much of, but that don't mean I'll sell it cheap, besides, how do you mean that, son? And don't say the wrong thing or I'll knock out your teeth."

"I need to run uptown," says George. "It'll take me about an hour."

"And what am I doing while you're seeing the sights?"

"You're watching the door of that gallery and telling me if an attractive woman walks out, a young woman with brown hair."

"All I do is sit on this damn bench," Hailey says, "but okay, you can give me some of that money up front."

George hands him a five dollar bill, "I'll bring you fifteen more in an hour."

"Make it twenty," says Hailey. "I might get bored, and I hate getting bored."

"Twenty." George holds out his hand. Hailey shakes it.

"Fine," says Hailey, lifting a tin of Copenhagen from his jacket pocket. He taps the tin of tobacco against his hand, pulls out a pinch and puts it between cheek and gum. Spits. "Brunette?" he checks. George nods. "Get moving. And this better be some kind of crime… 'cause I hate getting bored."

"No crime," says George. Hailey watches George. "You ever put yourself in a position," George asks, "with a woman where you know you're just going to lose, but you keep wanting to push it until it happens… even if it's the wrong thing?"

Hailey spits again. "That's about the only way I've spent my time with women. Done a few stints upstate 'cause of the problems women have got me into…". Hailey looks at the door to the Tait Gallery. "Sometimes a good crime will help. If you get caught, that is… gives you time to think, being upstate." Hailey considers George, spits tobacco juice, "Clock's ticking."

"Where's an uptown train?"

Hailey points over his shoulder, "Houston and Varick… go west a few blocks."

George looks at the door of the Tait Gallery.

Hailey laughs, "She got you good," coughing, "why God gave 'em pussies."

King Hailey is still on the park bench one hour later. George had crossed town to get his wallet. George assumed the man would be gone and Lilly too. "Hey," George hands the man a twenty dollar bill. "Sorry…."

"You take liberties, kid."

"I had to run a few places. Got my wallet."

"Good thing," Hailey looks at him.

George pulls out another ten, but Hailey waves it off. "Keep it. I've got nothing better to do. I saw a few women go in and come back out," King Hailey adjusts his cowboy hat, "only one was a brunette. I wouldn't call her 'pretty', and I figure you wouldn't either."

"Yeah," says George, pulling out the Tiffany's box.

"How'd this one get your panties in a knot? Banging some other guy?"

"No," says George, "I am the other guy."

Hailey laughs. "Forget it, she ain't picking you. She's already had her fun." He looks off, "They'll do that… and once they start running, they forget how to stop. Ten to one she's not looking for anything but what you already gave her." King Hailey gets to his feet, adjusts his jacket, dusts his pants with the back of his hand. "Sometimes life is all Mondays."

"I've never much liked Mondays."

"That's the point, kid. I don't know you and I'm heading to shoot some pool and have myself a nice vodka and Dr. Pepper, but I can tell you that some women are nothing but Mondays." Hailey looks across the street at the Tait Gallery, "She good in the sack?"

"Sure… I mean, yes."

"That makes it tough," says Hailey, "but that doesn't turn a Monday into a Sunday."

A GIRL CAN'T BE CHOOSY

George smokes a cigarette on the bench. Dressed in her black cocktail dress, Lilly walks out of the Tait Gallery and adjusts her sunglasses, carrying her purse and carry-all. She pauses in front of a shoe boutique and tilts her Givenchy hat. She pulls her pocketbook out of her bag and folds what looks like a check, slipping the check into the pocketbook and looping the bag over her shoulder. Lilly walks up West Broadway. Lilly's walk is less sashay, more a forward clump of her heeled feet. Lilly enters a restaurant with the words *I Tre Merli* on a black banner with three white crows. Lilly takes a seat at the bar, with George standing to the side of the bright doorway. Lilly removes her sunglasses and places them on the top of the bar. George walks up behind her.

This is one of those things he planned on not doing.

"One dirty martini," Lilly says to the bartender, "light on the dirt."

"Are you going to steal the glass?"

Lilly looks in the bar mirror. "You can sit down if you like, sailor."

George takes an empty barstool, "Bourbon Manhattan, splash of bitters." The bartender shakes Lilly's martini and pours the iced gin into a chilled martini glass. "Olives," Lilly says to the unspoken question, the bartender reaches to the garnish tray.

"You're all dolled up," George says. "Nice hat."

"Thanks. What brings you to this side of town?"

"Just walking. Nice day, felt like getting out."

"Don't you have a jealous typewriter at home?" She takes a sip of the martini. Her hands tremble.

"Dressed up for any reason?"

"There's no law against it." Lilly nods to the bartender. Perfect. She takes a second sip. "Did you follow me, George?"

"I thought you only drank martinis for courage? Before handing out gifts or whatever you call those packages of drugs." The words are bitter.

"You didn't answer my question, sailor... did you follow me?"

"I was curious."

Lilly laughs, "Curious George... isn't that funny? You were curious... just like the monkey in the jungle... so you went for a walk to SoHo?"

"I was curious why you didn't say good-bye this morning? Why you snuck out?"

Lilly sips her drink. "How suspicious of you... you really did follow me. I guess that's what I get for having a boyfriend... I get the jealous type."

"Why did you sneak out?"

"I didn't sneak out... I left."

"You could have said good-bye..."

"Ciao," Lilly says. "How's that? *CHI... AH... OW.*" She smiles, winks.

"Stop it."

"Maybe I can't handle the intimacy, George. Is that what you think? Do you want to be my shrink... you could be my first-ever jealous-boyfriend shrink?"

This is an excellent time to shut-up, a great moment for George to sip his cocktail and let it all drift away, order an appetizer, make small talk. Calm himself with liquor. George takes a pull of bourbon.

"The truth is," says Lilly, "I had a prior appointment."

"How much did Tait pay you?"

Lilly runs a trembling finger around the rim of her martini glass, takes out the olive and nibbles it. "My grandmother is very ill. A girl can't always be choosy."

"There are better ways to make money. What do you think he's going to do with those photos? He will sell them."

"Yes," Lilly says, "I assume that's why I was paid, because others will pay him."

"And you're okay with that?" George presses the knuckles of his free hand against the hand holding the stem of the glass. It feels like a year since they stood on the platform at the Empire State Building and looked down on Manhattan.

"It was very nice last night… very passionate. Let's not ruin it."

"Passionate? Like with Salvatore? Let me guess… you don't want to be predictable?"

"Last night was not like with Salvatore."

"I hope it wasn't."

"Because I am going to marry Salvatore."

"Marry him? Since when?"

"Since he proposed. I mean, that's how it usually works, right, sailor? Except when I say yes, I mean it… unlike some of us sitting here in this overpriced watering hole."

"When did this all happen?"

"A few days ago. I think you were busy entertaining your now ex-fiancée."

"Then why last night?" George watches Lilly. "Why yesterday? The whole day together… the night?"

"You were sad." She takes a deep sip of her martini. "That's all, really. I wanted you to have a great day."

"Is that what you do… sleep with sad men? If so, you have your work cut out."

"Stop it. I told you romance was dangerous…"

"You're right, Lilly, romance is dangerous, but not for you. You stay away from that trap." George motions to the bartender, drops two twenty dollar bills on the bar. "Another martini for the lady and make it the way she likes it, dry and cold with a little dirt."

"Very funny. You're quick, sailor. I'm sure the surfers in your story will say very quick and very witty things to each other."

George looks at Lilly.

"I do like you," Lilly says, putting on a cheerful smile.

"Just like you like any guy that pays for your gin." George turns to the bartender, "I'd watch that glass in her hand. They have a way of disappearing."

George stands on West Broadway, looking up toward Washington Square Park. He reaches into his pocket for his Zippo and smokes; he pulls out the gift-wrapped sky blue box with white ribbon from Tiffany's.

Lilly was right about one thing. It was time to get to work.

Lilly waits until the bartender has taken himself to the opposite end of the bar, talking with a waitress. She slips the empty martini glass into her bag, leaves George's money on the bar and walks out. The bartender is losing an empty glass, but he's getting a very nice tip. He's being handsomely paid. Lilly has nothing to feel bad about with Tait and those ridiculous photographs. In fact, if she is being honest with herself, she has to admit it was fun. She liked it. In fact, she liked it a bit too much, but that is her secret and she is allowed to have secrets, particularly on a beautiful day in SoHo. Lilly was surprised Tait had invited Verreaux, who never went out in the daylight, not to mention Leonard Karlson, her angry gentleman caller. But again, they only saw what they could never have for themselves, and if Leonard Karlson got a thrill, Lilly was paid twice for it, once their first evening and now on this perfect afternoon. Lilly needed a bite of food, something special to celebrate. Dressed to the nines, why not go down to Balthazar?

And fuck George. Really.

When George walks out of the Red Devil parlor three hours later, he has a clear bandage that is slathered in Polysporin and taped on his left bicep, covering a hula girl with a green grass skirt and rosy cheeks and heavy-lashed eyes. It's a piece of flash. His first tattoo.

George takes a right instead of a left and goes into Max Fish for a glass of whiskey. Then it's time to park his butt in front of his typewriter and finish Mick's project.

And fuck Lilly. Really.

GOLD-DIGGER

George hasn't seen Lilly in a few weeks, except for one day when she was walking up Ludlow Street with Salvatore; they were holding hands and looking very much in love. Good for her. Nicolette had phoned George to tell him she was back in Los Angeles and his clothes and assorted belongings were in boxes and had been delivered to his parents' house in Studio City. His mother said they would be in the garage, Nicki added. He could hear the mixture of disdain and hurt in her voice. He thanked her and asked about her work. She told him something about a screenwriter she was representing with a go project. The story was about two Irish brothers, etc.

Except for being in love with Lilly, George was lucky, happy and content that Lilly was out of his life. George sat in his rickety chair in the summer heat in Dave's apartment with the windows open above Stanton Street and tried not to keep looking at his tattoo of the hula girl in the mirror. He had to keep on his story about surfers. When he needed a break, he'd walk the puppy, who Lupe had named Isabella. After a lifetime in Los Angeles, George liked living in a neighborhood where you could walk everywhere and had no reason to get into a car. George would walk across the street to El Sombrero for a strong café con leche or a margarita to-go or he'd walk over to Los Aztecas on Allen Street for Mexican food that reminded him of L.A. or maybe up to the Turkish place on Houston. At night, he would usually go to the Diamond for a pint of Guinness and stay for a bourbon, but then head back to the L.E.S. early as the crowd picked up in the East Village bars.

George titled the screenplay *The Green Room* in a reference to the tube formed by the curl of the wave. George's lonely surfing boy and his lonely surfing girl would be pulled apart by events, but they would love each other against the wishes of their two surfing clans, much like Romeo and Juliet. They would die surfing.

George types at his desk. The back of his shoulders ache, and the room smells of Wite-Out correcting fluid. George tells himself that picking up a laptop might save himself a slow, toxic death bent over each white page of typing paper, wiping the tiny Wite-Out brush over a typo. A tapping at the glass reveals Lupe on the fire escape, with Lilly's parakeet on her hand. She waves for George to push open the window enough for her to crawl inside the apartment.

"Hey," says George, "be careful out there."

"Lilly went to the beach with that man. I told her I would feed Amanda."

"Wouldn't it be easier to go in her front door?"

Lupe shrugs. No key.

The white puppy tries to scale the window and get to Lupe, her tongue licking, paws scratching the wall below the sill.

Lupe does the delicate balance of holding the parakeet up on her hand, while scratching the puppy's ear. "Hey, Isabella."

"Do you need anything?"

"I'm okay," says Lupe, "but maybe Amanda wants to fly…" She holds the bird up, but the parakeet stays clenched to Lupe's finger, chirping and bobbing.

"You've been working hard," says Lupe, pointing to the typewriter and the stack of typed paper. "Why don't you get a computer?"

George shrugs. "I can't think that fast."

"You're weird," says Lupe. "Are you in school?"

"Sort of. I'm writing a story."

"Is it hard?"

"For a mujeri-whatever… for a playboy who's lazy," says George, "but we're getting there."

"Is it good?"

"I don't know."

"Will it make you rich?"

"I don't think so."

Lupe nods. "Is it for the movies? Lilly told me you write for the movies and are real famous."

"I'm not at all famous. Do you know where Australia is?"

Lupe shrugs like she doesn't want to admit to not knowing this place Australia. "I should go," she says, "I'm bothering you. My mother made me promise not to bother you."

"You never bother me. Maybe later we can have some ice cream?"

"Pineapple?"

"You got it." George takes the Tiffany box out of his desk drawer. "Can you put this on Lilly's bed for me? I think she'll want it."

"Okay," says Lupe. She climbs back over the sill and tentatively takes her way down the fire escape, with the parakeet on one hand, Tiffany's box in the other. Lupe looks up at George through the rusted metal of the fire escape stairs. "Do you love Lilly?"

"Lilly is a gold-digger."

"What's a gold-digger?" The parakeet flaps. Lupe calms the bird with a whisper.

"That's the kind of girl that only dates men who buy her lots of flowers and the most-expensive ice cream."

"Even if she doesn't love them?"

"You got it."

"I don't think Lilly is a gold-digger."

"Sure," he says, "probably not. That was a mean thing for me to say."

Lupe makes her way down the metal stairs and climbs in Lilly's window.

George looks down at the open window of Lilly's apartment. "Yes, you are."

JOKES & SHEILAS

Mick flips through George Nichol's script *The Green Room*. A row of female teenagers sit behind him, holding their portfolios. All the teenage girls are the correct height and weight for this casting and each has their composite card tucked into their book or handbag. Mute, patient, each girl is excited about this go-see because Mick has the reputation of making careers. He is known for selecting the girl with something unique that the other photographers missed. Each girl knows that there is some detail on her composite card that is not exactly correct, a bit of an exaggeration. Her feet are actually size ten, her breasts are not really 34-B, her legs are a few inches short, her hair is stripped of the dye and highlights, plain, common. Each girl weighs a bit extra on the scale most days. Or feels lucky that today is the right day of the month and she has been staying in at night and sleeping and is rested. She just has to control that desire to smile too much and talk because she's nervous.

Mick reads the title page and flips through the script, while George's eyes stray to the models poised in folding chairs against the wall. Mick holds up the script bound together with brass brads. "Is it brilliant?"

"Surfing and jokes and sheilas, just like you requested. Read it and let me know before you pay me the rest."

Mick removes a signed check from the pocket of his jeans and hands it to George. "I'll track you down after I read it through. You look rooted, mate. Been taking in the night life?"

"Just writing."

"Get some sleep." Mick slaps him on the back. "Give Lilly my best if you see her."

"I won't."

"You're in the same building, right?"

"She lives downstairs."

"I thought I caught a spark between you?"

"Sparks need gasoline."

One of the girls behind Mick taps her foot on the floor.

Mick says, "Lilly is Lilly."

"I'm going to stay in town for a few more weeks before Dave gets back, so let me know what you think. Call me at that number."

"I'll do it tomorrow," says Mick. "Who knows, but if we sell this one, I know some South Africans in J-town that are big on skiing."

"I actually know how to ski. I can write that one in my sleep."

"How's Nicolette? You stay in touch?"

The model's shoe goes TAP, TAP. The other girls stare ahead, trying to ignore her. George shrugs no.

Mick says, "Was it worth it, George? Maybe you should have stayed in L.A.?"

"Hey, I surfed for the first time. I wrote a script," George smiles, "and I got paid."

The impatient model stands behind Mick. "Excuse me."

"I've got to run," says George. "I've got a date with a little girl who likes ice cream."

"Excuse me," repeats the model, tapping Mick on the shoulder. "I'm talking to you." Mick turns to face her.

The model nods at the wall of patient women. "Some of us have schedules."

"Okay, sweetheart."

"I'm done waiting," the girl says. "I think you're an asshole." She struts to the elevator; her low-slung jeans snap with her hips and the clack of her heels.

Mick reaches into George's shirt pocket and removes George's pack of cigarettes.

"Don't mind if I do." George pulls out his Zippo. He lights each of them a smoke. Mick watches the young woman standing at the elevator, holding her portfolio. She stares at the closed elevator doors.

Mick hits the cigarette with a long drag, staring at the cigarette as if he just grew a sixth finger. "I thought I quit these evil things."

"You said that," says George, "but—" George shrugs. "It's tough."

"The flesh is weak," says Mick. He turns to the wall of mute, patient girls. "I'm sorry to keep you ladies waiting." Mick holds up the script, "I'm trying to get a movie off the ground. I'm sure you understand." Five heads nod in unison. The girl stands at the elevator, tapping her foot. "I owe each of you a favor," Mick says. "I'm doing a wedding catalog soon. If you aren't above it, give my agent a jingle and tell her to slot you in."

One girl raises her hand, "What about this job? You know, the editorial?"

Mick points to the girl standing at the elevator. "I'm afraid she's booked for that one." The girl doesn't want to turn around, but she hears each word. She is the focus of five sets of competitive eyes and Mick Tanner and that other guy, whoever he is. *Fuck you... you manipulative bastard,* she says to herself, but she smiles when she turns around and walks back toward Mick. She got the job.

PREDICTABLE

That afternoon, after putting Amanda back in her cage and placing the Tiffany's box on Lilly's duvet and making the bed for Lilly, Lupe went downstairs and did her math

85

homework with help from her mother, Yolanda. The mathematics tire Lupe, but Yolanda told her it was important to learn math if you wanted to learn other things, like how to become a veterinarian. Lupe had put fresh food in Amanda's cage, but she had spilled the first cup of birdseed and tried to pick up all the small seeds with her fingers. Some of the seeds had fallen in the cracks in the floor and Lupe had to get a knife from the kitchen and pry the seeds up. She was worried during her math homework that Lilly would think Lupe was not responsible enough to take care of Amanda. Lupe had to do a good job of taking care of Amanda until Lilly was ready, but she knew sometimes Lilly got mad for no reason and Lupe didn't want Lilly to get mad at her about spilling the birdseed. Lupe decided to go back up the fire escape and make sure the floor was clean and Amanda's cage was perfect.

Lupe taps at the open window of Lilly's apartment. The parakeet, Amanda, rings her brass bell with the point of her beak and flaps her wings. The bookshelf of empty martini glasses is blue in the shadows and the afternoon sunlight glows and ripples through the window glass, sparking the framed photograph of Lilly's grandparents on the ravaged bureau beside Lilly's lipstick and an ashtray packed with cigarette butts. The sunlight crease falls on the bed, now rumpled. Lilly is asleep in a tangle of bedsheet and duvet. Even though the window is open, Lupe pushes the frame higher, so she can fit under it without smudging her white jeans and pink T-shirt. Chocks of dried putty clack to the floor as the window inches up. Lupe is careful not to wake Lilly. Lupe wonders why Lilly would wrap herself in the heavy blanket? It's hot. The room smells like George's room, but with perfumes from the clothes across the floor that, sometimes Lupe folds for Lilly when the room gets real messy. Lupe steps off the fire-escape and reaches into the cage, touching Amanda, going, "Shhh-shhh," which makes Amanda tweet just once. Maybe Lilly has a fever? But then the man Lilly is going to marry, the handsome man, should be in the room too, holding a washcloth to Lilly's forehead like in the movies? Lupe never imagined she could grow up and be as beautiful as Lilly, but she hoped someday to be good at helping animals and she also prayed that someday she would have a handsome boyfriend, but he needed to be nice like George upstairs was nice. Lupe's mother was perfect, and Lupe had a perfect father. She wondered if it would be perfect for her when she became an adult. Her mother told her it was never perfect, but because her father was nice and handsome and kind and loved them, they were a very lucky family.

One of Lilly's feet, wrapped in black hose, sticks out from under the duvet. Lupe looks for the birdseed she spilled, hoping that none was left and Lilly wouldn't get mad at her or think she was bad at taking care of Amanda. Lupe sees a manila envelope on the floor, with black-and-white photographs sticking out of the envelope. Lupe doesn't know why she does this, but Lupe picks up the envelope. Maybe the envelope fell off the bureau? The photos are of a naked woman with a big black hat. The woman wears long pretty gloves. The woman is Lilly, holding a thin black stick. Lupe's stomach gets a twirling, not-good feeling. This is just dress-up. Lupe did dress up with her friends. Dress-up was fun sometimes in her mom's clothes. Lupe looks at the next photograph and her stomach feels bad. Lupe slips the photos back in the envelope. Lupe shouldn't have looked at the photographs. She just wanted to make sure Amanda was okay and the seeds weren't worse than she remembered on the floor and didn't need cleaning up. Lilly's foot in the sheer black hose pulls back under the duvet. Lilly groans. Lupe walks to the window and tries to step over the window sill, the wood creaks—

Dressed in a skirt and her black hose and a black brassiere, Lilly flies up, eyes red. Lupe is in front of her, scared.

"Get out!" Lilly hisses. "You fucking spic! Get out of my room!"

"Get the fuck out!" Lilly screams. "You thief!" Lilly glances at her bureau, her hands gripping and releasing the duvet. "Where's my eye-liner? Did you take anything?" Lilly makes fists, her breath hurried and short. "The coffee can." Lilly crawls off of the mattress, pushing away the duvet and digging into a drawer in her bureau. She pulls out a yellow can of Bustelo. Lupe's father and mother liked Bustelo too. Lupe is scared, but doesn't want to move or start to cry. Lilly touches something in the can and smiles to herself. "You," she talks to Lupe, "didn't get this yet, did you? How dare you come into my room?! How dare you?!" Lupe doesn't know what happened to Lilly, but Lupe steps onto the fire escape and knows she won't come back anymore. Lilly hates her now. Lupe can't cry yet until she gets to her mother, who will be cooking dinner. Lilly screams and it makes no sense. Lupe hears something shatter, like a plate. Lupe climbs down into her open window, sees her mother and runs in to her mother's arms.

Earlier that afternoon, Lilly's fiancé, Salvatore Kline, stood at the foot of the bed. Lilly was under the impression they were about to go out on the town for a leisurely lunch. She had just returned from a quick coffee with her publicist, Suzanna, about the possibility of working on a new magazine Suzanna was promoting. Lilly was wearing Suzanna's gray and black cap-toed pumps. Suzanna had insisted on lending them to her since Lilly mentioned they were very nice on a previous luncheon.

Sal stood in Lilly's doorway and handed Lilly the manila envelope.

"If you had asked me," Salvatore said, "I would have done what I could have done for you." Lilly looked down at the pretty straps of her heels and the way they accentuated her pretty feet. Sal had told her once that she had feet like a princess. "Instead," says Salvatore, "a man, not a friend, but a man that pretends to be a friend, shows me this." He dropped the envelope. "You have hurt my reputation." Salvatore walks into the hallway. "The woman I love would never do this… for any reason."

"I needed money. I didn't want to bother you."

"I could give you money. I know you like money, Lilly. I have heard other people talk and heard their thoughts about you, but I didn't want to believe it."

"Don't believe it then."

"You have no pride."

Lilly's phone rings.

"That must be your pimp." Salvatore holds the door. "I'm sorry, Lilly, I didn't mean to say that… but I have a reputation to manage. Even if I could forgive you…"

Lilly looks at him, "You can't forgive me, because of what other people think?"

Salvatore closes the door. Salvatore is gone.

Lilly unthreads the heel-straps and kicks off her shoes, first right, then left. The phone trills. It's an annoying fucking phone. The phone machine presents Lilly's pre-recorded greeting and she listens to her own voice and the imitation of the parakeet chirp. It seems like a long time ago that Lilly left Mr. Leonard Karlson on the street, screaming at her window, calling her filthy names.

The message on the phone is not an angry gentleman-caller demanding fulfillment of a limited arrangement. The message on the phone is from Charlotte Vida Boxner. Lilly's paternal grandmother, Lillian the First, passed away last night in New Orleans.

Lilly's mother doesn't know the complete details, but asks Lilly to call her as soon as possible.

LUCKY GIRL

Lupe skips rope. George walks up, holding two Froze-Fruit ice cream bars.

Lupe's eyes are red. She asks, "Pineapple?" George nods, "Yep."

Lilly screams and something breaks, *Maybe,* thinks Lupe, *another plate.* Lupe knows a girl whose mother throws plates when she is mad.

A toaster flies through Lilly's open window, hits the fire escape and clanks down the metal stairs, sparking on the steps and guardrail. Two men playing cards at a collapsible table pick up the table and move it toward the corner of Orchard Street, outside a restaurant with brown paper over the windows in the process of renovation. Workers are moving in and out with kitchen equipment wrapped in more brown paper and plastic safety wrap. Lilly stands at the open window and pushes out her TV. It drops to the empty sidewalk, where it explodes into chunks of plastic, fragments of glass tubing and colored wires. George tosses his untouched ice cream into the trash.

Lupe says, "Lilly is mad."

"No kidding," says George. "Excuse me." He takes Lupe and moves her down the block, "Stand here and make sure no one walks under her window."

Lilly's telephone flies through her other window, peppering the cement with glass slivers. People on the sidewalk pause at the street corners and look for the cause of the exploding noise of breakage. A man stops at the entrance of the African-American barbershop across Stanton. A plate sails out the window, wobbling like a Frisbee, and shatters on the street. A woman on Stanton Street yells, "She's crazy up there!"

Lilly's jewelry box spins out the window. George cuts his eyes up at anything falling his way. The jewelry box smashes. He picks up Lilly's engraved locket, puts it in his pocket. "Be careful," he says to a young man standing in the doorway of Arlene's Grocery, holding an electric sander. The young man nods his head as if this is a normal thing. The dented birdcage crashes out the window and bounces, sparking off the fire escape and windmilling to the cement. George runs into the building and up the stairs. He hammers on Lilly's door, "Lilly! Open up! It's George—"

A door inside Lilly's apartment slams. George goes up to his room and turns to find Lupe behind him, watching him. George says, "Fire escape," and they enter his apartment. George climbs out on the fire escape and climbs down. Lupe says, "Amanda?"

"If she throws out the bird, at least it can fly."

George presses up the window jam of the shattered window. Broken glass is everywhere, clothes are strewn in strands, dishes and jars of food are smashed against the wall. The bookshelf of martini glasses, untouched, shines in a shield of sunlight.

George picks up a torn photograph from the floor, a nude of Lilly in the Givenchy hat, black gloves, holding the cigarette holder. George knocks on the bathroom door. "Lilly, you okay?" He picks up a second photograph, a third.

A chirp and George turns to the window ledge. The parakeet flies out the window, lands on the edge of the fire escape, flaps again and is off into the open air.

The bathroom door opens. "Hello, sailor." Lilly stands behind George, her face puffy, eyes red. Lilly wears a black T-shirt, skirt and hose. She slips on the cap-toed pumps. Looks at her feet and says, "Pretty." Her black T-shirt says "The Cure." A tight smile crosses Lilly's face. She walks to the sink and draws a glass of tap water. Her hands shake. George looks at The Cure concert dates on the back of Lilly's T-shirt and waits for what will happen when Lilly turns.

"Water?" She holds out the glass. "I didn't break this one yet... or those..." Lilly stares at the rows of martini glasses on the bookshelf. "Each one has a story," she says to George. "They're not all pretty stories... but some were pretty fun." Lilly holds up the glass of tap water. She tucks a strand of hair behind her ear, "I hate to be a bad hostess, but it seems I threw the champagne against the wall." Lilly nods to a huge wet stain on the wall; shards of a green champagne bottle lay on the floor.

"I don't need any champagne."

"That's comforting." Lilly stares at the glass of tap water in her hand and stares as if the glass has something written on it. Lilly's fingers grip the glass tight. She puts the glass on the bureau and picks up a lipstick. She picks up a shard of broken mirror and holds the shard up, pouts and paints her lips. Lilly kisses the shard of glass, tossing it out the window. The broken shard spins flashing sun at George's eyes.

"There are people down there," he says.

"Fuck 'em."

"Bad day?"

She looks around her apartment, "What could you possibly be referring to?"

He pulls out a pack of smokes, taps the pack against the heel of his palm and offers Lilly a smoke. She takes it. Her lips tremble as she inhales on the lit cigarette.

"You seem upset."

"Yes," says Lilly. "I'll say it a thousand times, you're very quick."

He lights himself a cigarette, waving the lit cigarette toward the shelf of martini glasses. "Saving those for a special occasion?"

She exhales a lazy smoke ring into the glittery shield of sunlight. "I'll get to them, but right now I need a break, so to speak."

"So to speak," says George. He walks to the window. Grains of scrabbly glass are crunchy under his wing-tips. Down below, on Stanton Street, the parakeet flutters on the sidewalk. Lupe walks toward the tiny bird with her hands open. The parakeet's wings flap as the bird hops to the door of Arlene's Grocery. Lupe looks up at Lilly's window. George waves. Lupe waves back, shading her eyes and pointing to Amanda as the parakeet flaps over Lupe's head. It flies toward the hat boutique on the corner. The bird flits in curlicues at the storefront window.

Lilly says, "My grandmother died."

George looks back at Lilly, "I'm so sorry. Are you okay?"

"Salvatore said he wanted to take care of me then he left." Lilly looks at her cigarette. "Just because of some stupid photographs. It's not even, I mean, they are a little porny. But so what?"

"Romance is dangerous."

She looks up at him, her eyes rimmed with smears of mascara. "Fuck off."

"Is there anything I can do Lilly?"

"Who did he think he was signing on with anyway? He sure likes 'em wild when the lights go off."

"Maybe it's better this way?"

She picks up the photograph of her grandparents. The frame is cracked and sits on the edge of the mattress, "My grandmother…" Her shoulders shake. She places the photograph on her bureau, her trembling hands pick up the eyeliner. She wipes her eyes with her T-shirt and attempts to apply the eyeliner to her eyes, smearing it.

"Lilly," George takes the eyeliner from her hand.

Her smeared eyes watch him. "What do you know? You don't know anything."

"I know you loved your grandmother."

A sheering whine of tire and brake rip through the air as a fender slams into something. The impact slumps in George's gut. "Lupe!" George can't think of anything but what he doesn't want to see: Lupe on the cement at the corner, a Honda coupe, hazards blinking, a circle of onlookers constricting around the quiet, still body of the girl. George looks for Lilly's telephone, remembers it went out the window. Upstairs. "Lilly," he points. "Get to Lupe."

One flight up. Dave's. The puppy nips at George's socks. "Yeah," George says into the rotary-dial. "The corner of Ludlow and Stanton. It's serious. A little girl…"

George gets to the accident site. Lupe's father kneels beside the girl and strokes her hair. Lupe is conscious but in shock. Lilly stands off to the side, smoking a cigarette with her arms tight at her stomach.

"I called an ambulance," George tells Luis. A siren wails. George touches Lupe's shoulder. "Hey."

"Amanda," Lupe's eyes watch him. George has no clue, but nods yes, sure, yes.

The ambulance crawls close. EMTs push people out of the way and muscle in with a stretcher and a body brace.

"Here they come." George takes Lupe's hand. She squeezes his hand. "I'll bring you some pineapple ice cream." George steps back and lets the EMTs close.

Luis motions to the thrift store on Orchard. "Could you tell Bennie? He can find Lupe's mother? I'll go with Lupe."

"Where are they taking her?"

Luis turns to an EMT.

Lilly finishes her cigarette. The EMTs secure Lupe in the stretcher, protect her neck and spine with a brace and inject something for pain. "This kid," a sweating EMT with a rugged TV-actor face says to the crowd, "is tough!" The crowd claps. George puts his arm around Lilly. Her body tenses. "I think she might be all right."

"She'll be all right." Lilly pulls away.

"I'm going to Benigno's. You want to come with me?" But Lilly just walks toward the entrance of 101 Stanton, where the remains of her belongings are on the sidewalk. George asks, "Is there anything I can do?"

Lilly picks up her phone from the sidewalk, inspects it. "Yes?"

"Is there anything I can do?" George repeats. "About your grandmother?"

"Yes, George," says Lilly. "There is something you can do. You can make her come back alive. Can you do that for me, George?"

"Like I said, I'm sorry."

"Sorry doesn't feed the bulldog," says Lilly. Someone has moved the birdcage off the sidewalk, standing it against the street-level door of the building. Lilly looks up to her window and shakes her head at the parakeet on her window sill. "The little coward came home."

George shields his eyes. "It's good Amanda found her way."

"Why is it good?"

George picks up the birdcage. "Lilly, I know you're upset."

"You do?" She pushes the birdcage away. "Leave that ugly thing."

"Lilly—"

"That's why I threw the cage out of the window, to get rid of it and its noisy prisoner. You," she says to the telephone, "might come in handy." She turns to George, "I'm warning you, if you carry that ugly cage up these stairs…"

"Lupe loves that bird."

"Do what you want with the cage," Lilly says. "I'm going to call Salvatore." Lilly watches the sidewalk. "I'm just going to have to insist that Mr. Yvan Tait return the negatives to our private photo party. Mr. Kline can forgive his amore one faux pas."

"We need to find Bennie at the thrift store and get word to Lupe's mom that her daughter is in the hospital."

"You take care of that one, sailor. The little girl has a fabulous father and fabulous mother. She's one lucky girl."

"Lucky? That lucky little girl just got hit by a car and could be paralyzed or worse." George stares at Lilly.

"I'm just saying the little girl has parents that care about her," says Lilly. "I really do love her, and I'm sure she will be okay."

"Sure?" asks George.

"Yes," says Lilly. "Lupe will be okay. I need to speak to Salvatore. That's first on the list."

"I'm sorry about your grandmother." George takes her by the arm. "But I wonder what she would think of you now."

He places the birdcage against the door and pulls the engraved locket from his pocket. "You threw this out the window." George opens the clasp and hooks it around Lilly's neck. He clasps the locket. "If Amanda flies back into your room, give her some water." George steps back and looks at Lilly as she watches the sidewalk. "You are predictable, and it has nothing to do with passion. Just admit what you are."

She looks into his eyes, "And what am I, George?"

He walks down the street.

She watches him walk toward Orchard Street. She lifts up the birdcage and carries it up into her apartment. The shelf of martini glasses shine. The parakeet is back on the window ledge, chirping. Lilly stares at it. "I can't believe some hungry cat hasn't found you yet."

RULES

The parakeet hops right into the cage. Lilly walks to the bookshelf of martini glasses and takes two glasses, filling one with water and one with bird seed, placing both glasses in the cage. "There," she says to the parakeet, "see, I'm not a bad hostess."

She runs her finger along the ridge of the bookshelf of empty glasses. "They're not all pretty stories, but some were pretty fun."

She takes the edge of the bookcase and twists, pulling the case with all her strength, leveraging her shoulder to tilt the large shelf off balance, pain shooting down her arm. The shelves of cocktail glasses twirl as cones clack and split, collide in the air and explode in rapid exchanges on the wood floor. Lilly kicks at the fragments of glass like a child kicking at a puddle of sparkling water, three tiny specks of glass stick in her legs. Blood spots spread. She falls back on the bed.

"Oh, Lillian. Grandma…" Gasping, Lilly sits up and stands then sits again. She reaches down and plucks the tiny shards of glass from her skin. She was done crying, but now she cries again. Her body aches in her chest, burns in her throat. Lilly takes off the locket George clasped around her neck, the locket from her grandmother. Lilly opens the locket and reads, "To my darling granddaughter, Lilly, with love from Lillian the First." Lilly smiles to herself, imitating Sherwood from the counter at Tiffany's. "Very tasteful." It was nice of darling George, her writer that lives upstairs. Lilly plugs her phone into the wall. She might as well make the call. Get it over with. Her mood isn't going to improve. George is right. Lilly is what she is and nothing is going to change her, not tomorrow, not ever. Lilly takes money from men she doesn't much like, even from men she doesn't like at all. Leonard Karlson paid Lilly for the chance to use her with his eyes, to own Lilly in his ugly thoughts. Lilly took the money. Lilly accepted the new arrangement. Lilly had bent the truth when she talked with George about her past. Lilly had slept with one of her clients. Yvan Tait had set it up. Just another escort job, but the man was good-looking and he was strong in the bank account and he kept on the subject and his offers increased over the evening as they shared a delicious dinner at Nobu and Lilly drank a bit too much sake. It was Lilly that watched herself from a distance and counted each increase in his offer and watched her confident refusal to spread her legs for this man but then…. Fuck a man for a load of cash? Why not? She was free!

She was a wild thing. Just like Holly Golightly. Just like Audrey—only she wasn't like Audrey at all. Help orphans? She walked away from a little girl that helped her. A girl who was lying on a stretcher in an ambulance with flashing lights.

Lilly gets a bottle of peroxide from under her sink and rolls down her black hose, dabbing at the cuts with the stinging peroxide dipped in Kleenex. She sits on the edge of the bed. The cuts are just small nicks. She rolls the hose back up to her waist and wipes her face with an edge of wet bath towel, wipes away the smeared mascara.

There is a scratching at the front of Lilly's apartment door. Lilly navigates the carpet of broken glass, which makes a loud crunching under her shoes, and opens the door. Facing the empty hall, Lilly jumps as George's puppy licks her toes. "Oh," she picks up the white puppy and presses the puppy against her chest, "Hello, Poochie. How did you get loose?" Lilly puts her face near the puppy and the puppy licks her. "Uggh!" but Lilly holds onto the wiggling puppy. "Where am I going to put you?" Lilly looks at the room, the floor covered in shards, glass dust, thick slivers, tongues of jagged glass, elliptical half-moons, broken, sheer, ragged. "Here," Lilly puts the puppy on the bed. "I'm sure you have a name, Poochie," she says, "but just stay. Okay? Stay." The puppy collapses, excited to be on the bed. Lilly picks up a shard of mirror, evaluates herself. "You," she says over her shoulder to the puppy, "are happy, huh?" The puppy wags her tail. "I guess the smart writer was right." The puppy looks at her. "You know what I mean." Lilly holds the phone. "I guess I don't get to wake up in a big diamond," Lilly tells the puppy, "and know I'm in love."

The puppy leans forward on the unsteady white ocean of mattress and putters toward Lilly. She presses the dog onto the mattress. "Stay," she orders. "Geez, you've got a mind of your own. If you didn't know better, you'd fall right onto the glass."

Lilly's phone rings. The sound startles her. She drops the phone and sends glass flying. Lilly picks up the telephone.

"Hello?"

"Lilly?"

Salvatore.

"I have decided I must forgive you."

The puppy rolls on her back, shows her belly, her tail tucked between her legs. Lilly smiles, wiping her eyes, and looks at the photograph of her grandparents.

"Lilly?" Salvatore says. "Are you listening to me?"

"I'm listening," says Lilly. "I was just happy for a second."

"I've decided I must forgive you."

"Forgive me for what?"

"I think you know what I mean."

"Yes," says Lilly. "I know what you mean. My bad behavior. And you mentioned your reputation."

"I live in a world that has rules. Those rules must be followed."

"I shouldn't have posed for the photographs." Lilly looks at the photograph of her grandparents. "It was stupid, Sal. I would never do it again."

"I would hope not," says Salvatore. The puppy watches Lilly.

"But I will do something stupid again," Lilly tells Salvatore. "I can promise you. I'm just that kind of girl."

"You can be anything with me, Lilly. I will protect you."

"It's not about protection," says Lilly. "All my stories aren't pretty, but some were pretty fun. And some will be pretty fun. Do you know what I mean?"

"Lilly," says Salvatore. "I spoke with Yvan Tait about those photographs. He agreed to sell me the negatives. It was a simple arrangement."

Lilly laughs, "I'm telling you about me, Sal. I don't really care about those photographs, or anymore arrangements with Mr. Tait." The wedge of sunlight falls on the foam of broken glass, the spray of sparkle and white reflects the window light, the carpet of glass dust and white walls. Lilly cradles the phone against her black The Cure T-shirt. She sits on the bed and pets the white puppy, rubbing the white puppy's belly. Sunlight burns the glass blue, rose, lavender, slivering rays of crystal; the shiver and sheen of colors are reflected through the glass. Lillian the First is gone, a car honks, warning someone to pay attention. Lilly hears the normal voices on the street. She has to accept it. Lillian the First is gone. Lilly was a lucky girl too. Lillian the First was there one day to tell Lee Ann Boxner she would see a sign and know she was in love. Lillian the First was there for Lee Ann, when Lee Ann needed her to tell her that her life would change fast. Lilly needed to know that one day her future would be new and exciting. Someday Lilly would be free. Lillian the First taught her granddaughter that love was not a distant thing, but a gift for Lee Ann, a gift that Lilly would unwrap one afternoon in the sunlight. Lilly touches the locket around her neck.

"Lilly?" Salvatore says. "We need to resolve this."

Lilly, on the edge of the bed, holds the phone to her ear, rubs the puppy's belly again and looks around the glittering room. The white room is a diamond of broken glass. This is Lilly's diamond and Salvatore is on the phone. Lillian the First was right. Lilly is in love, but not with Salvatore. "Just like Tiffany's," she says. Her grandmother was gone, but her grandmother told Lilly the truth. "One big diamond." Lilly tickles the puppy's stomach. The puppy rolls over. The poor thing could have cut her paws on the shattered glass that littered the floor like ice. Lilly scratches the puppy's ears. Lilly says, "And there's even room to hang my hammock, or ride a unicorn." Lilly wipes her eyes. Her beautiful grandmother is gone. Lilly's eyes tear, but this is okay. Lilly lets herself cry for her grandmother. Dear and perfect Lillian the First who always loved her.

"Lilly," asks Salvatore. "What is this about diamonds? Did you say something about a unicorn? Lilly are you listening to me? I'm offering you a second chance, but you must know that this can't happen again. Nothing like this. Ever. My world has rules."

"My world has rules too." Lilly crunches on the shining carpet of glass to the window, balancing on her pumps and looking down at the intersection where Lupe was struck by the car. "I just forgot the rules, Sal."

"Lilly," Salvatore continues, "I'm confident you could learn to live with me, Lilly. I know you're not like other girls."

"Maybe not. But maybe I'm not so different."

"I love you, Lilly. I want you to be my wife."

"I don't think that would be a good idea."

"I can offer you everything."

"That's what I thought a few seconds ago, but things change."

"Life doesn't change in a few seconds," Salvatore says. "Let's put this behind us."

"I can't," says Lilly. "That's not what my grandmother is telling me to do."

"But I thought your grandmother..."

"My grandmother passed away." Lilly looks around at the sun-splashed room of broken glass, "but it looks like she left me with a diamond bigger than any in Tiffany's."

"You're in shock. Let me come over and get you. You can stay with me."

"That's very kind, but I don't think so."

"Are you saying it is finished between us?"

"I'm afraid so." Lilly says, "You're better off, Sal. Trust me. Ciao." She gives the phone a kiss and places the phone in the cradle.

ESPECIALLY THIS

George stands in front of the Cabrini Medical Center on East 19th Street. He taps out a Lucky and lights up. This is exactly why he needs to cut down on his smoking, so he can smoke this cigarette and enjoy it. A taxi pulls up to the entrance and Lilly steps from the taxi, wearing her green sneakers, dark blue Levi's and the jersey T-shirt with the No.13. George's white puppy blinks and wiggles in Lilly's leather shoulder bag. "Hey, sailor." Lilly looks at the cigarette. "You smoke too much."

"I've been told that," says George. "What's up? Salvatore didn't like your offer?"

"Surprise, surprise, it seems he wanted me back."

"That's good news. Good for you."

Lilly puts the leather bag on the ground and lets the puppy crawl out. The puppy stumbles to George and sniffs his foot.

"Can I have one?" Lilly motions to the cigarette. George hands her the pack and his Zippo then picks up the puppy.

Lilly exhales a perfect smoke O. "You know second-hand smoke is dangerous."

"I'll keep that in mind."

"I'm afraid we're going to have to start thinking about the puppy now..."

"We?" George looks at Lilly

"You and me."

"What about Salvatore? You said he wanted you back?"

"You know me," says Lilly. "I don't like being predictable." Lilly reaches into the pocket of her jeans and removes a thick envelope. "Here," she hands the envelope to George. "It's from the coffee can." George puts the puppy down and takes the envelope. He flips through the wad of green bills. "This is a lot of money."

Lilly pets the puppy.

"Did you hear me? Lilly, this is a lot of money."

"Over three thousand dollars, sailor. Give it to Lupe's parents." Lilly looks up at the hospital. "I bet this is pricey." Lilly takes a drag on her smoke. "Room service must add up."

George holds the envelope. "Don't you need some?"

"Don't want the money. You need me to spell it out or what?"

"Got it."

"How's Lupe?"

"They're monitoring her. She has a concussion and two broken ribs and a deep bruise on her hip. They have to keep an eye on her. They have to watch for any internal complications and make sure she is okay with the concussion, but the doctor said Lupe was very lucky, and everyone says she is strong."

"Thank God," says Lilly. "I can't cry anymore."

"They have a florist here. You want to get Lupe flowers?"

"Sure," says Lilly.

"Sure?" asks George.

"I mean, yes, George Nichols, I would love to go buy Lupe some flowers."

Lilly rubs the puppy behind her ears. "Your animal tried to escape, but she only made it down one floor."

"I must have left the door open. Everything happened fast."

"My grandmother told me everything big happens fast."

George scratches the puppy's ear, "Everything?"

"Everything," says Lilly. She steps forward and looks up at George. "Especially this." Lilly presses her body tight against George, kissing him.

George pulls back, "Lilly, what happened with Salvatore?"

"He wanted to get married," says Lilly, "I didn't."

"Why not?" asks George. "I thought Salvatore was a great catch?"

"It felt like I was making a good deal on a car." She takes George's arm and walks him toward the automatic glass entrance doors. "Isn't this the most ridiculous thing you've ever seen, sailor?"

"What?"

"I fell for the poor writer upstairs," says Lilly. "Just like in the movie."

PERFECT

Lupe was allowed to leave the hospital forty-eight hours later. Her ribs were wrapped, and her parents, Yolanda and Luis, took turns reading stories to her on the sofa in their apartment. She promised her parents she would stay off the fire escape. Lilly gave Lupe a key to her apartment and reminded her to knock. Still, Lilly and George took to spending their nights upstairs until Dave got back from his tour. Lilly swept the glass out of her apartment and cleaned it up. The photo of her grandparents was on the bureau. Her old television and VCR and the bookcase of martini glasses were gone, but Lilly was done delivering packages for Verreaux. Lilly didn't know what she was going to do now, but it would be a normal job, maybe in a restaurant or even a business office. George suggested that Lilly should come out and stay with him in Los Angeles, once he got himself set up in his own apartment. Lillian the First was right, that's for sure. Everything important in life happens fast.

Maybe it was finishing with Verreaux and Tait, but Lilly decides she wants to give up the other Lilly completely. Lilly and George walk into Benigno's. Nancy Sinatra's "Sugar Town" plays on the radio. Lilly carries the whole outfit: the black cocktail dress, the Givenchy hat with scarf, the white gloves, everything but the cigarette holder, which had been her grandmother's.

"Are you sure?"

"Yes, George. I am sure."

Lilly takes what Bennie offers. George stands outside the vintage store, smoking a cigarette. The white puppy, on a blue leash in a blue harness, barks at a pigeon. George looks at the store across from Benigno's. Two men in goggles, faces covered with white plaster dust, eat out of styrofoam containers and drink bottles of soda. The store is gutted. A sign says a new restaurant will open soon, please be patient with the mess.

Benigno walks out with Lilly. "Hey Lilly, you know a good lawyer?" He looks embarrassed. "This asshole landlord is trying to move me off my lease so they can turn this place into a club or some shit."

"I could talk to someone," says Lilly. "I'd rather not, but I will if you're in trouble."

Bennie waves it off. "Fuck it. I'll work it out. I've got a contract, right?"

"You want lunch?" George points up the street. "We can bring something back?"

Bennie shakes his head, pats his stomach. "I've got a new lady friend. She's slimming me down." He runs his thumb along the waist-belt of his slacks. "Getting me back to my fighting weight."

Lilly and George walk up Orchard, holding hands. Silver planes cross the blue sky.

Bennie hangs the black cocktail dress on a mannequin, placing the black Givenchy hat on the mannequin's head. Lilly should have haggled more about the price. Bennie almost tossed in an extra twenty-dollar bill when he paid her, but times are tight.

Benigno's vintage store was closed within three months. The landlord broke the lease, and Bennie had to find work hawking leather jackets at the storefront on the corner of Orchard and Stanton. The Bargain District changed just like Salvatore predicted.

George took a flight back to Los Angeles in September to hunt for a job and an apartment.

Lilly followed George at the end of December, in time to celebrate the New Year with a bottle of champagne. Her clothes, scarves, candlesticks, mirrors, make-up, and shoes were packed in her green plaid suitcase and a yellow American Tourister she found at a thrift store in the East Village. The Los Angeles apartment was a one-bedroom rental in Silver Lake. Lilly had never learned to drive a car. First her mother forbade it, worried about the boys, then driving a car fell off the list of tasks once Lilly arrived in New York City.

Los Angeles would be easy, like a vacation. Lilly had survived in New York City. Lilly would learn to drive. She was in love. Los Angeles had the beach and palm trees and sunlight. Life would be perfect.

AT THE DIAMOND: SCOUT HARRIS

Scout Harris pours tequila into a metal shaker, counting one-two-three for each one-ounce shot, topping the iced mixture with more tequila. Scout looks into the mirror above the register. He's going cold turkey tonight on the hootch. He stares into the mirror, psyching himself up with some cold Clint Eastwood mirror-face. His eyes crinkle. He is a killer standing under the desert sun, a serape covering his silver six-shooters, a thin cigar gripped in his white teeth. Scout flips the metal shaker and catches it, shaking the shaker above his shoulder, watching his blue eyes give himself a cold killer gaze in the reflecting glass. Fucking limit-spouts. The kid owner, Jon Domogarow, instituted the limit-spouts one week ago. Scout admits it was thoughtful of Jon not to put limit-spouts on the cheap well liquors. At least he could pour the cheap shit heavy.

This night, May 5th, is the one-year anniversary of the day Scout's life went into the toilet. Scout had been in a band called Johnson State. Scout had been playing tunes with his friend, Billy, since they were in high school. The band had a few changes in the line-up, but Billy and Scout were the constants. The band had lined up a recording deal and were about to hit the studio when Billy overdosed on heroin. One year ago, May 5th, two weeks after Billy swore to Scout he had cleaned up and wouldn't touch the shit—it was all going to be about the band and making the most of their big break and finishing up the new tracks and living the dream they had shared since setting up their amps in Billy's parents' garage in Richmond, Virginia.

Scout shakes the tumbler of Cuervo and lines up five shot glasses in front of two dudes and three chicks sitting on stools, smoking cigarettes and drinking iced mugs of Honey Lager. Scout pours the tequila, chilled, dosed with a touch of triple sec and Rose's lime juice. One of the girls, the hotter of the three, a blonde in a tube-top with her hair tickling her cheekbones, reminds Scout of a small Viking maiden with lip gloss and almost-white icey blue eyes. Viking Maiden goes, "What's this?" at the shots. Scout doesn't think he's seen her in the Diamond Pub before, and Scout's memory is good on the subject of girls in the Diamond. One of the guys Scout knows goes, "Scout, rock on!" and all five lift their shots. Viking Maiden gets off her stool. She's about five-foot-three, wearing boot jeans cut into fringe and brown boots with a big heel. Her eyes are on Scout. Viking Maiden goes, "Where's your shot?" And the guy Scout knows goes, "C'mon, Scout, do one with us, brother!" But this is the one-year anniversary of Billy putting on the blue suit, and Scout says, "No, you go ahead. It's on me."

One year ago, Billy put the needle in his arm for the last time.

Viking Maiden's eyes are on Scout. "Are you dealing with something?"

Scout says, "Drink your drink." And the others tap glasses and the loud guy—Scout can't remember his name—goes, "Happy Cinco de Mayo!" and they shoot the liquor down, except for Viking Maiden, who just holds her shot and watches Scout as Zeppelin's "The Immigrant Song" hits the juke. "Vodka soda!" some other dude yells over the noise, holding an empty glass over one of the chick's shoulders, his head turned back at his buddies, waiting to see if anyone else needs a drink.

Scout takes the glass, puts it down, grabs a clean glass and puts ice in the glass. "Any flavor?" The guy waves off the question, and Scout pulls out the well vodka, loading up the drink and hitting it with soda from the soda gun and a wedge of lime from the fruit tray. The bottle shakes in Scout's hand. The bottle must be a shaking bottle 'cause Scout's hand is fine until he tilts it this or that way, then the nerves up and down the sky touch his arm, wrist and hand and the bottle goes haywire from two decades of heavy boozing. Scout clocks the clock with his eyes. 11:00 p.m. Closing time is five hours away, which ain't nothing, but the weirdness of the clock mocking you like sunlight with birds and a sky that has his hands shaking, the clock crawling with numbers and talking to you about where you weren't when your best friend bit it on dope. Scout hasn't had a day free from liquor for a long time. Fuck it. Scout puts the soda gun back in the rubber grip over the sink, where you dip glasses to cleanse them in blue solution. The same blue solution Scout wipes through his hair. In the men's bathroom, his damp hands run more Dax wax in his hair. He has a cigarette in his teeth, and the gel is stained by dust in the bathroom light. His cheeks hawk-sharp, Scout is back behind the cherry-wood bar, making a shot of chilled dirt. A regular named Ralph asks for tequila. It's tempting, but Scout is going to be sober all night. "Three fifty," Scout says to some guy, taking the five spot for a seven-and-seven. The guy turns away and Scout hits the register. Five fucking hours left. Five fucking hours. Cold turkey in the Diamond… Scout puts the buck-fifty tip in the empty beer mug beside the register. He turns around for the next customer and finds Viking Maiden standing with her tiny white fist around the shot glass of tequila. Scout goes, "What's your deal?" Viking Maiden shrugs and squints at him through the cigarette smoke. "Just waiting for you," she says. Scout looks at the dirt bottles, pulls out an American Spirit, snapping a match packet open, bending the match backward and snapping it across the flint. He waves the lit match across the white paper cylinder lip of his smoke and drops the packet of matches on the top of the cherry-wood bar. "You can wait all night." Scout walks past the tequila bottles that might as well have his face on each label, whispering his name and grinning at him and throwing tough-guy killer-look movie star mirror-faces. Scout's cut cheekbones, greasy Dax-ed up brown hair and blue eyes watch him from the gold and white bottles of tequila. "Have a drink on me!" AC/DC screams on the juke. Scout doesn't give a shit anymore that Billy put on the blue suit and took their band into the oven. Scout's throat is a pale V beneath his corduroy shirt, with cigarette smoke curling past his face. "You're a fucking asshole, Billy." Scout watches his own face in each bottle. The bottles of dirt call Scout out. "Quitter, chickenshit." Scout won't listen. Billy is gone. Viking Maiden is game. Maybe tonight's not the night to hold back. Scout needs to lock it down. This stray is throwing him heavy wet-eye, the shot glass of tequila in her white fingers. She watches him. She wants to throw her legs up for him right fucking now… RFN, maybe take her downstairs where Jon Domogarow keeps the kegs. Do her against the wall. The bottles of tequila whisper, *"She wants it, bro. Billy made his choice, no reason you should suffer for his bad."*

Viking Maiden says, "You're shaking."

"It's been a long year."

"Going cold turkey?" Viking Maiden places her shot on the bar. Her friends lost in conversation, strands of cigarette smoke threading down from the ceiling to their mouths, people standing, talking or shooting pool around the glowing red Budweiser canopy-light over the pool table. One girl with a tight Izod striped shirt that stops halfway down her flat stomach eyes herself in the bar mirror while her boyfriend feeds the jukebox dollar bills.

"You taking it easy?" pushes Viking Maiden.

"That's the plan."

"Are you celebrating something?"

"The other thing," goes Scout.

"Mourning," Viking Maiden adjusts her top, placing her white-blue eyes right on Scout. She knows what's up. Some guy in a Mermaid Festival T-shirt at the end of the bar waves an empty beer pitcher. "You're one of the dudes from Johnson State. The one that didn't O.D.," Viking Maiden says. "I saw you guys a couple of times." She asks, "What inspires you? I've always wondered how people got from thinking about it to, you know, doing it? Spend their lives as artists…"

Scout says nothing.

Viking Maiden flips the white blond hair from her white-blue eyes. "Did you always want to be an artist?"

"I just wanted to play my guitar like I had a big cock." This was Scout's stock line, but it was a good one. Cut to the chase. "I mean the biggest cock."

Viking Maiden eyes him. Scout wants to smile. He looks at her shot of tequila on the cherry-wood bar. Viking Maiden says, "That must've been easy."

Scout goes, "Yeah," gives the bar a wipe, takes a hit from his cigarette. "Listen, I was in Johnson State… but…" His voice trails off, he exhales, eyes on Viking Maiden. "My best friend died. That's all that matters."

Scout walks to the end of the crowded bar, takes the empty pitcher from the dude in the Mermaid Festival T and fills it with Molson Gold, tapping in the sale on the register and dishing back change. It was a long time ago today that Scout told himself this May 5th was a good day for him to take a break from the hootch. He'd do it in Billy's honor. Yeah, in Billy's honor or maybe because Billy fucked them all up and drinking tonight was sick, and Scout didn't want to face a hangover and the skull-face of Billy in his blue suit holding a microphone and mocking Scout with Scout's lyrics, Scout's words in his own face from the dead place where Billy hung out now, singing the same words Scout and Billy worked into tunes. The van stopped and the crowd got noisy and stamped their feet and clapped and cheered, waiting for the show. Their last night playing live was like yesterday. The gig rocked hard, and the next afternoon, after telling Scout he was cool, Billy went thrift store shopping in Williamsburg with his junkie girlfriend and copped this blue suit and also copped some dope and took Johnson State's record deal into the oven.

Viking Maiden's eyes are ice-blue diamonds, her shoulders white. She says, "Let's have one shot. You and me, Scout. I liked that song you guys did 'Kissing Kasia.' Let's have one shot for that song."

Scout looks at the shot in front of Viking Maiden. "Kissing Kasia" didn't suck. The tune was about a time Scout fucked up large and hurt a girl he shouldn't have hurt, and lost her. He might have blown it in real life, but at least he made something work in that tune. Didn't even know if the girl, Kasia, had heard the song… they didn't talk anymore. She was around as far as he knew, living in Manhattan, he figured, hanging out with Mr. Payback, the dude she picked to bail with after Scout kicked her to the curb.

Scout reaches for the bottle of dirt and pours himself two fingers in a rocks glass. Viking Maiden holds up her shot glass. They finish the round in one blast. Scout shivers.

Metallica's "Nothing Else Matters" kicks in.

Viking Maiden wipes her lips and shows Scout her prettiest smile. "Let's have one more," she says, loud enough to get over the guitar intro. "Just one." Viking Maiden has a nice, small, round, high ass; her tits are perky. Scout is warm with tequila. He could roll that tube of stretchy material down to Viking Maiden's waist and suck on her nipples while she talks to the ceiling.

This is why it is so hard to go cold turkey in the Diamond. Scout pours tequila into the metal shaker, squirts in some Rose's and triple sec, shaking the mixture over ice to chill it. Metallica lifts the smoke-filled crowd. Billy put on the blue suit. Billy left Scout with nothing except nights at the Diamond. Billy took away Johnson State, took away their chance. Viking Maiden's eyes burn. Billy's skull-face watches Scout from the label on the tequila bottle in Scout's hand. Billy's skull-face says, *Deal with it, bro. Take the stray and leave the rest behind!*"

2. Book Mouse

TUCKED IN, SNORING

I got a postcard the other day from a regular of mine back when I worked at the Diamond Pub. George Nichols. The dude from Cali that dated this hot party-chick Lilly, a Diamond regular who once pulled me into a three-way down Avenue A after-hours in a bar called "Spoon." I forget her friend's name, a cute blond stray that looked good licking Oban single-malt off Lilly's tits. That night was something I kept to myself back when George talked about Lilly and shit. The postcard said something about George wanting to catch some music, because he was rolling back to New York for a visit and needed my cell. The dude not figuring that a cell phone is out of my reach RFN. But broke isn't so bad right now… bigger things on people's minds. Today is September 11, 2001, Tuesday night, and I'm uptown on 106th Street, sipping tequila in the Black Clock Lounge. I used to work as a bartender down in the East Village, but I left my gig at the Diamond Pub, after getting punched out by a friendly regular, a good dude, can't remember his name, that decided to hand me a smack-down one night when I was extra hammered and talking shit at him about some stray he had a crush on that I had boned and told him was skanky because she borrowed money from me, and we both knew she wasn't paying it back but heading off to score. My name is Scout Harris. My given name is Scott, but my dad always called me Scout, as in Indian Scout. We used to watch Westerns together when I was a kid. My favorite part was when the cowboys would jump on their horses and wave their hats and say, "Let's ride!" My dad gave me a cowboy hat for Christmas one year. My mom said I used to walk around the house all day, waving the hat and yelling, "Let's ride!" which basically has been my approach to life, except somewhere the hat became a guitar and the guitar became a bottle of tequila.

Today was so fucked up.

Megan tricked me into taking this journal and promising to use it over a year ago. I kept putting it off, then figured I'd give it a try tonight. If nothing else, Megan will blow me in gratitude, but then she'd do that anyway if I bothered to grab the subway downtown to her apartment filled with purple pillows. I'd do it, but I'm crashing at the Senator's pad, the Fat Mexican's crib, the apartment of Ralph Villalobos. The Black Clock TV news says you can't get south of 14th street unless you can prove you live down there, which I don't. Police barricades locked off downtown after the attack on the World Trade Center. New York City is a warzone.

Those had to be some long minutes if you were trapped today, choking on melting carpet and plastic and metal, bodies pushing you toward the broken windows as you tried to breathe.

Today was no joke.

And I'm handling it my way: drinking tequila, drinking cold dirt. I'm sure somewhere someone is writing a song about today, but I sure as shit couldn't do it now.

Megan told me that writing in this thing would help me deal with my issues. How lame is that? My issues? My issues are right in my face, Megan. I'm broke. I live on the Fat Mexican's floor. I haven't picked up a guitar in years. I was a bartender, which isn't anything great after you've done it for a few months, but now I work in a boatyard in a job so lame I think I'm one or two notches below a rent-a-cop. I wear an official-looking tri-cornered hat that makes it clear I'm some kind of tool along with a "uniform" that is really just store-bought blue Dickie work clothes. I have a nightstick in a drawer in a fish-stinking shed at the edge of the dock, where I park my ass on a stool and stare at boat-rigging that clinks in the wind, trash that floats down the Hudson River and count the construction cranes on the New Jersey side, waiting for the clock hand to reach the end of my shift. Sometimes when I'm very hung-over, I puke in the plastic wastebasket and dump the goop onto the condoms, styrofoam cups, plastic straws, and soda cans that coagulate in the black mossy water under the dock.

I get a paycheck, taxes withheld. Back at the Diamond Pub, I walked out of the bar in the hours before dawn, locking the metal gate with a pocket of cash and a hot stray tapping her fingernails on my arm, watching me with drunk, horny eyes.

Back then, most mornings were spent looking down at a naked stray, while the metal storefront grates on Clinton Street in the L.E.S. scraped their way open, letting you know the day had lifted and you could crash after a good fuck.

But I shouldn't be surprised, these days were waiting for me. Back when I worked at the Diamond, I knew I could only push it for so long and the day would push back. That day would come and give me a fist to the jaw. "Fuck you. You're fucked, bro!" I hid in the night, but I couldn't hide forever.

Speaking of suicidal towel-heads, I remember leaving the Diamond on quiet nights and stopping at the only open bodega on Houston, picking up a few cans of Ballantine Ale and a triple-X magazine two-pack. The man that held the late-night shift at the bodega was Syrian. He asked me if I could get him a job on an American military ship. Right. This guy was a terrorist. He copped to it. Told me he was at war with America. We would argue as the sun creased the edges of the city. He smiled a lot and would walk outside with me and shake my hand. It sounds strange and kind of fucked up after today, but I used to walk toward his screen of bullet-proof glass in the bodega with an extra kick in my tired legs after my Diamond shift, knowing I had a pocketful of money for porn and beer, knowing it was almost time to sleep and knowing my friend would be there and we would argue about who was right and who was wrong. I used to think about turning him in, but it didn't feel like a cool thing. It felt un-American to turn some dude into the cops just because he talked a bunch of shit at night. If I did that during my shifts at the bar, I'd be on the phone to the 9th Precinct on Avenue C every evening. I don't know what happened to the Syrian. One night I showed up to spend my hard-earned, smoke-stained twenty dollar bill, and he was gone.

After today, I'd make that phone call to the precinct, but after today, everything is going to be different.

I slammed back a beer at the Dublin House across from the boat dock, post-work, watching the old drunks watch the planes slam into the WTC on the bar TV. Then I walked up to the Fat Mexican's crib and we stared at the news. Imagine walking into work, holding a bagel and a cup of coffee, sitting at your desk, flipping through a *New York Post*, day-dreaming about a pay-raise or playing hoops at lunch out on the park or dreaming about asking out that hot stray down the hall. Seconds go *zip-zip-zip*, and before you know it, shit is fucked and you face a decision with no answer. Do you stand in the room breathing boiling carpet or do you ask that pretty girl for her hand and jump into the blue sky?

I was on the phone in the fish shed at the boat dock this morning, shaking from a tequila hangover, calling friends to figure out if everyone was okay. The landline was fucked, but I borrowed this boat-dude's cell. He owed me a favor 'cause I caught him buying coke from a bike messenger and let it slide.

Most cells weren't working today. One of the main antennas was on one of the towers, but his cell, for some reason, had service. I called everyone. I'm seriously glad I didn't have any friends that had to face those long minutes. Most people I know in this city work at night. They were tucked in, snoring when the shit went down.

THE Y2K MONSTERS

Megan Bathe handed me this journal New Year's Day, 2000. This was about six months before the friendly regular kicked my grid in and I woke up passed out and bleeding downstairs at the Diamond, where Jon Domogarow keeps the kegs of beer. A sewer rat crawled toward my face but wobbled off when I sat up and scraped the dried blood from my nose, mouth, and eyes. I had been drinking heavily for months, but every other night, the regulars at the Diamond would help me out the door into a taxi, not hold me up against the pool table and punch me into putty. It was the end of one century and the beginning of the next hundred years of shit. In the scope of things, I remember thinking, *I'll be dust soon enough so why should I care about a new century?* The Y2K monsters were going to get us anyway—attack of the machines and all that media bullshit. I ignored Megan's journal and continued to work at the Diamond, drinking and banging strays. I told Megan I'd get around to writing something in her leather journal, but I didn't. It was hard to deal with reality. Everything was going crash-and-burn. This was not what I had expected.

The year 2000 was science fiction; 2000 would never happen, and when it did, I'd be crazy-fucking rich, with a few platinum albums and some very cool gear, like a private jet and a monster house, playing my tunes in distant cities—unwinding at the end of the ride in Malibu or the Hamptons, St. Bart's or Mozambique. Instead, the new century started just like every other miserable year, except more fucked. I was older and hustling for ways to keep my head above the river of shit, still popping beers and pouring shots, working my shifts at the Diamond, which I couldn't face without getting hammered. I was burnt, but I couldn't say no to the tax-free tips. Each night gave me a roll of twenties. Alcoholic jerk-offs wagged fingers in my face and shouted for drinks, while I wiped up soggy napkins with Jon Domogarow on my case half the time about comping and pouring too heavy. I'd be slopping wet ashtrays with ash-soaked rags, mopping the pissed bathroom floors, boozing whiners boring the shit out of me with idiotic bullshit about the band, dribbling their spare wrinkled dollars and clattering change on the bar while they spit crap from their mouths. What happened to Johnson State? I'll tell you what happened. Our lead singer offed himself, that's what fucking happened. He can't sing when he's dead. That's what's getting in the way of our gigs. Death. That's why we never got the tracks down and the label never got behind our debut major-label CD. Death got in the fucking way. Some nights at the Diamond it took every bit of control to not swing a bottle of Absolut in a perfect arc at the square head of some dumb motherfucker who thought his drink wasn't strong enough, cold enough, cheap enough. Don't get me wrong, the Diamond was good to me, but at the end of the century, I was at the end of my rope and my feet were dangling. The script had flipped, and I was no longer the hip guitarist grabbing a few shifts before the big deal went down and I flew off to collect bags of money and watch girls play with each other backstage after Johnson State's stadium gigs, first supporting, then headlining. By the time the machines took over at Y2K, I was supposed to be walking into the Diamond for a quick pint of Saranac before ambling over to the waiting limo for a Tri-State airport run or catching a taxi to a photo shoot, interview, or exclusive party. Rather than getting the shit kicked out of me by a regular from my own bar, I was supposed to be the dude the regulars in the Diamond slap on the back, grinning and asking me if I have a chance to join them for one quick frosty and some gossip about my supermodel girlfriend.

Or they would ask me which band I hate or if I could pony up the skinny on the obscure lyrics to our big new radio hit. I was supposed to be a superstar, striding in my boots from one century into the next century, trailing a strand of cigarette smoke, a bottle of high-end dirt in one ring-jeweled fist. I was supposed to be in the studio re-editing our first greatest-hits compilation, which was a bit early, but because we switched labels as we built speed and had to generate product to complete our contract, we left the old label behind in our dust. Maybe we'd be cranking out some early-year B-side compilation just 'cause Johnson State was too wiped out from our first world tour to create any new material. We needed a break after taking those MTV awards (and almost the Grammy in the Rock category, if the judges hadn't wimped out). Sure, we might be in a brief detox stint for "nervous exhaustion," but we were going to be rocking it hard and deserved the down time. There were a lot of ways it was going to play for me by the year 2000. I remember walking through New York City during the blizzard of 1996, wearing two jackets, a knit cap and a scarf wrapped around my neck, with a good dirt buzz keeping me warm. Flea and Kiedis walked past me in the L.E.S., and I said, "Just fucking wait, bro..." They stamped their feet in the snow, and I told them to remember the name Johnson State. Flea and Kiedis nodded sort of polite, probably thinking I should leave them alone, but I wanted to give them props for their music and let them know I was nipping at their heels with my band. I pointed them up the street in the direction of Avenue C to this vegan place. Life was good, but then Billy put on the blue suit, and by the new century, I was still at the Diamond, counting tips, drinking through my shifts and changing those singles and five-spots into twenties, trying hard to ignore that you can't always get what you want. But sometimes, if you try real hard, you end up at dawn with a tequila bottle in one hand and some stray holding onto your leather belt, guiding your drunk ass down Avenue A.

By the time the new century rolled out and the Y2K monsters forgot to attack, I wasn't in the studio working out a killer album or even a filler album, I was standing behind the same fucking bar on East 6th Street, a cigarette in one hand and a wet rag in the other hand, wiping the ass-crack of dirty ashtrays while animals attacked stupid humans on the bar TV.

Death fucked Johnson State. Then I went into a slow—but then kind of speeded-up—crash-and-burn. That was the deal.

I held onto this journal. Megan told me it was about some book idea she had planned, something she called the "Document of Time Project." Some deal that was supposed to make us famous but sounded like the grade-school project of a spoiled girl with too much time on her hands. I kept the journal and lied to Megan that I'd use it like a diary. I couldn't face dragging this motherfucker into the Diamond, couldn't face explaining it or trying to do it... but I didn't toss the journal into the trash. I held onto it. And after the shit that happened today, I've got nowhere to go, so I'm giving it a try.

THE SONG ABOUT THE GIRL

I might have left the Diamond gig earlier, but it was hard to say no to the tax-free cash. Every dawn, I walked home with a roll of twenties in my Levi's. That roll was like having done something real, making the nut, bringing home the bacon. The weird thing was that soon I just wanted to give the cash away, spend it on anything, which is what I did, tipping heavy and buying shit I couldn't afford and didn't need or even want, like expensive amps and a new acoustic guitar I never played and couldn't drag up the energy to sell off, swap, or even give away. In addition to having no career when Megan first handed me this leather journal, I was bored shitless and on the verge of losing my sublet on Clinton Street. When I first moved into that part of town, no one wanted to live there, but the neighborhood was changing and the guy I rented from woke up one morning, shook his head and figured out he could make a shitload of cake if he sold some of his properties or upped his rent. Besides being greedy and not a complete idiot, my landlord was an antagonistic asshole. I had stayed under his radar, and then one day I wasn't under his radar—I was in the crosshairs. My timing isn't always good, and I missed one month's rent, thanks to a cocaine and strip-bar binge that depleted my envelope of twenties, fifties, and hundreds. My landlord expressed his tenseness by turning off my electricity. I ran a cord out my door into the hall to light my TV. My refrigerator stank. I duct-taped it shut. I still had hot water in the shower and heat cranking from the pipes. I ate in diners or sitting on a barstool at the Diamond. At dawn, I would snake a couple cold beers from the Diamond and carry them back to the apartment and sit in the glow of the TV and look at the guitars I still owned and hadn't sold, but never played. I took a part-time gig at a guitar shop on Ludlow, talking fuzz and chorus and wah-wah pedals with other freaks. Yapping about string gauges, digital delays, gigs and the advantages and disadvantages of different clubs and venues, who was cool and who charged you for every beer and raped you out of any money you might earn at your gig. I did a good job of pretending I still cared when some kid would roll up all stunned I had been the axe in Johnson State. The kid would squint at me, going back in time to a smoke-filled dungeon where he peered between the weaving bodies and heads of the crowd at Scout Harris, playing his ass off. Or maybe the kid remembered that ghostly band photo on our one EP *Last Day,* when Billy thought it would be cool if he was half in the shadow, even though he was the lead singer. He didn't end up half-in-the-shadow, he ended up all in the shadow, and he loved the photo and so that was the EP cover. No one was messing with Billy once he was set on something. One night, after Billy took his blue suit death-trip and jumped in the oven, I got lit and taped a photograph of Billy over the shadow of Billy on the EP.

"That one tune was great," the kid said. "You know… that one?"

"We did a lot of tunes."

"You know… ?" the kid was practically pissing in his pants. "It got played on the college stations." He wasn't the first fan I'd run into who couldn't remember the name of the one tune Johnson State recorded that anyone really remembers, which tells you something about this country's educational system or the kind of losers that liked our music.

"I don't know." I tried to get back to whatever menial task I was doing that day in the guitar shop, putting string packets on hooks on a particle-board wall or sweeping a floor. Something. Maybe staring in the waste basket beside the urinal looking for my career.

The kid wouldn't give up. "The song about the girl?"

The song about the girl? Half the songs in the history of rock & roll were about the girl. Fucking moron. I finally did what I always do and gave up. I said, "Kissing Kasia."

"Oh, my God!" The kid started wiggling. "That song was rad. My girlfriend in high school was named Karen, and it was her favorite song. I told her I would write her a song someday too, but I just played your song, dude."

"Okay." It was time to dust that wedge of dirt behind the front door. You know that place no one wants to clean? I was ready to clean it. Anything was better than strolling down memory lane with this idiot.

"Except when I played it to her, I sang it 'Kissing Karen.'" The kid was fucking happy.

"Good move," I said. "I think you owe me some royalties."

He stared at me, figuring out if I was serious. I began to soften to the kid when I realized he was just stupid. The kid asked, "Was she a real chick?"

"I don't remember."

"You don't?"

"No, I think she was real, but we never really know, do we?"

The kid said, "No, but that's cool."

"What's cool?" I asked him.

"I don't know." He was lost, looked kind of bummed.

I said, "Good." This should toughen him up for the rest of his sad fucking life. "Whatever happened to Karen?" I asked, not giving a shit.

"Who?"

Who?! Your fucking girlfriend, you dumb-fuck! But I said, "You know, that girlfriend you had that you were just talking about a few seconds ago? Karen?"

"She went off to college and dumped me for some dude."

I patted him on the shoulder, "A real cunt, huh?"

The kid was shocked. "No, she was great. We just grew apart."

Jesus. This didn't help my mood. When I was this retard's age, if a girl dumped you, you didn't say dumb shit like, "We grew apart." The fact was she still owed you money and she was fucking some other dude. If she dumped you, she was a cunt. If she dumped your friend or one of your drinking buddies, she was a cunt. If she dumped you, you didn't grow apart. That was the kind of shit you said when you dumped her ass, not the other way around.

I remembered my first time working as a bartender. It was back when Billy and I had moved up to N.Y.C. and I was seeing Kasia. It was a private art gathering in SoHo, and I had only been in the city for about eight months. I poured wine, popped open beers and poured vodka and cranberry into plastic glasses next to a weathered guy with a Rod Stewart haircut. Both of us were in white shirts with black clip-on bow ties. Once the crowd quieted into their plastic cups of booze, we started talking about shit, and he was interested 'cause I played guitar. Turns out he had been the lead guitarist for Kansas or one of those other big 1970s stadium bands, maybe Foreigner. He had made a bundle of cash. The dude had to be rich, right? So why was he standing in a white shirt in SoHo in the mid-nineties, serving free liquor to a crowd of people staring at graffiti art? Turns out he'd shot his whole wad on blow. All of it. Snorted it up his nose. And I didn't know that day— feeling pity for that sad fucker—someday I'd be staring at myself in that same mirror. The difference was that I didn't snort my career up my nose. My career bailed in an urn filled with my best friend's ashes. I hadn't made a fortune and lost it. I hadn't done shit. I had a minor-label EP jewel box with my dead friend's face taped over a shadow.

MEGAN BATHE

No, the guitar noise chat and the all-night shifts at the Diamond didn't soothe me by the time the new century showed up and the robots forgot to attack. Not much was soothing me when Megan handed me the journal, bound in leather, and asked me to write down my thoughts. It did sometimes help me to fuck Megan, so I didn't hand the book back and tell her to fuck off. Instead, I promised the big-titted stray I would give the journal a shot. The problem was that my thoughts were bad and I didn't want to spend more time with my thoughts. "But that's the point," Megan had said to me. "You need to come to terms with what's going on inside you, Scout, so it doesn't control you."

I'd known Megan for a while before I fucked her. My waiting list of strays to bang was long back then and I was busy, but one night, it happened. She got on my nerves, and next thing, we were going at it in the Diamond behind locked doors after closing.

"You need," Megan said when she handed me the journal, "to come to terms with Billy's passing. You need to make peace with yourself, Scout, and with Billy."

I like Megan best when I'm fucking her, and she's looking at me like she's in love. There is just one moment there where—for one quick second—she is quiet and not giving me advice and pointing out how I screwed up.

I first met Megan when Billy was alive. It was right before we signed the deal, because I remember she was at the Bowery Bar the night we all went out to celebrate. I saw her walking down 2nd Avenue past Paul's, the hamburger spot just south of St. Mark's Place.

Megan looked kind of sad and lonely, and I figured I'd bring her along with the band; one extra stray is cool. She had already been in the Diamond one night when I was bored and the place was empty. This was after a night when Billy Corgan and Marilyn Manson had come in with this loud, kind of scary woman who I thought was about to throw a bottle at me, but she turned out to be Courtney Love and actually tipped me, which was more than those other two did, although they didn't drink either—not that that's an excuse. I comped Megan a vodka-cran. She was wearing a pink Chanel suit, which was not the kind of outfit one expected in the Diamond. Jon Domogarow's Boston terrier sat on the steps huffing and puffing. The dog looked like a black-and-white frog, but the dog was cool, kind of like some tiny Yoda. I half expected the Frog Yoda to start telling me about the Force and my duty to save the Republic. The dog was famous around the East Village because it would sit in the doorway and stroke its penis with its paw, big eyes bulging in its frog skull. Girls would walk down 6th Street and coo and cajole the animal as it sat back on its humped tail, staring at the big world, stroking off. One day after opening the bar around six, two strays came into the bar and lifted up their shirts, flashing the dog. Something about bars in the East Village and girls raising their skirts, pulling up their tops… it reminds me of the time a girl snuck down the steps when I was changing the kegs in the basement and lifted her dress, showing me her shaved pussy because she liked one of our Johnson State tunes on the subject of the waxed snatch. And it did make your shift go fast, these girls flashing you, then sipping cocktails and watching you with glazed calm.

I kept telling myself I was going to get back into music, but I wasn't and didn't. I just drank, listened to the jukebox and followed the night. Megan would ask me about my life and always seemed to have answers for everything, like she had it all figured out and I was just the idiot that couldn't get a move-on. I'd watch her pick up younger boys. It was no big deal to me. She had been a shy girl once on 2nd Avenue, holding some dessert box of pastry crumbs, but Megan got over her shyness, and now, she'd prowl the Diamond, find her prey and drag them out into the dark and use them to help her get to sleep.

Before we hooked up, I never thought about fucking her, I mean, it crossed my mind, but it never stuck. Megan was a full-on Diamond regular when we hooked up. It was a dead night, closing time. She was drunk, throwing me some sloppy drunk-stray wet-eye, that glistening look chicks give when you're basically in there. You've got the chick nailed and fucking her is just your call. The vibe has happened, the connection made, she's yours if you want her. Megan told me to lock the tavern door, which I did because I was going to do it anyway. The bar was empty, and it was a few minutes short of four in the morning. I wiped the bar and flipped up the stools onto the top of the bar and began to mop. L7 on the juke. Megan got behind me and squeezed my ass, her face flushed, eyes crooked from vodka. I moved Megan in front of me and slipped the mop handle between her thighs, pushing up her skirt, reaching around and stroking the mop handle like I was jerking off her fake cock. "Oh my," she said, looking down at her mop-handle dick, "It looks like we have a situation."

"It's those breasts. They're so big," I said, not caring at all about her tits, but I was bored, it was late and Megan kept telling me I should be writing songs again. She used the word *situation* a few times and a few more times, and I told her politely to shut-up. "You use that word too much." Megan could have told me to fuck off, but she didn't. Megan just watched me stroke the mop handle, her eyes glazed.

It was on.

Megan unbuttoned me in a flash and had my cock in her mouth before the mop handle hit the floor. I got hard and she took me deep in her mouth, gasping, gagging, committed. Megan traced her fingers on the single word tatted on my groin, above my throbbing cock: *Concentrate!* I looked down at her breasts wide and pale in her black bra, Megan's brown hair falling around her shoulders, tickling my stomach and legs as she worked to keep my cock deep in her throat. Megan didn't look like she needed oxygen. I yanked off her top and unclipped her bra, her eyes never leaving my hard-on. She got back to sucking me off, and I watched the dogs playing poker in the wood frames screwed to the wall, the jukebox moving into the back-log of tunes paid for by regulars long gone after last call. Rob Zombie's "Dragula" was a perfect stripper tune for Megan sucking my cock. Megan was good. She wasn't too busy. When I was ready, I pulled my cock out of her pretty mouth and splashed a load of cum into her parted lips, her eyes locked on my cock circled by her delicate hands. She let the cum dribble down her chin, then wiped a finger along the spillage and ran the glossy finger over each of her nipples.

I offered Megan a final Cosmo. She accepted. I poured myself a hefty glass of dirt.

That's when Megan told me about her difficult relationship with her father. Her family was from Provo, Utah, but moved around often and she spent high school in San Diego, California. She called herself a "Jack Mormon," explaining over her pink cocktail as she reapplied her lipstick that she was born Mormon, but didn't practice. Megan was a piece of work. It started to make more sense to me as she sat in her bra and panties on the barstool and sipped her cocktail, in no rush to get back in her dress. Sometimes Megan would take the boys home or work something else out, like the night she gave Baron a blow-job in the women's restroom. I'd usually have my own thing going on, but Megan had one sure way to get me. She would start talking to me about the band and ask why I wasn't playing music. This turned into talk about me being a quitter. "Like your dad, right?" she'd ask, and I'd kick myself for talking to her about family history, her face reflecting the jukebox light, the haze of tequila, the noise of the Diamond jammed with people on my night off, Megan's bitchy smile, like she knew my dark core and what messed with me at night when I wasn't drunk enough to sleep. She'd glance to the door. "You can come over if you want," she'd say. "I don't have anything real important to do." And I'd be sitting there, too buzzed, but going in my head, *It's three in the fucking morning, who has anything to do?* Megan would say, "Come on. You've had enough tequila."

Megan was a good ride. I liked her, but Billy was gone and time crawled and I kept hitting the dirt. Then I got beat up by one of the regulars. I remember saying something, and I remember the first punch coming at me. Jon Domogarow saw the other punches. I woke up down in the Diamond basement, passed out with dried blood on my face and a wet bar towel on the cement floor, next to the kegs of beer. Jon had put a pillow under my head and wrapped me in a blanket. The rat crawled toward me. It was time to get out of the Diamond.

IF I SHOT JUNK

September 13, 2001, Ralph's pad: My head gets fucked when I start thinking about the way things were going and how things got where they are right fucking now. It's not that things have ended, but that's what I keep fighting in my head: THE END. That can't be the deal already? I'm 35 years old and that sounds old enough to have got something going. It can't be THE END. I have no clue what comes after THE END. I hurt myself last night at the Black Clock, drinking too many glasses of tequila, telling myself to walk across the street and make it up the five flights to the Fat Mexican's. Instead, I just drank, checking out the new bartender, named Rio, raising my hand whenever my glass was dry. Today sucked at the boat dock. At my lunch break, I stood at the door of the Dublin House on 79th, my skull and gut screaming for a Bloody Mary, fucked up, but a sweet plan.

I had two Bloody Marys fast and dragged my ass down Broadway for a slice of pizza.

After work, I picked up a pint of Sauza Especial and a bumper of Bud and KFC three-piece box on my way back to the Fat Mexican's.

When we were flat broke, Billy and I used to sit back with our beers and talk about the tricks of staying alive low on the rock-star food-chain: scamming for food and a place to crash and a way to cop more beers. We'd talk about Plan A, which was being a full-on rock star, versus Plan B, which was making some kind of living with your music, versus Plan C, which was where we wanted to think we were, which was followed by Plan D, which meant doing whatever we had to do next and didn't want to do, like get dishwashing jobs or paint some apartment for cash, versus whatever followed Plan D and was worse than living in cheap apartments, hustling for music gigs around Manhattan and aiming for a record deal you could almost taste… all the way to THE END. The plans got worse the further down the alphabet you fell. The joke was that, at the end of the road, was Plan Z. Plan Z was the final plan—before THE END. We figured living in a homeless shelter on your forty-fifth birthday was Plan X, so Plan Z was seriously fucked. Plan Z was a shotgun to the mouth after too many nights curled on a steam vent. The trick was where to get the shotgun. In Plan Z, you're not Kurt Cobain. You're broke. Plan Z was bad, so far down, you weren't making it back up.

If Plan A was being a full-on rock star and Plan B was making a living with my guitar and putting out critically respected tunes for a small, but committed label and still headlining major gigs and Plan C was right now and Plan D was painting apartments for cash, the drop off from Plan D was steep. I'm far enough down the alphabet now. I think I'm at Plan M. I think Plan O puts me in the crappy shack where I sit all day at the 79th Street Boat Basin, except I'll be sleeping there too on a mattress made out of Filet O' Fish and Big Mac containers stuffed into a garbage bag. My blanket will be a raincoat that smells of puke, and I'll be digging clothes from the dumpster. Plan M is as far as I want to go toward Plan Z. It's time to crawl back toward the fresh air.

If you followed the music scene, you might have heard of our band, Johnson State. We were a buzz. We were almost there, but we didn't happen. We were close to breaking big or blowing up as the A&R guys said while they shuffled around us like buzzards, flapping their Italian fabric and spitting at us and staring in our eyes, waving paper in our grids. It was going to be our year. Then Billy put on the blue suit.

Things always change, right, Billy?

I almost wish I was a junkie this week. I'd just get high, scrounge some money and score some shit, instead of being a normal booze-exhausted ex-bartender, hustling for spending cash and digging in a stack of boxes half a mile from Ground Zero. If I was a junkie, I could have slept through the whole day Tuesday, or better, got loaded and stared at that severe clear sky and talked to myself about how wild and perfect and beautiful life could be if it wasn't soiled with bad vibes and violence and sadness and greed and hate. But I don't do dope. Not Tuesday, not Wednesday, not today. Instead, I worked one more fucking day, this one an early shift at the 79th Street Boat Basin, with a night stick in my hand like some TV cop if he was played by Kid Rock with a wicked tequila migraine. I got out of my fish shack in the afternoon and nursed a cold one at the Dublin House, joining the old drunks as they sat with their glasses of legal poison and watched the passenger planes penetrate the North and South Towers, murdering thousands of innocent people. We sipped our hootch and waited while those poor fuckers that didn't get toasted in seconds from airplane fuel or ripped into smears from fragments of jetplane got to leap from boiling rooms or dissolve in the collapsing skyscrapers. People vaporized when they hit the street. One beer turned into three. People dropping like water balloons in my skull. I did the same thing yesterday, only after I got warmed up, I grabbed a downtown train. I had a plan yesterday, but I didn't plan on finding the Book Mouse. I figured I'd hit my storage facility then walk south of 14th Street to K.L.'s restaurant/bar at Downing and Varick in the West Village. I would shake Kenny's hand and chit-chat with the very hot, very bored waitresses that, for some not-good reason, never try to fuck me. I had an urge to be around friends. I didn't want to go cross-town to the Diamond. I'd do that later with a bunch of records to sell from my storage unit, make some cash and check in with Jon. Then I'd see how people were doing at the Diamond Pub, the whole deal, but

Kenny's was a straight shot on the subway, and I wouldn't get too loaded and I'd be back uptown in time to catch some sleep, if you can call it that, on Ralph's floor. I figured the biggest problem at Kenny's would be listening to the business suits who didn't get killed talk about the attacks as if the attacks were some kind of big football game, a sporting gig to be analyzed and critiqued, like the Jets lost a big one to the Dolphins. The West Village has never been my scene. If it wasn't for Kenny's and Don Hill's—back when they had the Clit Club on Thursday nights or maybe an old Western at the Film Forum—I'd never go near the place. Now that I live uptown, I sure as shit don't need to ride a subway all the way downtown to hear more assholes make asshole talk. But it would be good to hang with Kenny tonight and smoke a few cigarettes, sip a glass of high-end dirt, chow on some Korean shortribs and check out the hot waitresses that always act friendly and bored, and never try to fuck me. Also I knew Kenny would run me a tab.

The TV keeps telling me that volunteers are lining up at Ground Zero, digging in the wreckage, calling out for survivors. I can't imagine what anyone is going to find digging in that hole of ghosts, except cell phones ringing and maybe some severed hands and worse.

I wish Billy was here for this shit, except for one bad move, Billy would be here right now.

Billy survived a fucked-up family life. Billy handled it. Billy's mom ran off when we were in junior-high and Billy's brother was a psychopath and Billy's dad was one notch up from my dad in flat-out failure, but Billy didn't whine. Billy got me playing music and got me in that van on the road to New York City. Billy made Johnson State.

And Billy took Johnson State away.

You'd think a childhood spent watching your dad swill down his pain would have left me bottle shy, but all afternoon, after the Bloodys, I was counting on a big glass of tequila, my hangover screaming for hair-of-the-dog. My drinking has always been aggressive, which was cool when it worked. But it's not working. My drinking days are behind me. I just don't want to know it. There is a lightbulb blinking off and on in a square room, plaster peeling from the water-stained ceiling. Sirens and flashing neon give the square room a kind of cool hard-core vibe, but it's not cool at all. I'm crashed out on a stained mattress in a cheap motel. I can't pay for food and couldn't even eat the food if the plate was in front of me. I've spent my last few bucks on a pint of white dirt. I look down on myself on that stained mattress. I'm bloated, starved, my eyes shut tight. If I was snoring, I'd be passed out, but I'm not snoring. I'm clenched tight, praying the bottle of white dirt isn't empty. I've got to wake up, and when I wake up, I don't want to be that guy I'm looking down on, Billy. I don't want to be that sweaty wreck, shaking from withdrawal, scared shitless, trapped in my skin, Billy. I saw the fear in your eyes when the dope ran out. Fucking trapped. I saw the death sentence. When it took too long for you to score, it was ugly to watch. Billy, it was in your eyes. I should have done something, should have pulled you back to Plan Z… problem was I figured we were way up the alphabet, not down at THE END. I figured we had time, but we didn't have any left. Our time was gone.

THE BOOK MOUSE

I've put a dent into the pint of dirt and feel good. Time is spinning ahead and behind me like Time was tossed from a moving car, bouncing on the highway. Time is breaking up like road-trip sunlight on your windshield, shimmering off the side-view. Creases of Time shine on the face of the Econoline's crappy cassette player in the dashboard. Time is all around me, but I can't touch it, Billy. Still, I've got more of Time than some people this week. I won't whine. The tequila takes the edge off. I started to talk about going down to Kenny Lee's restaurant and my storage facility yesterday, Wednesday. I made the storage unit, but I couldn't make it south of 14th Street deeper into the West Village to Kenny Lee's restaurant. You need I.D. to prove you live south of 14th. This was the borderline, protecting the massive crime scene at Ground Zero, while the rescuers worked and trucks hauled debris and the searchers searched for survivors. Tonight the guitar noise in my skull tells me to go to the Black Clock and see if Rio is working, but instead, I'm going to sip this pint of Sauza and ease back this bumper of Bud, just hang tight and scribble for Megan. Last night I hit the dirt hard, really rocked the boat, right after getting back from the storage facility and telling myself I wouldn't put myself in a coma. I got my eyes taped onto the curve of Rio's fine ass and the tequila went down like apple juice. Rio comped me a few, but I did my own damage. Like I said, I moved uptown because I needed a change— any kind of change and fast from the Diamond scene and all the East Village corner bars, where I was pals with the bartenders because I had comped them heavy or fucked them or both. I knew everyone, but when you drink tequila to get sober, you know you're either having one hell of a good ride or you are in a first-class seat to a fucked-up place. I had both going hard when that regular smacked my grid into a bloody mess. The electricity was out on my Clinton Street crib and things were not looking sweet. The Fat Mexican had settled some divorce issues and moved uptown, taking a job I still don't understand with these business professors. The Fat Mexican made a bid to straighten his shit up after his ex took everything except the limp dick in his hand while he cried, looking at their wedding photo and trying to get a hard-on. I watched my bloody face in the Diamond mirror, had three shots of vodka, washed up in the Men's and figured it was time get out of Dodge.

It was hard to let go of my gig at the Diamond, but the 79th Street Boat Basin was advertising for a flunky who could look intimidating and was reasonably reliable. I'm skinny, but tall and I can do a good psycho face, so they gave me a shirt with epaulets, a walkie-talkie and my nightstick and my perky cap. I don't have real guns in the arm department, but I learned in the mosh pit and on stage how to puff out my chest. When I want to, I can use the killer Clint Eastwood face for real. My eyes can get dudes to back off. A guy named Anders hired me at the Boat Basin. Anders gives me my paycheck.

I noticed sheets of paper yesterday in the subway and on streetlights. The news stations today show hospitals with walls pasted with Xeroxed smiling faces of people that didn't make it out of Tuesday, smiling faces of people hoisting their children, posing next to their favorite dog or cat or raising pieces of cake, prepping for a swing with a softball bat or a stroke of the tennis racket or standing with their new skis in the white snow, faces of people sitting in front of the Christmas tree, faces copied onto computer paper and taped all over the city. If you didn't know better, New York looks like the city is about to have a big party or maybe start a new holiday and the city wants to make sure you don't miss it. Then you figure out the city is having a funeral.

Before I got hammered on Wednesday night and watched Rio's ass until I was blind, I took the train down to my storage facility on 17th Street. The plan was to dig through my boxes and cannibalize my record collection and sell off some wax to the local dealers. I had racks and racks of records in my old Clinton Street crib. I know a few guys that will pay real money.

Remember the song "Kissing Kasia"? Our best cut. The song you did perfect, Billy. The tune on our EP that helped get us the deal with Fingerline. I can remember so many things about Kasia, but I can't remember kissing Kasia. No memory. The memory bank is empty. Can't even remember if I liked kissing her, but I guess I did. I went out with the girl for two years. The reason I'm thinking about all this, Billy, is that I was in my storage facility yesterday staring at the Book Mouse. The song "Kissing Kasia" stuck in my head. What happened was that, digging through the boxes, looking for that wax to sell, I came across an object I didn't expect, a voodoo surprise, as soft as a rabbit-foot charm in blond gold. The Book Mouse spun me, Billy. Dead as a nail and as alive as if the scissors were still in my hand and the petal of Kasia's blood was still on the tip of my finger from ten years ago in my Hell's Kitchen apartment.

Have you ever had the past jump right into the present? Not just a memory that takes you back in time but an actual thing dropped right into your hands from the machine whirring up in the gasoline sky? It sounds bogus, but that was the deal yesterday. Time folded around me like a blanket or like water when you jump high off the cliff or platform and shoot feet-first to the bottom. That gasoline sky spit the gold coin right into my hand. I was tripping. All I could do was look in my hand at the Book Mouse and shiver. What was this?

I stared in my hand at the coin of Kasia's gold pubes.

A tuft—a pad that made me think of a mouse…

Kasia Crocetti.

This was the gold coin of her pubic hair I snipped one afternoon in the Hell's Kitchen apartment ten years ago. The tuft of hair felt warm, but I knew it wasn't, just the fever of my hangover and the effort of lifting boxes up and down in my storage cell. I clipped Kasia's pubes down that afternoon but nicked her with the scissors. We had painted the whole apartment that weekend with a fresh coat of white paint. I put the gold pad of her hair into my bartender's guide and forgot about it. Ten years the Book Mouse waited for me.

I never committed, just called Kasia when it was time to hook up for drinks and fucking after the sun went away for the day. And Kasia let me get away with it. I remember wanting Kasia to stand up to me and make it clear in my own head what I wanted, but Kasia helped me fuck it all up by not telling me to fuck off. Kasia would see me walking up Broadway near Lincoln Center with another girl, like that one time with the actress after dinner and a movie, and Kasia would get mad and we wouldn't see each other for a week. But then she would be back at my apartment door in her jeans with the ripped knees and cowboy boots, her leotard dance top and her long gold hair. It's weird I can't remember kissing Kasia, but ten years is a long time.

I'M DIFFERENT

I sat in my fish shed at the Boat Basin again today. For anyone that hasn't done this kind of thing to earn a few dollars, this is a great way to spend Saturday: cramped in an office that smells of moldy river, while your head screams with a drink logic that a sixer of Dominican beer would help the pint of tequila and bumper of Bud coast you down.

I'm back at Ralph's now, watching the sun fade in a blue sky. I'm just not right in the skull. The Book Mouse dropped into my open hand. For ten fast years the tuft of Kasia's trimmed pubic hair nestled in my *Mr. Boston Official Bartender's Guide*. Kasia left me for Mr. Payback because she had to leave me. I made Kasia leave me. I fucked it up again and again. I kicked that girl to the curb, when all she wanted was to stand beside me and hold my hand. Screwing it up with Kasia wasn't the worst thing I've done, but, like I said, it stung ten years ago when the dust cleared and I realized Kasia was gone.

They've opened the city south of 14th Street and I'm toying with that subway ride down to Kenny Lee's restaurant, but as I sit here—sipping chocolate milk, kicking it on Ralph's floor, leaning against the sofa, trying to do Megan's journal gig, keeping one eye on Ralph's cat, that piss balloon covered in fur—who walks in the door but the Fat Mexican himself. Ralph shows up after some flag-football game in Riverside Park with graduate business students. Flag-football? Graduate business students? *And I thought my day sucked?* Did I tell you the cat's name? Fabio. It was a while back that Ralph and his then-wife paid a chunk of money for the swollen Tribble, traveling upstate by train in the dead, dark winter to a high-end Persian cat dealer who gave the Fat Mexican and his wife a certificate that told them why they just got ripped off buying an animal so overbred it needed vitamin shots and regular acupuncture treatments to keep from shitting orange strings of crap all over its furry legs. After the divorce, Ralph got stuck with the large dreadlocked gerbil. His ex just took their daughter, Chloe, and whatever savings Ralph hadn't tanked in his lame

110

dot.com company.

After his game of flag-football, Ralph rips himself open a manly bottle of non-alcoholic Cutter's beer. He stands over me, my jeans and cat-kicking boots as I lean against his sofa, my ass parked on a part of his floor not stained by pale splotches of cat piss. I'm smoking a cigarette.

"How's that going?" Ralph points at Megan's journal.

"What do you mean? Aren't you doing this too?"

Ralph sips his Cutters.

"You know, for Megan?" I say. "Didn't she give you one of these?" I hold up the leather journal of scribbled and blank pages.

"I'm using a digital recording device," the Fat Mexican says to me. He reaches into a hi-tech satchel filled with business books in bright covers with big letters like cereal boxes or porn videos and pulls out a small metal James Bond thingamajig. "Sony makes this," Ralph explains. "It's cutting edge. You can download clips onto your PC and e-mail them, if you've got a fast modem. Soon you'll be able to Bluetooth them."

I have no idea what he's talking about, except for the part where he's not spending all his time scribbling in a journal. The Senator gets some James Bond gadget, while I have to lug this leather book all over the place? I knew Ralph had been yanked into Megan's project or D.O.T. gig, but I figured everyone who got involved had two things in common: one, they had shot a load of cum on Megan's big tits, and two, they had to waste all their time writing in a journal. The Fat Mexican wasn't writing in a journal. The Fat Mexican was talking, like into a tape recorder! How hard was that?

"That's fucked up." I'm wondering if Ralph has any real beers in the fridge. Maybe one or two nestled down in the vegetable drawer under his array of diet shakes. "Why don't we switch? I'll talk into your James Bond toy and you can use my high-tech pen and write on this super-rare designer paper. This journal is way cool. Very old-school."

The Fat Mexican, standing in his sweats and Troy Aikman Dallas Cowboys jersey, just grins, bubbles his non-alcoholic malt beverage, burps and wipes his lips. "No thanks."

"You got any real beer?"

Ralph waves toward the kitchen. "Have at it, roomie."

I give him a look. Where did this dude learn to be a host?

He goes, "I didn't buy any. If that's what you're asking."

I give the Fat Mexican a quick annoyed glance then let it slide, faking the humbleness of the brave artist who doesn't need a hand up during hard times, but what I'm really thinking is, *Stock the fucking fridge, bro!*

These are the pleasures of couch-surfing. I've got the Fat Mex sucking down his piss-bubbles of non-alcoholic beer, while his cat, Fabio, dangles a spiked willy over my sleeping bag and Ralph checks up on his 401K or whatever he does puttering around on his computer. And here I am, his friend, guarding the last dry and clean pillow in the apartment and asking for nothing but a twelve-pack of beer and a shot or two of dirt?

"I'm on the wagon," says Ralph. "You need some money for a six-pack?"

I wave him off. I'm an adult. I can buy my own booze. "Sure," I turn on a dime and hold out my hand. "Need anything from down at the bodega?"

"Some jalapeno chips," says the Fat Mexican. He reaches toward the cat and I swear I taste vomit in the back of my throat as the Senator scratches the tangled mullet of Fabio's head fur. "Megan told me she thought it would be better if you wrote in the journal," says Ralph.

My look must have been what the fuck? Ralph's wallet opens and my hand closes on the ten spot.

"She said it would get you back into making music." Ralph grins. "Megan is sharp."

"Megan is a whore." I can't believe that cunt is trying to control me from down in her overpriced railroad apartment on East 12th. "That chick doesn't know shit."

Then Ralph goes, "Megan told me George is working on her project, too. He's back in L.A. The thing with Lilly didn't work out." And I go: "Yeah, I heard that news. Can't say it surprised me. But I'm pretty sure Megan is using this lame D.O.T. idea to keep her hooks into all of us dudes from back-in-the-day. Guess she must be tired of banging all that younger East Village cock."

I lugged the sixer of El Presidents back upstairs, two bags of jalapeno chips on top of the green bottles. The Fat Mexican's TV is saying how the remains of victims are getting ambulanced up from Ground Zero to the Jacob Javits Center. I ripped one bottle open and had a gurgle, just to ease the edge. I can't believe I haven't made it back downtown since Wednesday. I still have the albums I pulled out before the Book Mouse stunned me. GNR's *Appetite for Destruction*, Motorhead's *Eat the Rich*, Lemonheads' *Lovey*, the Minutemen's *Double Nickel on a Dime*. I didn't find that first Jane's Addiction. I bet I could get some cash for that. I found Megadeth's *Killing Is My Business* and *Business Is Good* and Alice in Chains' *Dirt*, the Chili Peppers' *Mother's Milk* and Jon Spencer's *Extra Wide*, which was a favorite at the Diamond. Plus I found the Butthole Surfers' *Independent Worm Saloon* and that's when my hand hit the pebble-leather cover of *Mr. Boston Official Bartender's Guide.*

I remember Kasia's tits. They were so awesome, her mom even bragged about them to me and made sure I noticed them. She said, "Look at Kasia's bust!" (Like I could avoid it?) I remember her Levi's with the holes in the knees. I remember the black lace bustier she wore under white T-shirts. I remember pulling down her bikini underwear on that ratty sofa in Hell's Kitchen or when she undressed for me on my futon in the corner by my guitars.

I opened the bartender's guide on Wednesday, September 12, and the Book Mouse dropped into my hand.

I remember a whole lot. I just can't remember kissing Kasia.

I sat at Ralph's computer and worked on a letter to Kasia. Like I said, I'm new to this computer shit, but the technology is cool. I would have used it before, but I never had a reason. I'm old-school, analog, didn't even have a cordless phone on Clinton Street. A CD player, sure, but I listened to wax most days and nights.

```
SENT FROM: rvillalobos@earthspring.com
SEND TO: kasia_crocetti@windosync.net
SUBJECT: Long Time - from Scout Harris
MESSAGE: Kasia,
Hey, it's me. Scout.
I know it's been a long time. (Don't be mad.
I just want to see if you are okay.) Tuesday
was crazy, right? Are you in new york? Call me.
I am here. Hope you are safe.
Scout Harris

P.S. don't be mad. I'm different.
```

I read the message and checked it out with Ralph, added his phone number, and then he told me which button to hit, so I pressed "SEND" and my note to Kasia shot off into computer space. Yeah, I'm different: I'm homeless, broke, and completely fucked by dull days in my fish shed at the boat dock, hungover, waiting for a paycheck to get me another bottle. My skull flutters with porn images of Kasia. I'm trying to keep my eyes off the televisions all over Manhattan. I don't want to watch those two planes slam into the skyscrapers filled with people. The Book Mouse slipped into my open hand Wednesday, and I hope Kasia Crocetti is okay. I want to make sure Kasia wasn't in the wrong place Tuesday. But part of writing her that computer letter was a different thing, wondering if Kasia was still hot and might want to hang out. I didn't want that computer letter to spook her, but my mind was jumpy. A cigarette was burning a blue strand of smoke in my fingers on the dock, while planes slammed into the World Trade Center over and over again. Orange waves of fiery gasoline spill down the stairs and through the ceiling and across the floor like a ship sinking in a red ocean.

I typed that letter and hit "SEND." Every word I typed was lame. I can deal with that. My mind is some kind of crazed guitar solo with shitloads of screeching feedback. This terrible week is winding down.

Yeah, I'm different, Kasia.

No, I'm the same, just more fucked up. I'm putting this pen down.

Hey, I'm back again, and it's Monday. I didn't write in this thing at all yesterday, but I'll tell you why. Something big happened.

I had dinner with Kasia.

I kissed Kasia.

Like I said, I'm not down with all this computer shit, but on Saturday, I told the Fat Mexican what I wanted to do after the Book Mouse slid into my hand. I asked Ralph if there was some way we could use a computer to track down a chick I hadn't seen in years. Kasia was probably still with Payback, living in some Crate & Barrel-packed condo in Chelsea with cocker spaniels and maybe one or two kids. But I can't whine about the past. I was the kind of dude that deserved what I got. You act like I acted and you will get a Mr. Payback at your door. Trust me. Billy, you got your Mr. Payback big time, holding your blue suit on a hanger with a tiny balloon in the pocket.

Ralph said, "You want to go back and try to fix the past with this lady?"

"I'm not trying to fix anything," I said. "I just want to check in after the whole 9/11 crap, make sure she's okay. Besides, she was hot, what's wrong with checking in with hot chicks from the past? Is there something wrong with that?" I realized I was sounding kind of defensive, which is probably why the Senator just dropped the subject.

Ralph said, "Let's google her."

"Yeah, that's the idea, but we have to find her first."

Ralph laughed, "Scout, Google is a search engine on the web."

"*Riiiight*," I said. "You totally lost me after you said Scout."

Ralph broke it down, there's this thing on the computer. It's called a search engine. You just put some word or name in a box on the screen and hit "GO" and it hunts for anything that relates to the word or name you typed into the box. I asked Ralph to search for Johnson State and couldn't believe when a bunch of what the Senator called "hits" popped up. Yeah, great, these hits were basically every shit review our band ever got, playing our hearts out in dives, rambling around in that smelly van, but there were also a few good reviews from some 'zines and three obituaries on Billy's death.

What really blew me away and even got a whistle from the Senator were some photographs from that Fingerline benefit we did at Woodstock. There we were! Ralph did what he called "a download," and there were Billy, Josh, Jacob, and myself, cranking it up in front of a sweaty crowd. Some shirtless dude was crowd surfing in front of the stage, with a big draped JOHNSON STATE banner behind Josh as he hammered his kit.

I thought of all the chicks I'd hooked up with who had these computers in their apartments, sitting on a kitchen table or something. I could have been googled! This Internet was heavy duty.

"We have one thing going for us," said Ralph. "Her unique name, 'Kasia Crocetti'"

We googled Kasia and got a hit, an e-mail address for a high-school reunion. Ralph pointed out it could easily be the same girl if Kasia went to high school in New Jersey. My Kasia did go to high-school in New Jersey. Could there be two Kasias in the Garden State?

Ralph showed me how to type out the e-mail letter. Ralph found it funny that I had no clue how to use the machine, and I had to point out to him that I could put a guitar in his hands and he could tap it like a monkey, but it might take him a while to figure out how to play one hook I could dream up in my sleep.

I paced up and down Broadway all Saturday afternoon, trying not to go into the Black Clock and stare at Rio's ass or go into Cannon's Pub and look up some strays and spend money I didn't have and get drunk too early. There was a new Kim's Video uptown, so I wandered that direction and went into the shop and flipped CD jewel boxes. I promised myself that, if Kasia wrote back and we talked, I'm going to be different. I'm going to be honest about my feelings and not jerk her around just to get in her pants.

I met the Fat Mexican back at his pad. He brought a pizza. He's a cool dude. I've got to say that for the Senator. And before I can eat my third slice of pepperoni, the Fat Mexican is in front of his computer, yapping at me about how he needed to get himself a faster LSD line or some shit. *Click, whiz* and Ralph went, "She wrote you back."

I looked on the screen and there was a letter addressed to me: Scout Harris. The letter was from Kasia. I couldn't believe it! She was in New York. She had just got off a bus from Montana. She was living in Montana. Livingstone, Montana? Well, Kasia always did look good in cowboy boots and Levi's, particularly with her shirt on the floor of my Hell's Kitchen apartment. Kasia's computer letter told me she was in New Jersey. She put her parents' phone number in the letter. My hands shook and it wasn't entirely from the booze. I picked up Ralph's phone. It was that easy. I called Kasia Crocetti.

I called Kasia, and we talked for two hours. 1) Kasia had left Mr. Payback and 2) We were meeting Sunday night for dinner.

It happened that fast.

I owed Ralph a glass of dirt. I didn't have much cash but convinced him to walk downstairs and buy us a few rounds at the Black Clock. It was Saturday night.

Ralph and I grabbed barstools. Rio was working and popped me a Bud and Ralph some Euro non-alcoholic beer. You know what goes down? Ralph falls in love with Rio. I'm not kidding. It takes three minutes. Who knows, maybe he's done jerking off to photos of his ex-wife. Maybe he's ready to get back in the game. As for me, I'm going upstairs to rub one out with the image of a naked Kasia in front of my eyes. The images are all ten years old and hazy, but if the booze doesn't hit me too hard, I'll get there. Kasia had a rocking little body and my skull remembers that I used to get to use it.

VARIEGATED

Kasia pushes open the door of Kenny Lee's on Sunday night, leaning her shoulder into it. The weather has turned nippy and Kasia has a scarf looped around her neck and her lush blond hair. She's wearing Levi 501s, just like ten years ago, and a plushy velvet green shirt that buttons up the front, with the top two buttons unfastened and the plushy velvet green shirt's collar pulled out over the collar of her tan buckskin jacket. Kasia unzips the jacket and looks around the restaurant, sees me at the bar, blinks, not wearing glasses, must be contacts, and smiles, waving. I hold up the Budweiser I've been nursing for forty-five minutes. A big uncontrollable goofball grin slams my grid. The funny thing is that I had planned on a few tequila shots to warm me up and get me in the groove, but once I walked into Kenny's, I changed my mind. I wanted to see Kasia without dirt in my skull. I'm flying from adrenaline and the beer is nothing but a bottle to hold in my nervous hand, while a Spirit burns in the ashtray. I've been tossing Clint Eastwood face everywhere I look, including the bar mirror, and my face feels stuck in a squint and cold killer grimace. But seeing Kasia rips that cold killer gaze away and I'm smiling. Kasia. Her smile is just like I remember her smile, and she makes her way through the crowded tables.

Kasia gives me a peck on the cheek, her eyes pale blue. She runs a finger down my black RAMONES T. "You wore that for me?"

I look into her eyes, hug her. She crushes up against me, and I remember how Kasia fit. I'm totally into the honesty gig, being a straight-shooter, the new Scout. This Scout is different, but I have no idea what she means by the RAMONES T-shirt. "Yeah," I say. I look sheepish and kind of embarrassed, which is easy since I have no clue what she's talking about. All kinds of back history could be associated with this T. Did we catch the band together, then have a fight on the sidewalk... did I fuck her in the balcony of the venue? I can't remember.

"That was a great show." Kasia pulls out a pack of Camel Lights. "Where's Kenny?" she looks around. "I can't wait to see him. It's been years."

I'd bet ten dollars Kenny is downstairs in his basement office, smoking cigarettes and practicing tricks with his Zippo to impress the hot waitresses... or reading dense books and writing poems. He told me the paperwork and long hours of running a restaurant/bar will kill you. When I was working at the Diamond, a regular asked me if I wanted to partner with him and start a bar in the East Village. I remember standing in the packed Diamond and all I saw was Billy looking back at me from the regular's face. Billy was letting me know an obvious fact: owning a bar would destroy me.

"I think he's in the office." Kasia nods and then I say, "I probably should have started my own bar." This is a lie. I'm nervous. This honesty gig is not easy. Kasia smiles, watching me. Fuck it. Do it right or don't do it.

"When did we see the Ramones?" I ask. "I don't remember."

Kasia shrugs off her buckskin jacket and the green plushy shirt billows and I can see one of her pale breasts cupped in a purple bra. I get my gaze clocked back to her bright eyes.

"I thought you said you were different?" She taps herself out a cigarette. I light it with my Zippo. Kasia inhales and exhales a thin stream of smoke.

"I am different."

"Then stop checking me out."

"I don't know if I can do that. I'm not completely different."

"You don't remember the Ramones show? Well, you look good anyway, despite what you've done to your brain."

"Forgetting things keeps my head peaceful. It's kind of a Zen deal."

"Yeah," she laughs. "You've always been very Zen, Scout."

"Remind me."

"It was at Roseland. I bought you the tickets for your birthday."

"Thanks," I say. "Before I get you a drink, can I apologize RFN for what a dickhead I was back when we were hanging out?"

"RFN," Kasia laughs, "Right fucking now, I haven't heard that one for a while." She thinks it over. "At least you were always honest."

The honesty gig. I guess Kasia was right about that part: I was an honest slut. I was an honest dickhead. "That's not good enough," I say, but Kasia is right. I did have a code, some kind of system of honor, lame as it was if you were a chick and tried to have a relationship with me. I was honest. Still. I start to say more, but Kasia touches my lips with two fingers. I stop talking. She motions to the bartender, Mike, a handsome actor, flipping a dry bar cloth against the leg of his jeans, in the corner. "Can I order a drink first?" Kasia asks. "You don't have to apologize. I did some bad stuff too."

Mike asks, "What can I get you guys?"

Kasia orders a glass of Sauvignon Blanc. I tap the bar with my empty beer bottle. Mike pours Kasia her wine and cracks me a second bottle of Bud, knocks his knuckles on the bar top. "That's on me, Scout."

She taps her wine glass against my beer bottle. I have apologized, or tried, and now I have no clue what to talk about with Kasia. Ten years. It hits me hard why I used to hook up with girls when I drank. This conversation business is tricky. My tongue was thick in my mouth, throat dry. I felt like the Fat Mexican when it came to dealing with women after his divorce, whipped before I even gave it a shot. I took a long guzzle of beer.

Kasia says, "You still have your hair. I thought you might be fat and bald."

I stroke my free hand down my longish hair. Back then it would have been past shoulder length, now it dangled half-way down my neck, not quite enough to pull back in a pony-tail, but the sloppy vibe was cool when it fell across my eyes. I flash my bedroom eyes, tilt my chin down and accidentally slip right into a lame attempt at Johnny Depp mirror, pouting and trying to look vulnerable. I pull out fast.

Kasia likes my hair. I can see her pale blue eyes watching me. "I used to love your hair. Can I..." she reaches up and I tip my head and she takes some strands of my hair, rubs the hair between her fingers, smoothing the hair like she's testing expensive fabric. She pinches my ear and laughs a small, embarrassed laugh. "Funny," she pauses to take a sip of wine and compose herself. "I remembered it more one color. Now, it's variegated."

Kasia's pretty fingers in my hair, tickling my ear, "What's that mean?" I'm sticking to my honesty gig. "Variegated?"

Kasia smiles again and her eyes look at me like I'm something she liked, lost, and found again. "*Variegated* means streaks." She lifts my hair close to my eyes. "There's strands of blond and brown, just subtle stuff, a strand of red, a bit of white."

"Gray?" I say, faking shock. "No fucking way."

Kasia brushes her fingers down the stubble on my chin. "I always liked it when you didn't shave."

"I know." I give her wolf eyes.

"Stop it," she says. "Just be yourself... be the different you."

"I'm glad I called." I work the honesty tip.

"It is nice," Kasia says. Warmth whistles up my spine, tingles in my skull. I'm aware of my own breathing. A shot of tequila would be right. I get a flash of hitting the "E" chord at the end of "Only Today." I wrote that song in the Hell's Kitchen pad after Billy and I got out of living in our van, cooking dinners on a butane stove in Tompkins Square. I met Kasia that same week in Central Park. She was roller-blading with some chick pal of hers and they were catching sun in bikinis in Sheep's Meadow, when Billy and I strolled up drinking bumpers of beer in paper sacks. I had my guitar and sat next to Kasia on the grass. I started playing Nirvana's "Smells Like Teen Spirit" all cheesy, like a lounge tune on my guitar. Kasia asked me to be quiet. We got to talking. I was in.

I don't order that shot of dirt. "I'm not bald," I say. Kasia sips her wine. "But I'm also not as skinny as I used to be." I squeeze the wedge of gut at my leather belt.

"That's nothing." She takes a drag of her cigarette, looks me up and down. "You could look worse."

Was it on?

I can't take Kasia back to my place because my place is a dry-cleaned sleeping bag that might have already been nailed with urine by that hairball Fabio. "Where are you staying?" I ask, the Depp mirror flickers on my grid, but I kill it and shift to standard Clint Eastwood, turn with my back to the bar and squint off at the entrance to the restaurant.

I let Kasia watch me for a moment, then I turn it off.

"With Amy," Kasia says. "She and her husband live on 23rd Street."

"That's cool." I let the silence burn, waiting for a great plan on some crash-pad option that will make sense to Kasia and not stress her out while walking us both hand-in-hand to that righteous moment when I get to roll down the leotard tights she must be wearing under her jeans. Yeah, I wait for the plan, but all I see in my skull is Fabio's mashed Persian cat grid staring at me with crossed eyes. I have no options. I'm hosed. No hotel, no cash, no keys to other pads, no chance of getting Kasia to ride a taxi one hundred blocks uptown to listen to the Fat Mexican snore in his bedroom while I try to fondle her on his sofa.

"Are you wearing tights? I remember you always wore green tights."

"They weren't always green," she says. "I had brown too, and maroon."

I hit off my cigarette, making sure a thick strand of my hair cuts across my eyes, I don't have anything to say, so I give her the hard down-tilt of the chin, the upward squint, hair across my face and exhale a thin stream of smoke, working basic tortured-rocker mirror.

I'm doing good for a dude without an empty tequila glass in front of me.

The news slams hard: I'm lost in Kasia.

I push this useless thought out of my skull. Stay focused. Work the honesty gig. Don't fall into mirror-lock. Hold back on the dirt. Nothing has to happen tonight. Any fool can fall in love this week after all the shit that's gone down. The trick is to get her legs in the air... no matter if it takes a week.

"It's not cold enough," she says.

"Cold enough? For what?"

"The tights," Kasia repeats. "Did you drop acid?"

"No," I work the full-on honesty. "I'm nervous."

She laughs. "Right."

The waitress asks, "Another drink?"

The waitress is attentive, professional, skinny, stylish and very bored—just another stray that doesn't want to fuck me. I don't think of fucking her right back at her, or since I'm doing the honesty gig, I think of fucking her, motion for another bottle of beer and a glass of wine for Kasia, and compliment myself on thinking about the fact I'm not seriously thinking about fucking the waitress just considering it, because I've got my focus on Kasia and have already told myself I won't fuck Kasia either. I'm a saint. I'm not thinking of fucking any of the women in the bar, even the women I'm thinking of fucking. "That's a nice shirt." I give a nod to the green, plushy shirt. Has an extra button de-buttoned? I thought it was two, but now it's three buttons down, the round curves of her breasts right there if another button goes—the hint of Kasia's pale shoulder as she adjusts the shirt. She looks down at herself, with a trace of blush on her cheeks—it could just be the nippy night air. Or she's hot for me and wants me to get on it fast.

I take a long thick strand of her hair and rub it lightly between my fingers, just like Kasia did with my hair.

Kasia blushes. "Stop it."

I lean over, take a whiff of Kasia's neck. "You smell the same."

Kasia pushes me away. "Okay, Romeo."

"Really. Is that the same perfume?"

"Cristalle, by Chanel. Same one." Kasia gives me a long look. "Scout," she says in that tone of voice you never want to hear from a woman. "It's not going to be like that, although I bet you want it to be."

"Be like what?"

"You know."

"You mean you don't want dinner?"

"I'm not talking about dinner." I am still the guy that hurt her.

"But we can make out, right?"

Kasia goes, "No! We can't make out. We're just having dinner."

"Are you seeing anyone?"

KISSING KASIA

Kasia tells me about some dude in Livingston, Montana, while I re-toss tortured rocker-dude mirror at her as her eyes drift down to my white leather jacket and she talks. He's a lawyer in big land deals with private companies, makes bundles of money, but she doesn't

117

really like the guy that much. He's just a friend. I don't ask her if she's fucking this friend. And Kasia doesn't cough it up, lets it ride. She doesn't respect what he does for a living, but won't go into it and I don't care.

"What happened with what's-his-name?" I ask. "Ten years is a long time to be together. I figured you two would get married, you know, all that."

I watch her as the waitress places menus down beside us. I remembered Kasia as the calm, soothing one, always patient. I was wrong. She tells me about her break-up with Payback. I listen. I've been wrong about her forever. My memory was wrong about her and I was probably wrong about her back when we were seeing each other. I made a big deal about her sweet character 'cause she liked me and I had it easy. But Kasia isn't just sweet, patient, and kind. Kasia has an edge and had it back then. I just took her for granted. The story she tells me is that she left Payback 'cause she caught him banging another chick. She admitted she had lost her desire for him and maybe pushed him into it, but it was done and she was still pissed off about him banging some woman when they were living together.

"I wanted kids," she says. "He didn't. I was tired of taking care of him all the time."

"I hate that guy," I add, helpfully. He had his ten-year run and now I want to hear about how his run failed. "Tell me everything. Really, Kasia, I am so totally on your side on this one."

"I'm sure you are."

"And don't leave out the part where you fuck him over good. That's going to be my favorite part."

She holds back a smile. I can tell she was no angel in this whole deal with Payback, but who is in any relationship, and anyway, I don't give a fuck: let Payback get his payback.

"You know," she says. "It used to bug me, but he acted like he was the one that introduced me to Los Lobos, but I saw them with you in Central Park that time."

"In the rain."

"In the rain."

"That fucker—stealing our memories!"

I remember taking a bath one night and listening to *Will the Wolf Survive,* while Kasia was studying for some college test. I usually took baths to Jane's Addiction or Alice in Chains or Metallica, but when Kasia was studying, I took baths to more calming tunes. I would sit in the bath for over an hour. I kept a spiral notebook in a plastic bag on the floor beside stacks of magazines, *Forced Exposure* and *Creem* and *Spin* and assorted porn mags. It was a good way to work. Let that hot water get your mind numb, listen to some other tunes and then drain the tub and scribble down lines about what was filling your skull. I might have been in the bath when I started "Kissing Kasia," but I think I worked that tune out on the bus ride home from Richmond, Virginia, after a fucked-up trip at Christmas, right after Kasia told me it was over and she was dating Payback. I was flat-broke and had to bum money from my folks to make it through a few months. This is never easy and Dad was still in his TV booze-swamp and Mom was worried about me and Kasia was gone, but that's when I wrote the best song I ever wrote.

"Did we ever take a bath together?"

"I don't know," she says. "But I remember you writing in the bath. You would yell out lyrics. I think my grades dropped when we started dating."

"Dating?"

Kasia's eyes are sad. "Do you still do that?"

"Do what... date?"

"Write songs in the bathtub?"

The honesty gig is in trouble. Write songs? I can't even hold a guitar in my hands without dry-heaving. "Not much."

"Do you have a band?" Kasia asks. "God," she looks shocked. "That was so rude of me not to ask about Billy? Are you—have you been okay?"

"Sure." I bail on the honesty gig for one second. "Great."

"And do you have a band?" Her eyes watch me. "You've got a new band?"

"Yes," I say, "I mean, no." I have no clue what to say 'cause I don't have a clue what to say. "Billy died…" I drain my bottle of beer.

"Didn't Billy… a few years ago?" Kasia looks at me.

"Almost four," I say. "I'll get back to music, but it fucks with my head."

She places her hand over mine. "You were best friends, Scout. It's understandable."

But this is the shit that is really fucking with me. "Fuck Billy. He did it to himself." I look Kasia in the eyes. "I don't want to talk about this right now. Let's talk more about doofus and how he was a prick and how you dumped him for being a jerk."

"Okay." Kasia's pale blue eyes watch me.

"I just don't want to make a big deal about Billy and the whole deal. I haven't been playing music. Billy died. I didn't do a good job of keeping him from blowing it, but he's gone and he fucked himself and he fucked the band and he fucked me."

"Billy did what Billy did. You can't blame yourself."

"I don't blame myself." Not sure if this is honest. I didn't show up here on Sunday of this shitty week to talk about my dead friend and my dead band.

"Okay." Kasia touches my arm. Spirals of electricity shoot behind my eyes. I feel like I haven't had a woman touch me in way too long. "Let's order, okay?"

I cool down and take my eyes off the "100% agave, reposado Cazadores" and take my mind off of telling Mike to line up ten straight shots. Kasia and I order up a mess of stuff from K.L.'s menu, edamame and shrimp tempura, appetizers with eel and slices of fish wrapped in kelp, oyster rolls, raw strips of tuna marinated, fried calamari. Kasia tells me her friends know about this evening and want to hear about Scout Harris after all this time. Her friends remember how I put Kasia through the wringer. Kasia tells me about the first time she heard "Kissing Kasia" on the radio. I had sent her the EP, but she says she never got it. I'm sure Payback dropped it in the trash, but fuck him. Kenny comped us dessert and two extra glasses of wine. Kasia tells me that one of her close friends died of cancer and that it was rough for her. She was strong and took care of her friend, but then he died and she didn't have the strength anymore to take care of people. She says, "I should have called you when I heard about Billy. I always felt bad I wasn't there for you."

No biggie. Don't sweat it. I was busy drinking and whoring.

We talk more about Payback and the details on their crash-and-burn.

"That's great," I say. "But how does it feel now?"

"It was the right thing to do. We had screwed it up. Both of us. It wasn't going to be fixed. I had to leave."

"Sounds familiar," I say. "Once it's fucked up, it's hard to fix."

"Yep," says Kasia. "What a weird week." She tucks a strand of her blond hair behind her ear. "Here I am bitching about an ex-boyfriend and I should just be glad we're all alive… including him."

No one deserves what happened this week. It even turns out Payback had been at the base of the World Trade Center on Tuesday, but had got away.

"And seeing you," Kasia says. "That's something I didn't expect."

"I'll only try to kiss you if you want me to kiss you," I say, not even sure what I say when my mouth opens and words fall out. I'm going by gut.

Kasia says, "I'll let you know if I'm in the mood, which I won't be."

"Okay, but I'm glad I googled you."

"I am too," says Kasia. "Last time I saw you was at that bar in the East Village, the one you worked at…"

"The Diamond Pub."

"You were surrounded by young girls. I felt old, and I was only twenty seven."

"Sounds like that time…" How I can say something so pompous and full of shit. Sounds like that time? What the fuck is the matter with me? And I was the guy that wrote the songs for Johnson State?

Kasia reaches over and laces her hand in my hand. "I loved," she watches me with her pale blue eyes, "watching you play guitar."

We talk about what happened to Johnson State after Billy died. I tell her about the deal with Fingerline and the way we couldn't deliver the tracks and were a write-off.

"What have you been doing?"

"I kept working at the Diamond, juggled a few other stupid jobs." I kill my beer and roll the bottle on the bar, "Things went from bad to fucked. I wasn't going anywhere and I figured I had to get out of that scene, so I got a job uptown and now I'm crashing on a friend's floor up on the Westside at 108th Street."

"Where are you working?" Kasia asks me. "Another bar?"

I'd be way into not talking about this, but Kasia is waiting, so I say, "Security."

"What?" She doesn't think she heard me right.

It's so hard to believe, but I spit it out. "Security."

Security? Security against what? Garbage on the river? Terrorist attacks aimed at crappy little sailboats? "Security," I say for the third time, "you know, kind of watching stuff, making sure people don't break in, making sure people pay on time."

"You?" She laughs. "Where?"

"At the 79th Street Boat Basin."

Kasia puts her hand to her mouth. "Oh, my God, that's hilarious! Can I drop in for a visit? I'll be back in town next Tuesday."

"No, you can't."

"C'mon! Please? Amy asked me to come into town and babysit. She and Jim have tickets to some show at the Knitting Factory."

"The owners are tense," I lie. "They're not cool with people coming to see me."

"Do you wear a uniform?" Kasia's holding back giggles.

"I'm glad my complete failure is so much fucking fun for you," but I'm not tense.

The other waitress that never tries to fuck me walks up and asks, "Can I get you guys anything else to drink?"

"Two shots of tequila," says Kasia, "whatever brand Scout prefers. My treat."

"Okay," says the waitress. She looks at me, "Cazadores?"

"Sure," I say, "Couple cubes of ice."

"Got it." She sashays over to the bar, where Mike continues to flip his white bar towel against his jeans, look handsome and wait for a crowd to appear and make the clock turn fast.

"Do you come here a lot?" asks Kasia. "It's nice you and Ken have stayed friends."

"Kenny is about the last friend I have in town," I say. "I mean, there's Ralph uptown. He's definitely a stand-up guy. Hardy, of course. And Jon Domogarow, the kid that owns The Diamond, but I don't talk to anyone that plays music. I just let go of it. Kenny writes poetry. I drop in sometimes for readings and smoke and sit in the corner. It's very sexy. Yeah, I guess I have about four friends after all the years I've been in this city. I don't hang with musicians. That's my number one rule."

"Five if you count me," says Kasia. She squeezes my hand.

"You live in Montana," I say. "Besides, you're not a friend."

"I'm not your friend? Scout Harris, how can you say that?!" She takes my hand again. "So what am I? Just another ex-girlfriend?"

"No, you're not just another ex-girlfriend. You're something else."

"Why don't you talk to the other guys from Johnson State?"

"What's the point?"

"I can think of a few," says Kasia. "But let's drink some tequila first. This feels like a serious discussion, and I am not in the mood for a serious discussion, not after this week and not on my first night having dinner with the worst boyfriend a girl ever had... ever."

"Ouch. Ever is such a long time."

Kasia looks at me.

You broke my heart too, Kasia, but I don't say it. This honesty gig I've got myself into is like not drinking. It sounds really good until you start doing it—or not doing it—and then not doing it just wears you down.

Lucky for me I wasn't not drinking and the waitress returns with two shot glasses of 100 percent agave dirt. I put the glass under my nose and let the fragrance of wisdom and truth and the high sails of the gods rustle my brain.

I didn't suggest the high-end dirt and had done a remarkable job by my standards at not already dipping into the liquid fuel. I fought the urge when I first walked into the bar, but didn't think about it more than five times once Kasia had walked her bouncy walk across the floor and slipped out of her buckskin jacket as her plushy green shirt billowed, and I caught a glance of her white breast. Women know we're looking at their bodies all the time. They're not stupid. It must be a drag, but it must be hot too; the obviousness of the whole gig must make their pussies warm. Kasia wants me to notice her, and I have noticed from the moment she pushed open the door. My eyes have been locked on Kasia.

It was smart of me not to have any tequila. The dirt might have unleashed the mad noise in my skull, the edgy part of me that picked a fight with my favorite regular at the Diamond and got me down in the basement and covered with blood right before the rat waddled over for a snack of my face. Dirt can work for you and dirt can turn on you. Dirt triggers the demons and warriors fighting it out in the glass jar of your skull. Dirt is not for the weak, and dirt is not for the strong if they are feeling weak.

I was smart about the tequila, but I had let Kasia know I was down with fooling around with her. I played my hand too soon. Nervous. Idiot move. I should have listened to her and stuck with a colder Clint Eastwood mirror. She would have pushed and I would have watched the horizon and she would have pushed some more to get attention just like any stray. I had blown the deal before those first glasses of tequila were placed in front of us and Kasia lifted hers and tapped it against my glass and said, "Here's to you, Scout."

I was locked out.

Kasia was too elegant to put up with a slut like me.

I drank the tequila and ordered us another round.

JUST LIKE THIS

It's the next day and I can't remember how Kasia and I got outside of K.L.'s, leaning against the car with my hands up her unbuttoned, green, plushy shirt. I know we had about six shots of that high-end Cazadores reposado. At least I did, snagging one glass Kasia left on the bar when she begged off to the Women's head. I was backing the dirt with beer and we were both talking like mad. We were leaning against the car outside, and it was nippy, but not too cold. Kasia was talking about something, but we both knew the subject didn't matter, she was just talking until we got to the next stage, maybe she was talking about Amy's daughter's school or the lawyer that was just a friend in Montana—all I knew was that she didn't care about what she was saying. We were having a different conversation. Kasia leaned away from me, with the gentle lilt of her hips pointing up. She made the adjustment as my thigh moved between her thighs and she leaned back sitting against a Mercedes, and the cold of the metal shivered through her jeans. No, those silver buttons would pop fast. Kasia held her arms around her buckskin jacket and plushy green shirt, and she pressed forward against me. My hands went under her jacket and shirt to her naked hips. I touched her warm neck with my lips and unhooked her bra, and I couldn't believe I forgot how she kissed. Kasia kissed just like this.

I would do better with a guitar back in my playing days if I tried to put in words the kiss, but Kasia moved into the kiss like a rabbit about to nibble a piece of lettuce, her nose tickled my nose and her lips—forget the rabbit now—Kasia's soft warm lips, brushed red with lipstick, parted and her tongue flicked against my tongue as I pressed my hand across her round breasts, freeing her shirt back over her naked shoulders. Kasia adjusted her thighs so my leg could slip in between her legs and give her a grinding post. Her round breasts were warm. Her kisses were gentle, moving forward, pulling back. My hands slipped down to her hips; she pressed against me. Then Kasia pulled back against the cold Mercedes and shivered. Kasia Crocetti. I switched places so I was leaning against the cold Mercedes, and Kasia pressed her naked chest against me as if she was trying to get through me to the cold metal of the parked car. Our tongues flicked as Mike snapped his white bar towel while talking to Kenny Lee, people drank, the restaurant windows curtained, and the kitchen closed. Kasia's body was sparking and humming silent messages my body was tuned to capture. Her body hot against me, I lifted up my arms in my white leather jacket, the RAMONES T rolled up so our chests pressed warm and naked against each other on the cold Manhattan street. I was surprised the car alarms on Downing Street didn't explode as the universe tilted and rubbed and we pressed and whispered and kissed. My fingers traced under her arm, across the ripple of her sharp ribs and the slender slant of her hip. Her pussy burned behind the denim against my raised knee. I smelled the cigarette smoke and Cristalle in her thick blond hair, and I was back ten years. I was back again with Kasia, but I was new. I was different.

We were different.

Kasia allowed me to kiss her breasts on the sidewalk, running her fingers through my variegated hair before she pulled her shirt together and buttoned up as a couple walked down the cold street. K.L.'s restaurant door opened and two people walked out, talking, laughing, loopy, eyes glancing our way. Kasia and I were drunk. We kissed, not caring who watched us in the night.

Voices zoomed in and out as we concentrated on kissing before Kasia pulled back.

"I need to go."

"Okay," I held her hips with my hands and pressed my thigh hard against the V of her jeans. She looked at me.

"I missed you," I said. "I just want you to know that."

"You are different," said Kasia. "It's a good different."

"Can I see you again?"

"I need a taxi uptown." There was a weave to her whole body as her hands went into her back pockets and she gazed drunkenly at me and blinked.

"I'll walk you," I grabbed her ass, pulling her against me. I kissed her again. This is kissing Kasia. I let go of her, and she stepped back. "I didn't expect this," I said. "You know… this." My hand slides up to her shoulder, touches her blond hair.

"Making out," she said. "I thought I told you we couldn't do it."

"Yeah, you said that."

"Walk me," she took my hand and we headed to get a taxi. Way too fast for me, a yellow cab lets out a fare on the corner. I've stood on this corner for ten minutes and not even seen a taxi, but now, after ten years, I have a ripped, wet-eyed Kasia against my chest and the taxi is waiting. What the fuck is that about? "Want to stand here for a sec?" I ask before kissing her again on her lips.

"I can't," she pulls away. Kasia didn't want to slip into the wrong deal. The tequila hazed her pale blue eyes. She looked sad, but a little smile crossed her lips and she pressed up against me and kissed me fast, "Gotta go."

I wanted to be a gentleman. I had already undone Kasia's shirt and slipped off her bra in public, kissing her breasts on the street. I accepted my sleeping bag and the responsibility of helping Kasia stick by her plan to not get laid. "Okay." If this was being a gentleman, it flat-out bit, but I held the cab door and Kasia scooted in, zipping her buckskin jacket straight up to the neck, flipping back her long blond hair, cheeks flushed, her red lips swollen from the kissing she promised wouldn't happen. Kasia turned to me as I held the open door. "I'll call you." Kasia looked at me through the glass then faced forward as the taxi pulled into traffic.

The taxi drifted down Varick and made a left, heading back to Sixth Avenue, the Avenue of the Americas. I walked back toward K.L.'s, the curtains billowing as air rushed through the opening door and Mike reached for the bottle of tequila. I would have one shot before I got into the subway, got up to my sleeping bag and dealt with tomorrow's hangover. I had kissed Kasia. Ten years gone. Tuesday was not out of anyone's skull. Ground Zero burned and thousands of innocent people had disappeared in the severe clear sky. I watched a newscaster on the TV over the bar standing in the smoking wreckage interviewing a New York fireman on the rescue effort, the rescue effort with no one to rescue, the cleanup effort, the murder site, where the wreckage glowed in smoke. People were either fucked this week or they were covered in luck. My mind skipped to those people that had to jump from the skyscraper. I was glad I didn't know anyone in the WTC towers. Stories were repeated and retold, the man that leapt in perfect sky-dive form, the man that was supposed to have surfed down the building on slabs of crumbling cement, the dog that guided the blind man away from the collapsing cement and metal and suffocating fumes. Some of these stories would be real, some couldn't be real, time would tell. I sipped my tequila, while Kasia was almost up to Amy's with stories of making out with her bad ex-boyfriend from her innocent early twenties. How would I have jumped from those burning windows? Crying? Holding my eyes shut? Making a last joke? Or like a kid off a diving board into the blue swimming pool of cold water on a hot summer's day?

That's how I hope it felt for those poor fuckers, like a long dive into cold water.

The Book Mouse fell into my hand.

I kissed Kasia and she kissed me.

EMOTIONAL INTELLIGENCE

The days crawled since I kissed Kasia. I kept making myself not ring her up on the phone. Each night I put down a sixer of beer and a pint of dirt. Fabio nailed my sleeping bag on Tuesday, one week after 9/11. Each day at the boatdock was hell. Dull, hungover, bored as shit, I reminded myself not to call Kasia. Give her space.

Thursday night hits, and I call Kasia on her cell, using Ralph's line.

Kasia tells me Amy is going to run this open-mic benefit at a coffee shop in Chelsea. The plan is to get people to pay to watch all the performers each week and then donate the money to one of the funds for the families of the victims of last Tuesday's terrorist attack. Kasia volunteered me for the first night. Kasia says it can be acoustic and some people will read poetry and some people will do stand-up. "C'mon, Scout. It'll be fun."

"Okay," I say, "but how about if we go see this movie tomorrow at the Film Forum?"

There is silence. Kasia tells me she will be out at her parent's place in Jersey, but she'll be at Amy's on Saturday night. She's not sure about the movie. She's supposed to do something with Amy and it would be rude to spend the whole night out, but she can get away later for some food or something low-key.

We talk about the guy from Livingstone. Kasia spills that this Livingstone dude is in Manhattan. He is rich and flew into town to take Kasia to a benefit, some hyper-swank tuxedo party to raise money after 9/11. "Like what you'll be doing," Kasia says, "at Amy's open mic."

That's what I'll be doing, except I might help raise thirty bucks if I don't fall on my knees and puke in front of ten people in a coffee shop.

Kasia tells me she's looking forward to seeing me Saturday night. I don't ask her if she's fucking her friend from Livingstone. I don't need to ask. I don't want to hear Kasia say yes, and I don't want Kasia to lie to me. I suck it up and sign off as the Fat Mexican walks into the apartment. He wants to go down to the Black Clock. His treat.

I have two tumblers of Patrón, sipped slow and easy as Ralph nurses an O'Doul's non-alkie and watches Rio and listens to his heart thump.

After the second bottle of tepid piss, the Senator gets up the fire, and as Rio backs us up by placing a shot-glass upside down on the bar, Ralph asks Rio out for a coffee. Rio wasn't out on the street before we walked into the bar, so Rio didn't see Ralph hyperventilating and combing and re-combing his slicked black hair. Rio didn't see the nerves the Fat Mex was fighting, and I'm surprised because once Ralph moves into action, I have to give the wide dude credit. He works it strong and confident.

Rio adjusts the neckline of her black French-cut T-shirt, which is embossed with the silver word *EVIL*. I figure Rio is embarrassed and maybe a bit afraid of Ralph, but then her face gets all smiley and she gives Ralph some wet-eye and says, "Sure, when?"

I can't fucking believe it? The Fat Mexican pulls out a fancy pen and writes down Rio's phone number on a cocktail napkin, folds up the napkin and tucks it in the pocket of his striped suit shirt. His wide black slacks and his wide hydraulic thighs bound up the stairs two-at-a-time, the handrail creaking as he leaps and lands and leaps. I drag behind him, a tiny white fist squeezing my lungs, my black boots on the linoleum steps, my skull stuck on this business of playing music in front of people when I can't even play music alone in front of the fat, retarded cat Fabio. One solution would be to drink heavily and just wing it. Go for it with half a bottle of dirt in my gut. Throw some mirror and rage all RFN. That would be punk-rock, unless I crash and burn and end up as a lame bad joke with people laughing at me and shit, including Kasia. Billy has been dead long enough. It feels like yesterday, but it's not yesterday. Kasia wants to see me crawl out from my hiding place and sing a song for Amy's money-raising gig. The city is pulling together. Kasia might let me kiss each of her breasts after enough tequila, but Kasia won't let me fuck her until she knows she wants me. Kasia won't want me if I can't get up and play at least one song and contribute to the relief effort. It's not about the song, it's about helping out. Our city got attacked. Thousands of people were murdered. If Ralph can scramble up the guts to scam a date with Rio, I should be able to strum a few chords and sing a song, do my part, put a few dollars in the kitty for all the people that lost someone they loved while I sat in my fish shed and nursed a hangover and watched black smoke stain the sky. Besides, doing this gig might be the only way I get to fuck Kasia again.

I should fuck Megan.

That would let off steam. Then I wouldn't care that right now Kasia is all dolled up with some stooge at some Madison Square Garden event.

I should not fuck Megan.

I want Kasia and I should stick by Kasia. She is worth the time, effort, risk. The clock ticks slow on the wall, but that's my problem. Watching the Fat Mexican lope up the stairwell, I think of George Nichols dropping into town from Los Angeles. I meant to give Jon my phone number in case George dropped back into the Diamond.

I stretch out on the sour sleeping bag and try to make myself not listen or wait to smell the horse-piss leak Ralph unleashes in his white-tiled bathroom cubicle. For a nice little apartment, it's like sleeping in a men's room at a bus station. It's amazing the Fat Mexican doesn't dent the toilet. The sounds of such a monstrous stream will only get Fabio geared up for another attack on my nylon bag. I figured I'll call Jon at the Diamond and leave Ralph's phone number for George Nichols.

My tequila buzz takes me down for about one hour of sleep, and *BLAM!* I'm awake. Ralph snores in his bedroom. I get up and close the door. I take out the Guild and hold it, remembering all the time she's been in my arms, all the girls that have heard me play her at dawn with the ashtrays stuffed with butts and half-filled beers on the tables and floor. I put the acoustic back and pick up my Fender Mustang Strat. In the moon glow, I slam my shin against the coffee table and hold back from cursing the darkness. Fabio lumbers out of my way, meows and becomes a shadow on the window sill. I guess the buzz isn't really gone or maybe I'm half asleep. I tune the guitar in the dark. Hit the fridge and find a bottle of Presidente. I pop it open and take a long guzzle. I pluck a few notes of the Replacements' "Take Me Down to the Hospital," the silent room begging for a stack of amps. My skull flutters like a drive-in screen with images of the World Trade Center, the poor fuckers just black specks flicked from the burning sky-rise towers. I do what I always do when I need to get my feet on solid ground and start playing Bob Marley's "Redemption Song." My fingers are thick and slow, the guitar strings dull. I tap the strings light and whisper the words. I wouldn't call it singing, and I wouldn't call it playing guitar. My throat is scratchy. I sing about the pirates, the merchant ship, and the bottomless pit.

I finish the beer, my stomach in a knot, tapping my foot on one of the Senator's expensive rugs I try a few chords of "Kissing Kasia."

> *You found me on your rope and dropped me…*
> *Down into a different town, you dropped me…*
> *Kissing you, Kasia, wrapped in Hell's Kitchen*
> *Kissing you, Kasia, white hell and soft sheets…*
> *Hell in your kiss and hell on my feet. I'm going to miss…*
> *You, cold Kasia, while I'm walking the streets…*

Last thing I remember is trying to whisper all the words for "Highway to Hell." I wake up at 4:45 a.m., curled around my Stratocaster. Fabio stares at me through his dreadlocked mane of ratty hair and his crossed, slitted eyes. I must have dosed off because the red numbers on the Fat Mexican's television unit tell me it is 5:40 a.m. Fabio is back on the window sill, faint dawn in a pale square on Ralph's lacquered floor. I try to imagine myself at this open-mic benefit gig. My hands go into fists and press against my thighs. I'm curled on my side on the floor, wrapped in the cat-stained sleeping bag. Out the window are pale curtains with people behind them in rooms doing what they are supposed to do: drifting awake or sleeping—not sleeping it off, not wrecked with nerves. Their boots aren't beside their head. Their clothes aren't still on. They aren't thinking of a drink as the sun lifts over the island, imitating Western movie heroes and making tough faces in the mirror in front of girls they like, pretending they didn't fall into a bottle and quit.

Ralph's wide body shakes the frame of his bed as his snores ratchet past the closed door of his bedroom, counting Rios in his sleep.

I had kissed Kasia. That should have been enough. Kasia, that should have been enough, but now it was going up to the next level. I looked at my guitar in the moonlight. You'd think that Stratocaster was tied to a string that went from the kite of purple window right into my burned-out heart. I hated it, curled up on my side with nothing. The guitar was what I did to nail some stray, trick some filly into riding my cock. No, I loved that fucking guitar, and most of the guitars I owned since my first. I just couldn't love the guitars now 'cause I was tired. The nights are long when sleep leaves town. I should just pick the guitar back up and play each and every song I can remember until the sun hurts the glass and Ralph stumbles into the bathroom, his automatic coffee maker spitting black coffee.

At the Black Clock, after my third Patrón and Ralph's second O'Doul's, Rio's phone number is tucked safe in his shirt pocket. The Fat Mexican starts telling me about this interesting book he was reading about this thing the business professors call "EQ." I didn't get it at first, but then I got it. He meant like IQ, but this was emotional intelligence. This was about being intelligent about your emotions.

I stare at the black windows in the building across from Ralph's apartment. My head runs fast when I close my eyes, ghost images and lyrics from songs and chord progressions and weird characters half from TV, half from real life, skitter across my closed eyelids. No fucking wonder I get drunk every night. My skull flashes with fragments of visual images, like I'm dosed out on acid and wired by my veins to five different channels of noise. This isn't rest. Everything is wrong. The money I don't have, apartment I won't get, the band I don't jam with anymore or ever again and no one cares. I do what? Work in a boatyard? I tell myself to just uncurl, grimacing and locking my jaw and squinting at the fat Persian cat on the window glowing with dawn. Just get up and try the guitar one more time. Move your fingers on the strings. Pretend. Pretend you can do it. But I don't do it. I stay curled up on the floor. I'm doing a new mirror. I'm doing the Scout Harris mirror. This mirror is a natural, but it's not much fun.

If there is a thing called "emotional intelligence," I don't have enough of it in my system. I think I must have sweated it out, or flushed it out with dirt. The main thing is that it's all gone and I need a refill.

AVENUE OF KASIA

Friday hits and it's tough snaking more wax from my storage cell, but I need cash for tomorrow night. I filled the knapsack with every album I had left from Minor Threat, Black Flag, Butthole Surfers, Flat Duo Jets, you name it, my Metallica, Suicidal Tendencies, my Van Halen, AC/DC, Cheap Trick. Storm Troopers of Death. Tool. Pantera. C.O.C. Flipper. The Flesheaters. Social Distortion. Some Dylan, Springsteen. I bagged every album I figured I could swap for cash, celebrating the pillaging of my collection by getting myself a burger at Paul's for old time's sake. After the burger, I pushed away the thought of calling up Megan and caught the train back uptown.

It's Friday night, and I've been pacing the Fat Mexican's pad, sipping hits of dirt from a pint of Cuervo, nursing a bumper of Olde English 800. Tequila and malt liquor is not a good move, but I'm edgy. Tomorrow is one hundred miles away.

I pick up the guitar and try again, sweat trickling down my neck, fingers shaking. It's like playing guitar in the middle of the Lincoln Tunnel—noisy, polluted—too fucking loud to hear. I smoke a cigarette. I smoke a second cigarette. Fabio waddles back and forth. He gets bored and waddles close. I prod him with my socked foot. I get up close to his dish-plate face. "Did you sit on my guitar, you little fat fuck?"

"What?" The Senator asks from the bathtub. Cigar smoke drifts from the misting room of tile and porcelain. Ralph reads a pink paper called *The Financial Times*. I can see his hairy legs, his feet red from the hot bubble bath. I look away. For a man who has made and lost a lot of money, Ralph is only in his mid-thirties. He has dark skin, is very stylish in a business way. He carries his weight like some kind of athlete. I still remember the first night he walked into the Diamond Pub, looking so Wall Street, young, confident. He looked like someone about to be very rich. According to his ex-girlfriend, Kathleen, way back when I was banging her and not living on Ralph's floor, Ralph is a handsome man. Kathleen told me this with a calm look on her face, even though Ralph had burned her bad by running off and marrying that friend of hers, Caryn Hwang.

The Fat Mexican paid for that mistake.

"Were you saying something?" Ralph's voice rolls from the bathroom in billows of cigar smoke.

"Nothing, you Hefty Hombre… I was just talking to your cat."

Ralph laughs a deep, rich laugh. He has a good attitude for a dude that has gone through grief. I've got it figured that he keeps me in his apartment 'cause it makes his own deal look normal. He may have lost everything, but at least he's not me.

126

"Scout, why don't you pull out your guitar and play something?"

I look at my guitar case. "What do you think I am, some Fat Mexican's personal music bitch?"

That was a dumb question.

"Yes, that's exactly what I think you are. Do you know any Jobim?"

"I don't play spic," I say, wondering if he's got any beer in the fridge.

"Antonio Carlos Jobim is Portuguese," Ralph splashes his wide body in the tub of bubbles. "Samba music. How about some reggae? You ever play any Marley?"

"No," I lie.

"Play anything," the Fat Mexican splashes in his tub. "Just play something."

Fabio crawls up on my guitar case, slit eyes tracking me as he waddles. "I would, your Fat Highness, but your ugly cat is crashed out on my guitar. I don't want to bother it."

Ralph laughs, splashing water as a bloom of cigar smoke drifts from the bathroom door. "You're chickenshit, Scout, just plain chickenshit."

Fabio stares at me. The hairball does one of those cat-stretch maneuvers—pressing out its ratty paws—and scrapes my guitar case, kneading the case like he's prepping himself for a long snooze. If the Senator wasn't in earshot, I might give the dim animal a serious boot. "You want something on the stereo?"

"Go for it. Would you like a cigar? I've got some new Davidoff's in the humidor."

By humidor, the Fat Mexican means the small wood box near his Bose stereo. He snips pieces of carrot and puts them in the box. They help keep the cigars fresh, I guess. I was rolling my own Spirits when I first moved up here and I kept the pack of shag in his box of carrot snippings, but I got lazy and went back to paying for pre-rolled smokes. "I'm cool." I tap a cigarette from my pack. I flip through the Fat Mexican's CDs. I don't recognize most of it. Rueben Blades, Gloria Estefan, some jazz I recognize, some reggae, some rock. I pull out that guy Thelonious Monk because I like his hat. I slip the disc into the system.

The Senator is in a good mood, thinking about his coffee date with Rio. He takes me out to Rosita's Cuban-Chinese restaurant on Broadway. We walk right past the Black Clock on the way back to the apartment. I was sure Ralph was going to want to peek in, but it turns out he talked to Rio that day on the phone and knew she wasn't working. This means my free dinner is not going to be followed by free drinks. I pony up for three bottles of Presidente and plan on a restless night of non-sleep. I've got two fingers of dirt in a pint bottle tucked in my duffel bag upstairs, so little left it's almost not worth the taste. Tomorrow I'll see Kasia and it wouldn't hurt to hit my shift at the boat dock without a hangover, maybe bring my guitar and strum a few songs, practice for the benefit.

I spend the whole black night staring at the ceiling. I might have nailed an hour of exhausted sleep-like blankness as the sun warmed the cracks of sky between the buildings. After a hot shower that makes my eyes tear from exhaustion, I slip into my blue Dickie work pants and my blue Dickie work shirt and hoof it to the subway to get down to the dock and sit on my ass and do nothing, tapping my nightstick against the desk and flipping through the Saturday edition of the New York Post, my N.Y.C. Park Department hat tilted on my head.

I keep forgetting my sunglasses. I tip the peaked bill of my N.Y. Parks cap down over my red eyes and take micro-snoozes, waking with a jolt when the dock creaks. On the other side of the river, New Jersey construction sites face New York like huge resting insects waiting to crawl into Manhattan.

That night I take the number one train down to K.L.'s. The Fat Mexican leaves his place with me on his way to meet Rio. Their coffee date has turned into a movie and dinner. Rio apparently can go see a movie with a complete stranger, while Kasia's schedule is tight. I get dinner, no movie. I ignore the part in my skull that wants to think about the lawyer friend who might still be in town and the cause of an understandable deception where Kasia makes plans with me, but might be fucking him, even though she says she doesn't like him. She could be riding his cock RFN. I can't blame her. I'm a bad decision myself.

The Fat Mexican looked suave in a charcoal sport coat over a black sweater. He had a leather overcoat draped on his arm. His hair was gelled and he smelled like a man of substance, a man with a job and an apartment, tucking away his cell phone, telling me he was late. Ralph offered me money, but I told him I was okay. He handed me a twenty-dollar bill anyway and we walked to Broadway, where I hit the downtown train and he walked up the block toward some pricey French restaurant.

Kenny works the bar. The place is crowded. He slides me a Bud.

"I'll also take a Cazadores. Two ice cubes."

Ken gives me a look that says *this one's not on me.* "Don't worry. I've got some money and I'll get you back for last weekend. You did me a solid." I'm meeting Kasia in SoHo at a local hang called Milady's.

Dinner with Kasia flies and before you know it, we're on the Avenue of the Americas, tugging at each other's clothes in a spray of headlights.

Kasia's lips flutter on my chest, her pubic bone grinding against my fingers. We are supposed to be looking for a taxi so Kasia can go back to Amy's. The weather is icy, with snow sprinkling down from the charcoal sky. Kasia unbuttons the last three buttons of my flannel shirt. She looks up at me. Her eyelids are heavy.

I slip two fingers into her pussy.

"Oh!" she says.

This is another thing I forgot, the surprised sound she makes as you enter her.

Kasia undoes the buckle of my belt and pops open my Levi's, slipping her cold fingers around my hard, warm cock.

My hands slip around Kasia's ass, sliding under her cotton bikini briefs, her flared black slacks pushed down her thighs. She does the same to me. I am focused. It's about this time that snow flakes fall from the black sky. Kasia's cowboy shirt is unsnapped, her wife-beater pushed up, her breasts pale in the streetlight. We stand against a brick wall, balanced, with both our pants pushed down, our hands on each other in the cold, slashed with car light, kissing. We can't stop kissing. Kasia rocks against my hand and moans. Kasia rides the palm of my hand, grinding, arching her back and telling me, "No, no, no." She nibbles my neck. I lift her up and hold her on my forearm, my hand reaching through her legs, cradling her ass. She rubs back and forth on the cradle of my arm, clenching my leather jacket. The cold wind burns my naked ass. Cars on Sixth Avenue go *beep! beep!*

"We can't do this," she whispers in my ear.

She looks down at me and sees my tattoo, *Concentrate!*

It's done in heavy ink right above the natural tuft of my pubic hair and my angry, desperate, aching cock.

"Oh, my God," she says in surprise. "Wow..."

"I love you," I whisper in her ear.

Headlights crease her in go-go stripes and speckles of snow catch in her blond hair. What a stupid thing to say.

"Oh, my God," she rides the cradle of my arm.

"I want to fuck you."

"No," she says, her back against the brick wall, her legs wrapped around my waist, her face splashed by headlights as a car slams a divot on Sixth Avenue.

"I have to go." She struggles, pressing my arm down with her boots, searching to hit the cement, using the weight of her body until I lower her. She wiggles up her pants.

I stand on the Avenue of the Americas, my hard cock out of my jeans in the white falling snow. "No—that's fucked."

"Really?" she laughs.

Kasia is happy, and I figure she's right. She can't fuck me on the street.

Fuck, I say to myself, fuck, fuck, fuck!

The cold is bitter, but the loose speckles of snow falling are a blanket. Fucking Kasia on the street couldn't make this night more perfect.

Kasia pulls her knit cap from her jacket pocket, rewraps her scarf around her neck, zipping up her buckskin jacket.

She takes my hand and we walk up the block. I flag a taxi and we kiss, the yellow car idling beside our warm bodies.

Kasia looks up at the sky, snow falling in waves. "I can't believe we almost had sex on the Avenue of the Americas."

"I'm going to call this the 'Avenue of Kasia.'"

"You're a goof." She leans in for one quick good-bye kiss.

"Later," I say, closing the cab door. Kasia gives me a half-wave then faces forward as the taxi pulls up the Avenue of Kasia.

I ride the train uptown.

I know why I feel free and fine and not worried about tomorrow, not afraid. It's just Kasia. She's back. I kissed Kasia. Kasia kissed me. It was all starting over. Kasia wasn't history. Kasia was back.

But the night wasn't over and I'm getting ahead of myself, jumping right to the part of the evening where we scraped naked together on the street on our second night out. Before almost having sex on the sidewalk of that busy boulevard on that cold snowy night, Kasia and I had hamburgers at Milady's, a local SoHo dive with a pool table and a good jukebox. Kasia said, "I told Amy you would sing at the open-mic benefit."

My stomach dropped—the knot un-twirling then recoiling tight. "Yeah?"

"Scout, it's the thing to do, but if you don't want to do it, don't do it."

"No—"

"If it's beneath you to play at a small benefit, I get it." She didn't mean it. That was obvious. It was a small event, but this was about contributing, helping out, doing our part. This was about fighting back at the terrorists that attacked our city.

"It's not beneath me." This was tough. It wasn't beneath me. The scary fucking truth was that I didn't know if I could do it.

"You don't have to play, if you don't want to." Kasia's pale blue eyes watched me.

"You'd think it was cool, though, right? If I played a song?"

"Yes," said Kasia. "I would think it was cool."

How could I escape this deal? Me, sitting with my guitar in my shaking hands, people coughing as I adjust the mic and try to do something I can't even do in front of a cat.

"What would you sing?" Kasia asked me.

"I know some Carpenter tunes."

"Don't be an asshole, just play one of your songs."

"I haven't played anything since Billy."

"Since Billy died?" Kasia touched my hand. "Why not, Scout?"

"I don't know."

"You've got to try," Kasia said. "Just play anything." She looked like she was about to get teary.

I'm the fucked up one. "How about 'Puff the Magic Dragon'?"

Kasia rolled her eyes, "Okay, sure, play 'Puff the Magic Dragon.' I don't care what you play, just show up and play a song and help out—or don't. I'm just asking you," Kasia said, "to come to Amy's benefit and play. Do you want to play music and help or not?"

"Yes," I said, figuring I would figure it out. I couldn't say no. "Count me in."

"Great," Kasia didn't smile. "I'm glad. Do you want a shot of tequila?"

"We drank tequila last time," I said, "and I took off your shirt on the street."

"I know," said Kasia. She got up and walked to the bar.

One hour later we stood on the corner of the Avenue of Kasia and I closed the taxi door with fingers warm from her pussy. Kasia watched me through the taxi glass for the second time since the Book Mouse had dropped into my hand. I waved to her and began to walk through the light falling snow. I looked up at the tossed specks of white filtering down from the black sky. Everything was good. The only problem was that I had promised Kasia I would sing and play guitar at Amy's event. I hadn't promised to drink. I had promised to play music. I had even promised "Kissing Kasia." I hadn't promised to drink and that was all I remembered about rock & roll: how to tilt back the bottle and dream.

LAST NIGHT

But I didn't go home, instead, after the long, slow subway haul back uptown, I walk out of the 110th Street station one-hundred percent sure that I'm going to nestle onto my floor space and crash out for the final few hours of the evening. But one-hundred percent sure means different things to different people, and even though I'm the new, different Scout Harris, I put back two dirts in the Black Clock, then call Megan's apartment from the pay phone. I get her answering machine, her pre-recorded, professional Megan voice. This makes sense since it is two in the morning. I tell the machine who I am and that I'm writing in her journal non-stop and that she owes me a favor. That's when Megan picks up the phone and goes, "What's the favor?"

With the hard, cold plastic phone against my ear, I say with the lips that are still rosy from kissing Kasia, "I want to fuck you."

Silence.

I've crossed the dirt borderline. I'm not the same dude from downtown, not even the same dude who watched the subway doors clack open and close on the uptown local, not even the same dude whose cheeks are burning from the frosty night. I'm not the same dude who still had the scent of Kasia on his fingers, the smell of cigarette smoke in her lush blond hair, mixed with her perfume on my chest from when she kissed me.

"Where are you?"

"I'm uptown at the Black Clock Lounge."

"Where?"

"Up on 106th Street and Amsterdam."

"Oh, c'mon, Scout?!" I might as well have said I was in Pittsburg. "Do you know what time it is?"

"It's time for you to suck my cock."

"I have to work tomorrow."

"Work? I thought your dad supported you?" Sarcastic insults worked great on Megan, a smart move if I wanted her to fuck me.

"I've scheduled appointments on the Document of Time project."

"The what?"

"The D.O.T," Megan says, as if talking to a kid in nursery school. "We're building momentum." It's on. I grin at my reflection in the glass front of the Black Clock. "You know," she explains, "the Document of Time project is the reason you're writing in that journal. I'm creating an autobiographical history of the people from the Diamond Pub."

"Who cares about the Diamond Pub? I thought I was writing in this thing because it was going to help me fix myself or deal with my issues or however the fuck you put it? Besides, if we're all doing the work of writing down shit for you, then how are you the one that's creating anything?"

"You're so scared of life, Scout. I can't believe I never saw this quality in you before? This is not the path I would have expected you to choose."

"Fuck off," I reply.

"I'm producing the project," she says. "I'm the creative force guiding the project to fruition."

"What a load of bullshit." I own this chick. "Do you want to get laid or not?"

"You're such a gentleman," Megan says back, gamely trying to twist her shiny spoiled-girl bitch-knife in my back. "How could I turn down such an elegant offer?"

"Probably," I said, "if you had someone else to fuck you, but since it is two in the morning and you are alone, I figure you'll take the deal."

"I have pilates in the afternoon."

"Oh, forget it then." I grin at myself in the glass window facing out on Amsterdam Avenue and the swirling snow. I sigh as if I'm about to hang up the phone, which I'm not, since I know we're not done.

"Fuck you," the little slut says back to me. "I'm sorry I have commitments. I'm sorry I don't sit in a boatyard all day waiting until I can get drunk."

"That's not nice. That's a mean thing to say, you little stray. Now, do you want to bend over on your pretty little bed of pillows and get fucked hard or not?" As the Fat Mexican would say, this was a good strategy: insult, tempt, repeat.

"I think you're drunk."

"Of course I'm drunk. Why else would I be calling you at this time of night? Just cover the cab fare and I'll hike it down to the East Village."

Longer silence.

"Fine. I'll meet you at the Diamond," she says, "and don't call me a *stray*."

"Sure, whatever," I say, "but don't keep me waiting."

"Or what? You won't let me pay for the cab or you won't let me let you fuck me?"

"Nice. You're fun when you're bitchy, you little cunt."

"I hope you don't talk to all your girls like this." I can almost hear her smile.

"I always talk special to you, Megan." I give her name a bit of a strum. "This journal is messing with me. I just thought it would be fun to pop down and hang out. You know."

"Yeah," says Megan, "I know."

"And not wake up on Ralph's floor."

"Poor baby," Megan says. "Get in the taxi. You're wasting time."

Her phone clicks dead. Except for the one-hundred blocks of downtown travel, this is old times. This is how we always hooked up: drunk and insulting. It's the same deal: get naked and fuck each other on her stack of purple pillows. Then I shoot a load on her face, on her tits or on her expensive linen, depending on my mood. Megan would moan and babble through the whole gig, and I'd wake up at noon and my head would hurt like a motherfucker.

I never thought about my head until it was too late. I never thought about tomorrow until it was too late. Tonight was the same deal. I thought about Kasia as the taxi headed down the FDR, snowflakes swirling against the taxi glass. Kasia was asleep or drinking a late-night cup of herbal tea with Amy, coming down off our night on the cold sidewalk. I wasn't coming down at all. I was riding it hard. I had grabbed a tallboy of Olde English 800 from a bodega and was pounding the malt liquor in the taxi, and a glass of dirt at the Diamond would be the ticket. No reason to come down. Not yet. That could happen later.

I wake up the next morning on Megan's pricey bed with the big pine headboard and the predictable stack of pillows in different shades of purple. Megan snores beside me. Megan's snore is soft. Her exhale leaks in a timid whisper through her parted lips. It's almost cute. Then there's me. My body pulses, sour at the core, pasty tongue stuck inside my dry mouth. I'm fine. Good. Great. Then I'm not fine. I am way not fine. The top of my skull is cold sweating in the overheated bedroom; my dick is a tiny, bludgeoned, chafed pud. A cross of red fire burns in my forehead. The heating pipes click and spit. I remember nothing. My Levi's have been stepped out of in some kind of clumsy, drugged waltz. My Levi's wait for me in a wad and my shirt and white leather jacket are dropped in a lunatic weave that must have started at the bureau cluttered with Megan's assorted crap—framed photos of Megan arm-in-arm with people that love her, enameled boxes of earrings, a

131

litter of necklaces and bracelets. All I remember is slapping Megan's white ass with one hand, while my finger slipped into the tiny pink button of her anus. Just a porn memory that might not even be real. And now, morning. Glorious morning. Every drunk's least favorite time. What can you do? Fight the pain and tough it out. I wasn't going to make a big deal out of sunlight and the obligation to work at the boat dock. I definitely wasn't going to worry about whatever happened in my black-out. What happened, happened. It was cool. Streams of porn visuals ran through my skull. I clocked my spilled clothes on the floor. Megan sleeping curled in her lavender and purple. Memories of me and Megan weaving away from the red lights and noise of the Diamond in big steps as my hammered eyes goggle up and down Avenue A, my arm around her shoulders as she guides me to her apartment. It's hard to tell what is real and what is a dream leftover from some porn tape I played too many times on my VCR rig back on Clinton Street. The heat pipes click and spit and Megan sleeps. I'm sure I spanked her. Yes, the spanking is re-spooling in my skull. I might have fucked Megan in the ass, but there's also a good chance we stumbled in drunk and played around for a few moments and passed out. That wouldn't be bad. Or I hefted her small body and big tits up and let her sink onto my cock, sheathed in a condom, and let her ride herself silly into a gurgling, panting mess of pleasure. If I didn't at least do that, I was sort of a dick and I'd wasted the cash Megan spent on my cab fare. The little gal deserved to get fucked. It would be a drag if I had passed out. What bugged me was that I couldn't remember much beyond slapping Megan's ass, weaving on the street of honking and hurtling cars and then in rewind asking Annie at the Diamond for a second Tecate and a shot of cheap dirt. I take pride in this business of heavy drinking, and I remember last night that it was very cool to be down with the late scene at the Diamond Pub, hanging with the other risk-takers and folk who had the guts to live hard and break away from the chains of the daily nine-to-five. My date with Kasia was cool, but it was important that I didn't get locked into a pussy-whipped deal with an ex I wasn't even fucking yet. It was important to not lose my balls, while she was out with lawyer dudes from Montana. I needed to be the real Scout Harris, the Scout Harris Kasia had always wanted, right? Megan looked good: Her face was flushed, her lips were glossed and her eyes were watching me like I was the suave and handsome devil that held the key to her cunt. Only a coward would have stayed uptown and quit. I ordered an extra round from Annie. She nodded and reached into the stand-up Diamond fridge for a cold red can of Tecate.

I pull back the duvet. I squeeze Megan's big tits. She pulls up mid-snore and murmurs. I push her over onto her side. Her snore fades into that soft whistle of breath. I sniff her neck. I kiss her neck. It is amazing how this chick can swill vodka and still look pretty and smell delicious. The bed is fragrant from her pussy, ass, armpits, smeared shower lotion, shampoo fragrance, spritz of chick cologne, sweat and the cigarette-smoke scent of drinking late in a smoke-filled bar. All these smells filtered through her skin and made my cock hop. Time for a morning mount. I stroke my shaft until it gets real hard and then lip it into Megan. She talks to herself in her sleep, her eyes going open, hips moving with the thrusts of my unsheathed cock. Megan is really such a slut. I'll pull out, no problem. I get on my knees and fuck Megan hard and fast, my skull shrieking, the hangover waiting back in the dark, whispering my name. The clock on the wall tells me it is time to get Bloody Marys and fried eggs at Life Cafe. I have the afternoon shift at the boat basin, the afternoon shift, thank fucking God. Megan backs up against me, grasping her purple pillows against her tits, moaning, chewing on her wrists. She is very awake. I pull out and shoot a splash of jism on the pale white of her lower back, glossing the curve of her ass.

I wipe myself off with her bed sheet (lavender) and slip into my boxers and pull on my jeans. I sit on the edge of the bed and lace up my black boots.

Megan says, "You came inside me."

I pull on my shirt and jacket. I walk into her bathroom and splash water on my face. I don't look half bad. Shaky, shivering, but high from the morning fuck. "No, I didn't."

Megan, still on her stomach, watches me. She clutches a purple pillow against her pillowy tits. I point to the speckles of sperm on her back. I sit down and rub some jism with my finger and trace it across her rosy red mouth. "See this?"

"Last night."

Fucking last night?

"You weren't using anything either." Megan rolls over like a harp seal and rubs her scummed body up and down on the lavender sheets. "I'm ovulating."

Jesus. Why did I go to the Black Clock? Why didn't I walk up to Ralph's and embrace the cat-piss nylon puddle? Why didn't I wait for the brutal sun? "Okay. I get it. Bad move. But you're using something, right?"

"No, I'm not using anything and I'm not having another abortion." Megan's voice is ragged from the late night and smoky bar. "I've already had two."

"Okay," I say, "but they weren't 'cause of me."

"One time was."

Flashes, sparks, tremors, jolts of feedback hum and stringy licks of voices from last night bang in my skull. My skull is a fucking pinball machine. One Bloody Mary won't fix this hurt. Greasy eggs and hash browns won't fix this hurt. Nothing will fix this hangover. Ever. I sure hope Megan didn't get knocked up while I was in a tequila black-out. "When did I get you pregnant?" Cool out, chicks fix this problem all the time. I've been through it, was through it a long time back with Kasia. I just figured it wouldn't happen again.

"Right after Billy died, at the beginning, when we started seeing each other."

I sit on the bed and scrunch up a fist of purple duvet. "Why didn't you tell me?"

Megan pulls on a pink T-shirt wadded near the bed board. "Because I was in love with you. I didn't want to scare you away."

This was news. "In love with me? When?"

"Right after Billy died. Don't you remember that I was with you all the time?"

The insides of my arms and legs wriggle with twitches, spasms. The late-night shots of dirt siphon back up in waves through my itchy skin. I shiver. Alcohol withdrawal is what is going on. It sucks being me on Megan's bed right now blasted with panic. "I didn't even think you liked me very much," which isn't exactly true. I always figured Megan kind of liked me, but I didn't think she liked me enough to stick that word *love* on it.

Sitting up against her bedboard, Megan begins to cry. "Oh, Scout," her voice sounds different from the dolled up she-wolf slut-vibe voice she used last night. "Darling…." Tears run down her cheeks. She sniffles.

"I'm sorry," I put out my hand and touch her thigh.

Megan snort-laughs under her tears, "Right."

I pull my flannel shirt back off over my head in one move and hand it to her. She blows her nose in my shirt, looks at the wad of snot on my shirt and sniffles. "There are tissues in the bathroom," she says.

"That might have helped a few seconds ago."

Megan smiles. She is still Megan. Fuck it. I go into her lavender bathroom and grab the lavender box of Kleenex.

We kiss in the doorway, cold air blustering up the stairway shaft. Megan has dressed herself in cotton gray and red plaid pajama bottoms and the pink T-shirt. The T-shirt is tight on her big tits and she looks cute, rubbing her nose. The tears make her smiling face shiny. There is a pale light behind her from her apartment and I can see her unmade bed stacked with purple pillows. I like Megan more without her normal slathering of make-up, but I decide I like her best when she's crying. "Call me, you know," I say as we unclench and she looks up at me. "Call me if you need me for anything."

"Thanks," she puts her arms around my neck, pulling me toward her in a hug. "Keep writing in the journal." I almost think of walking back into her bedroom with her and curling up under the purple duvet. Megan and I could just curl up together, and if I got hard again, I could fuck her and squeeze her tits and look down at her tear-stained face and the boat dock could guard itself.

PUFF THE MAGIC DRAGON

After one uptown train, one egg sandwich and three Bloody Marys at Cannon's Pub, I stand in the shower at the Fat Mexican's pad, my red eyes tearing in the hot water. Megan will calm down. Megan will not want to be pregnant. Megan will do what has to be done. Megan cares about her project—her D.O.T., her "Document of Time." Megan doesn't want to have a child. Megan as a mother?

I towel off next to the phone machine. Ralph's scrawl is on a Post-It: "Call Kasia."

Did Kasia phone this morning? Did she phone late last night after she got to Amy's? And I was out banging Megan without using a condom, my head bleeding from a gold crown of dirt? Fuck. I drank the Bloody Marys so I wouldn't dry heave at the wet smell of the Hudson River. I drank the Bloody Marys to help face the herpes sore of my day job. I would need the buzz today if I was going to make my monthly nut. I drank the Bloody Marys just so this kind of surprise on a Post-It wouldn't spin me out.

I look into the long mirror on Ralph's brick wall. How was I going to play guitar and sing in front of real people?

I had to get sober. I had to get close to sober. I had six days before the benefit. I would take it easy tonight. Taper down. Have a few medicinal brews, a bedtime shot. Some heroin in the eyeball, maybe tape a strip of Valium under my tongue, snap my way through a box of whippets, drop some Ecstasy, snort some rails, dose on liquid acid, curl on the mattress in that blank white room in my skull and try not to think of the people at the benefit, the people that would look at me with big wide eyes, waiting for something to happen when I walked up to the microphone with my guitar. I almost ran down the steps to the Black Clock, but no, I'll just make it through the rest of the day after my shift, nurse a big glass of cold beer at the Dublin House and try not to look around at the old men drinking beside me on the barstools. I have to face sobering up now, or I am going to sit in front of the microphone and crash and burn and Kasia will see the truth. She will see the real Scout Harris. Yeah, I'll be different. I'll be a complete failure. Kasia will shield her eyes from the smoke and the flames and the wreckage. I have to get my shit together for Kasia. This is all about Kasia. I want her. The Book Mouse is a fishing lure floating on the blue water, and I am an ugly pickerel, pointing snout, sharp tiny teeth, sideways eyes, long hair flapping as I wiggle to the surface for that blond pad of tequila-gold pussy hair. I think of Shane McGowan, the ex-lead-singer for the Pogues and the Popes. That boozer had it easy. He didn't have to play guitar. He could just shake and scream in the microphone. Anyone can do that. Even Billy kept going past the point when eating cereal and tying his shoes was a daily challenge.

The phone rings. I watch it. It could be Kasia. I don't know if I like this idea, or it scares me shitless. I pick up the phone.

Megan.

"What time is that benefit?"

The three Bloody Marys funnel right up through my skull in a dizzy puff. The vodka evaporates. "What benefit?" I'm shaking.

"The one you told me about last night? I was on the phone with Tommy and Saetha and they were talking about going and telling everyone from the Diamond. It's great, Scout. We're going to get a real crowd."

"Megan... fuck!" I slam my hand against the wall.

Long silence. Her voice is small and pretendy, "I thought you'd like to have some friends for support?"

This was getting out of control. "Let me call you back," I lie. "I'm not sure of the date. Are you going to get one of those, get one of those morning after pills or whatever?"

"You need a prescription for those."

"Fucking get one."

"I'll probably be okay."

Here's where I step it up a notch. "You don't want to get pregnant, Megan."

"You don't know what I want," she says, sounding ready to fight with me like every other time we've taken a break from fucking to communicate with words.

"What about this whole journal project and all this stuff we're working on? What about the D.O.T.? Think about the fucking D.O.T. for fuck's sake?! I thought we were all going to get rich and famous off this gig?!" I am indignant. I haven't been spilling my guts on this thing just so Megan can drop it and go play mommy.

"I'm not going to get pregnant," Megan says, but I don't believe her. "I was just hysterical. Too much drinking last night. I took a Xanax."

"Great, Megan. That's great, but what does taking a Xanax have to do with anything? Like what does taking a Xanax have to do with getting pregnant?" I can't believe that only two hours ago I was hugging and kissing her. "I'm not hanging around as some kind of dad."

"I know, Scout, relax. I have a meeting and have to go, but get back to me about the show. I'm telling everyone and people are very excited."

"Don't tell anyone else," I say, "I'm not even sure it's happening, and I'm not even sure I'm playing any songs. It could just be a bunch of losers in a coffee shop shaking rattles and tambourines, doing spoken word and singing 'Puff the Magic Dragon.'"

"Puff the Magic Dragon" was stuck in my skull.

"You're a selfish dick," Megan says. "This is a benefit to raise money. You should be happy I decided to promote it. This money will help the victims…"

"Listen—"

"No, you listen, Scout. I might or might not be pregnant. I will find that out, but people all over this city are pulling together to try and make a difference after what happened. If you want to sing 'Puff the Magic Dragon,' sing 'Puff the Fucking Magic Dragon.' Just don't quit, and stop acting like it's such a challenge to pick up a guitar. Stop feeling sorry for yourself."

"You're a bitch." It feels like the right thing to say. Megan is a bitch. A Bloody Mary halo circles my head.

"Fuck you," she says. "Just get back to me with the date and time. I'll get a crowd of people and I'll call you the moment I have my period, so you don't have to sit in the boatyard and be accountable for your behavior."

"You know—" I go, but the phone is dead. Fucking cunt. I can't believe I told her about the benefit. Good, great, fucking brilliant. Everyone I know will show up. Perfect. I've got to slow way down on the booze. I've got to practice some tunes. "Puff the Magic Dragon" was a joke, but even that tune sounds tough to pull off when you're shaking from your spine to your fingertips. "Kissing Kasia" will be fucking impossible. I open the case and pull out my Guild and strum a few chords. "Puff the Magic Dragon lives by the sea…"

I place the guitar on Ralph's sofa, skip into the white-tiled bathroom, kneel in front of the toilet and puke.

SOBER

I've heard coming down from a real drinking habit can kill a person. This is a good excuse not to go cold turkey on the booze, but I also know I have to get a grip on the deal before walking into that coffee shop. George once quoted some writer and said,

"Sometimes one drink is just one drink too many." I figure that's what I need to do: get my mind focused on why I want to crank back on my boozing and get it under control. Part of it is money, but I am a walking example that poverty won't keep anyone from getting loaded. I'd seen Billy dance his way around being broke and still cop dope. And compared to heroin, booze is cheap. There's always someone who will front for some drinks and there's always a reason to justify spending what's in your pocket. Fuck the morning. I showed myself good at that trick last night. At least Megan paid for the taxi, but now she might be knocked up… a bun in the oven. It was too horrible to consider. It was enough to make you want a civilized bucket of tequila. I only had one chance to stay motivated and that one chance was Kasia. The Fat Mexican had a bottle of Absolut in his freezer. I washed the puke from my lips and brushed my teeth. I pulled the vodka bottle from the freezer and poured myself a shot and drank it. I picked up the phone and dialed the number at the Diamond. It was early, but Jon might be getting set for the day. I wanted to leave Ralph's number for George. Annie, the bartender, had said something about George, thought George might have stopped in looking for me.

The rotary phone at the Diamond rang and rang.

Here is my plan: keep my mind locked on Kasia. Practice the guitar, quiet fingers tapping the frets, take a few medicinal shots and beers, but keep my head quiet, strum and sing in a soft voice. The TV talks about a journalist in Florida who inhaled anthrax spores sent in an envelope. Death is in the air, but so is humiliation, and if I'm going to do my part—contribute and not fuck up in front of Kasia and everyone else—I need to be close to sober.

I get in my boatyard blue Dickies uniform and hit the streets. Time to muscle up for my security gig at the boatyard.

And the days and nights go like this…

Night One: two bumpers of Budweiser. I kill the final two fingers of the Fat Mexican's bottle of Patrón. Watch TV. VH1 has a special on the rise and fall of Def Leppard. I didn't know the drummer lost his arm in a car accident—walking around the English countryside, his arm in the grass. He learned to play with his feet on this homemade rig, using his one arm. This is good stuff. If the dude could play drums without an arm…

Morning Two: I sleep hard for two hours then pop awake. It's tough to get myself to the boatyard, but I make it, put down a buttered bagel and a black coffee and keep myself entertained with a copy of the *New York Post*.

Night Two: The Fat Mexican tells me about sleeping with Rio. He thinks this is the real deal. He doesn't use the word *love,* but I see the word flicker in his eyes. I make us both macaroni and cheese and pop Ralph a non-alcoholic Cutter's. He pulls a bottle of red wine off his wine rack. He opens the bottle, pours himself a glass, swirls the wine in his mouth and spits it out in the sink. I drink the rest of the bottle, looking out the window at the Black Clock Lounge. Ralph reads a business book with all three of his favorite words in the title: *Strategy, Organization,* and *Leadership.* It would be easy to walk into the Black Clock or over to Cannon's and get drunk, but I don't walk down the stairs. The wine will hold me. I pull out my guitar and practice "Redemption Song" and Sublime's "Wrong Way." I keep botching the chords, but it's easier if I don't try Johnson State songs.

Morning Three: It must be cutting back on the booze, because I wake up with a hard-on. (This usually only happens if I have a stray in bed, but this morning it's different.) I have a late shift at the boatyard. Ralph whistles out the door on his way to be the office bitch for these business professors that hired him. I pull a 1999 issue of Penthouse from my duffel bag. My cock is rock hard and my head doesn't hurt. I lock Fabio in Ralph's room. I go in the bathroom. The magazine has a pictorial of this chick that looks like one of the waitresses at K.L.'s that, for some not-good reason, never try to fuck me. The chick is skinny and wears red heels and a big floppy red hat. I start to take care of business, but my cock doesn't jump to it—kind of numb and desensitized, which surprises me. It hits me I want to look at a magazine stray that looks like Kasia. I flip through the mag with no luck, until I get to the pages of advertisements in the back—lots of photos of naked girls and lots of ads for erotic phone messages. Most of the girls have cocks, but one girl doesn't have a cock and looks just like Kasia used to look holding her breasts and arching her back. She has long blond hair. I remember the photo from a different ad. The photograph of the naked woman is probably about ten years old. I fire a load into the sink, tagging the faucet and the mirror. My left leg wiggles in a spasm. My right thigh cramps. I almost fall back into the bathtub and split my skull open. Instead, I limp around the Fat Mexican's apartment, with a towel wrapped around my waist and my hard cock sticking out. I try to put the Penthouse in the duffle bag, but my leg cramps when I crouch and the towel won't stay around my waist. I have to lower myself to the floor, with my cramped leg stretched out, then slide on my butt to the duffel. Fabio scratches and moans behind the locked door in Ralph's bedroom.

Night Three: I call Kasia on her cell phone. She tells me the lawyer friend from Livingstone, Montana, is still creeping around town. Kasia doesn't say more about the arrangement. I ring up Megan on her cell and ask how she's doing. Megan knows this is about her womb. She tells me she is on a date and it's not a good time to talk, but everyone is excited about the coffee house benefit. The big-titted skank even called some friend of hers named Suzanna to see about ratcheting up the publicity. Maybe turn this into a Johnson State reunion? I remind Megan that I haven't talked to Josh or Jacob in a few years and Billy is dead. There won't be a Johnson State reunion. Ever. We finish talking because Megan repeats she is on a date. I get the bottle of Absolut from the Fat Mexican's freezer and pour myself a big shot. Before I drink the shot of chilled vodka, I wrap a strip of brown masking tape around the cap of the bottle and write, "NO!" in black felt-tip on the tape. When I say I poured a big shot, I mean I filled one of the Senator's crystal rocks glasses to the brim. I take a swig then put in a few ice cubes. I need to make this stiff cocktail last me. I know this sounds fucked up, but I am cutting down. Trust me. VH1 has a special on Leif Garret, the one-time teen pin-up actor and party boy. Hammered, he wiped out and crashed his car and left his best friend paralyzed in a wheelchair for life. Leif doesn't seem stressed out about it, but maybe he's just acting tough.

I nurse the vodka. I do thirty push-ups, three sets of ten. I watch a rerun of *Cheers* and tell myself I can be the bartender that gets sober too, or at least, the bartender that doesn't get hammered every night.

Morning Four: Couldn't sleep. That one big mug of vodka made me want a second big mug of vodka. Three times I pulled out the bottle and read the word "NO!" in felt-tip on the tape around the screw-top. I didn't unpeel the tape. That tape was all that stood between me and Kasia's pale blue eyes watching me tremble and shake and walk off the stage, unable to play a tune, just another head case, another quitter. Last night I unpeeled the tape and poured one tablespoon of vodka in the crystal rocks glass. I re-taped the vodka bottle and put a second exclamation point by the word "NO!!" I sniffed the vodka in the glass. I put the glass with the tablespoon of vodka on Ralph's coffee table beside my sleeping bag. I didn't drink it. Fabio sat in the window sill at 5:00 a.m. I looked at my two guitars. My stomach hurt. I unlatched the case on my guitar. I held her sweet body on my chest and stared up at the ceiling, the thimble of clear vodka glowed in the rocks glass on the table.

Night Four: Bad day at the 79th Street boat basin. Anders tells me I might not have a job much longer, unless I get some kind of security certification. This security certification involves tests, written and physical, and some kind of city or state measurement sign-off. Anders won't be specific and won't pay for me to do it, might even start lining up a new guy, but nothing definite. Anders tells me not to worry, which makes me worry. After my shift, I walk to the Dublin House and order a small draft. I write the lyrics to "Kissing Kasia" on a napkin along with the chords, just to see if I can remember it. Back at the

Fat Mexican's pad, Ralph takes me out for noodle soup at Ollie's up near his office across from the Columbia University campus. I watch the college strays. Some of them clock me and toss college-chick wet-eye. I get heavy college-chick wet-eye from a punk chick with spiked hair. I drink two Tsingtao beers at the Chinese restaurant. Rio's got a shift at the Black Clock. Ralph wants company. The Hefty Spic doesn't want to look like a stalker. I drink two Budweisers at the Black Clock and leave Ralph talking to Rio. When I walk back to Ralph's pad, I am excited to find that Fabio has shot a stringer of piss on my pillow. I walk over to his tiny, plush cat bed and pull my cock out. The Persian watches me. I want to urinate right on the cat's pricey bed pillow, but I don't want to smell my own piss all night. I watch a VH1 special on heavy metal. Vince Neil from Mötley Crüe spins out drunk in a red sports car and kills one of his best friends. Nicki Sixx overdoses on dope. Is pronounced dead. Doesn't bite it. Checks out of the hospital only to go home and shoot up again. Very rock and roll.

Ralph doesn't come back to the apartment. The sun glimmers in a dark sky as I sweat through my T-shirt and boxers.

Morning Five: I wonder if the acid, ecstasy, and mushrooms I've ingested over the years have had a bad effect on my nerves? I feel testy. I had an early shift at the boatyard and was at the dock by 9:00 a.m. with two egg McMuffins and a big styrofoam mug of hot, tasteless coffee. I thought I was going to puke this morning, and I wasn't even hungover. Just those four medicinal beers—

Kasia hasn't called, but her friend, Amy, left a message on Ralph's machine telling me she put me on the flyer and announced this as my come-back performance after the end of Johnson State. This almost did send me into the bathroom gacking, but it doesn't thanks to my phenomenal restraint last night in the booze department. I get the food in my stomach. I see Anders fiddling with a cleat on the dock. I ask him what's up? He tells me to relax. He's lying through his teeth, but I don't give a fuck. Fuck Anders. Fuck the boatyard. I have no clue what I am going to do at this fucking benefit. Kasia wants her song, but I don't think I can pull it off. It's actually a tricky tune with this lead in, guitar teaser to the chorus. It was tricky shit for me back when I played all day long. Now, I don't play ever and my hands shake. After my shift, I walk up to the Dublin House and write down three songs on napkins, writing as much of the words and chords as I can remember. I figure I'll start with "Pretty Smooth" and then do a cover of Minor Threat's "Salad Days" and then, if I can pull it together, "Kissing Kasia." I might hold "Redemption Song" as a back-up. I scribble down the words to that first tune I wrote for my high-school love, a chick named Lauren Haylor... about her car stereo that got ripped off. The tune was called "Sorry." Can't believe I remember the words. I tear it up. I'm kind of stressed. I sip my big cold glass of Budweiser and try to imagine playing guitar in front of people. I stare at the white screen in my skull, but I can't see the image of me doing this thing. I just see Megan, Kasia, Kenny Lee, Hardy, Jon Domogarow, Amy, and the Diamond crowd all watching me in silence. I want to order just one sensible double tequila, but I pull myself out the door and walk into Central Park to find some ducks or trees to stare at while I cool out.

Night Five: I knock back one twelve-ounce Presidente and stare at the ceiling. I flip to VH1. Karen Carpenter dies from anorexia. This reminds me of the Sonic Youth tune about Karen Carpenter. I doze off and my dreams are so vivid I might as well be awake. In the morning I jump up, terrified, but the feeling passes. I'm not plummeting to my death, at least not RFN. My T-shirt is soaked with sweat, but I'm okay. Panic is normal. I'm an addict. That's the good news. The sweat and fear make sense.

Before I fell asleep last night, staring at Cheers on "MUTE," after the VH1 show ended, Kasia phones me at Ralph's and apologizes for being out of touch. I know and Kasia knows that being out of touch is another way of telling me she's been fucking her lawyer friend from Livingstone, Montana. Kasia's been fucking that stooge she doesn't like or respect, which tells you about everything you need to know about women. I guess they all grow up and have a moment where they take a stiff one from the enemy. It's been ten years, and I remind myself this isn't the same innocent Kasia who used to love me. I am one raw nerve. Kasia tells me she can't wait for the benefit and wonders if there will be a big crowd, and if so, how they'll fit in the coffee house? She asks me if I'm nervous. I tell her that I am nervous. We talk on the phone and it feels like there's no hurry and she's digging this bonding moment, and then suddenly, Kasia tells me she has to run, which we both know means dress for some kind of fancy dinner and ride the money-scented cock of the lawyer she doesn't respect.

I pull out Ralph's bottle of vodka and see the tape and the NO!! I unpeel the tape and pour two inches of vodka in a crystal rocks glass. I sit the glass on the coffee table. I pick up Fabio. This is the first time I've lifted the cat or really touched the animal. I pet Fabio. My hands tremble. The cat looks as if I'm about to throw it out the window. I put the cat on the sofa and unlatch my guitar case, lifting out the guitar. I play for Fabio. I sing "Kissing Kasia." Three times.

I think of Billy and put down the guitar.

I think of the World Trade Center and the people trapped in those long minutes.

I stretch out on the sleeping bag. A sofa cushion wrapped in a T-shirt is my pillow, since Fabio marked the original feather-down unit the Fat Mexican loaned me. The two inches of vodka reflect the moonlight. I leave the clear liquor in the glass.

I stare at the ceiling.

Morning Six: I wake up with a clear head and feel good. I stand up, cough once, race into Ralph's bathroom and dry heave until a dollop of bile drops in the toilet. I spit a few times and wipe my lips. It's all up from here…

Night Six: I take my Guild with me to the boatyard and sit on the edge of the dock in my blue Dickie workgear and peaked cap, even remembering my sunglasses. Maybe it's because I'm not hungover, but I play songs into the wind, facing the direction of Ground Zero… the Hole of Ghosts on the southern edge of Manhattan. I stand up and walk back and forth on the empty dock, playing the guitar like some knucklehead in an 80s metal-ballad MTV video. I look across the Hudson River to New Jersey, where I once practiced the fine craft of filing micro-fiche for eight bucks an hour when we were getting Johnson State going. I take a turn at Minor Threat's "Salad Days." I go into "Redemption Song" and Sublime's "Wrong Way." My body has sweated out some of the booze that has soaked and stewed my muscles and internal organs over the years of heavy drinking. I sit down and hang my legs off the edge of the dock and watch my black boots above the gray water. I pluck around on the guitar, and I see my old man back when I was a kid. He's watering the lawn in the backyard, holding the green garden hose and whistling Neil Diamond's "Crackling Rosie." This was before his accident and his own heavy drinking. He used to whistle a lot when I was a kid. He'd do yard work, and I'd sit on the wall with that first guitar he bought me. I try the chords and sing…

Anders walks up and tells me I'm fired.

I finish "Crackling Rosie," singing loud, staring past Anders at the state of New Jersey and the huge insects of machinery perched on the landfills across the dark river. Anders' slacks crackle in the breeze. Anders waits until I finish the tune. I ask Anders for my last paycheck. He is prepared and hands it over to me. I shake his hand. Anders looks at me and shakes his head, probably expecting rage or begging, violence or crying.

"It's been great." I grin, like we just finished a helicopter tour of an exotic island.

Anders has the whole thing worked out and doesn't want me coming back around and doing damage. Like I give a shit. Anders walks away. I play "Kissing Kasia" from start to finish alone on the dock. I have this feeling I hope I can capture for Megan. If I do, she might use some of the stuff I'm putting in the journal. Looking down the Hudson River, I figure, that the fish shed doesn't matter, the sleeping bag on the floor doesn't matter, and it doesn't matter too much that my favorite regular, the sweetest guy in the Diamond Pub, punched me out because I was a drunk asshole. It does matter what happened, just a few miles down the road, on Tuesday, September 11th. Those people didn't deserve going out that way. It also does matter that Billy chose to kill himself with his addiction. And it also does matter that I have a chance to play this song for Kasia and apologize for the way I treated her when she only wanted to enjoy what we get for a brief second, before the plane hits, before the floor gives out and the room fills with fire and we have to jump.

It also does matter that I'm scared about something as stupid as singing one fucking song. What has happened to me? I never thought I could become this lame.

According to the rules of rock and VH1, the only good thing I've done so far is not get drunk behind the wheel and kill or maim one of my friends.

I sit on the dock, my guitar beside me, my last paycheck in my pocket, and I know why I'm scared and I drink too much and fuck Megan when I'm thinking of Kasia. It hits me that it really is simple. I used to have something that mattered. I had it with Billy. We loved our music. We believed in our band. Now I'm alone. I am in high school again except Billy isn't around to buck me up and kick me in the ass. I've got to walk myself out of the maze of excuses and fear and obstacles that stopped me. I've got to do it myself. I'm not trying to be a hero. I'm just trying not to be a quitter. No one can help me—New Jersey to my right, New York to my left, the Hudson River rolling under my boots, my fingers strumming at the guitar, working out a series of chords. Here I am. I could use some of those business words Ralph is always talking about, those words on his books: *Leadership, Strategy....* I could definitely use that emotional intelligence. I could use some help with all this shit, but the fact is just that I'm too spooked to stand up at a microphone and do the one thing I'm supposed to be good at: make some noise. I wrote one song that was worth a shit, "Kissing Kasia," and I've never sang or played it for the one girl who was fucking supposed to hear it. I mean, she's heard it before on the radio or whatever, but that was Billy singing anyway, that wasn't me. And I'm the one that fucked up and gave her away and lost her.

I'm pathetic.

I don't even want to begin to face the fact I sing like shit. Billy was the singer in our band for a reason. He may have had attention deficit disorder and been high on heroin, but he could sing. I was the dude with the good stance, clean chops, good hair. Billy made the girls damp in their panties, even junked to the gills, he made the chicks wet with his voice.

I stretch back on the dock and look up at the sky. "Severe Clear" as they said on September 11th, not a cloud in the sky. I can't change what happened with Billy. I'm a fuck-up too. I loved the pussy and attention of being in the band, but I also loved writing the songs and playing them, developing them with the band. Sure, I loved the strokes I got at the Diamond, just like I loved the strokes I got for being in Johnson State, but the two things weren't the same. I don't want strokes. I'm fucked because I'm scared of failing, but okay, I'm scared. I might fuck up at the benefit. So what? I am a fuck-up. I just can't be a quitter.

I've got to crawl out from under the rock.

This isn't THE END. I still have *when.*

I tool around a few chord changes thinking of a word… *Severe Clear.* It hits me the pedal isn't tapped and the gas is still in the tank. I consider walking up to the Dublin for a celebratory I-just-got-fired beer and a napkin to write down some lyrics, but I don't need a bar. This is a beautiful day on the dock. I lost my job. I don't have to go anywhere, because I have nothing to do until I take the train down to Chelsea tonight to the empty coffee shop to listen to bad poetry, spoken word, and probably some musicians that aren't terrified and dry-heaving before they perform. I walk back past the moored boats and grab some McDonald's napkins from the fish shed along with a pen. I sit on the dock and begin…

What a day. It's so severe, little girl,
    You know what they said when they heard the news?

140

Turn off the songs that scare the town.
It's so severe, way too clear. When you walked out that door
On the 107th floor, too early, it was clear
Severe clear. Lovely girl I never knew
When I heard the news, the sky was severe.
The sky is clear. You can fly, you can walk
Away, today, but won't come home. I didn't know you, girl
Just lost you on a day that was severe, bright and way too clear.

Anders walks up with a big clean-cut scary-looking motherfucker. The scary-looking character is cut with muscles on muscles. His eyes are polite. He smiles at me. He has very handsome teeth. I'm trying to figure out these "Severe Clear" words. It's like a puzzle, figuring out how they can fit. I hand the big dude my peaked Parks Service hat and the keys to the fish shed. "The nightstick is in the top drawer," I tell him and Anders. I walk away. Anders says something, but I don't hear it and don't care. I can't pull off this song before tonight's gig, but it feels good to not be terrified, bored, vomiting, or drunk.

DOWNTOWN TRAIN

The doors of the No. 2 train open and a man steps on the train, holding a guitar. The man has lived a hard life and that hard life has stained the man's clothes, his face, but not his green eyes. His hair is slicked up and back. He is groomed, but his clothes are grimy. He has a hooded sweatshirt underneath a black suit jacket, a dingy once-white thermal under the hooded sweatshirt, baggy wool pants and work boots. The man could be in his early forties, with his face creased, soul patch and long sideburns. I'm wedged between two large women with shopping bags. My guitar case is upright between my legs. Brown cords clench the side of the case, the tattered flared bottoms of the pants are soaked in the scummy wetness of the train floor. These are my good-luck pants from back when Johnson State was still together. I remember when these pants were loose on my waist and I had to cinch my belt. Now the pants are tight. My shirt is a maroon paisley number with frayed elbows. I have on my white leather jacket. I keep my eyes trained on my black boots. The eyelets are ripped, the boots are cracked at the bottom of the eyelet row. I can see a patch of my gray sock. I don't want to look at the other loser in the train holding a guitar. I don't want to give him money, hear him play, sing. He unzips his padded guitar case, and I pray we get to the next stop fast and I can bail. But the express train has started making local stops in that way New York City subway trains just flip on you, and now I'm fucked. We're making all stops, and I'm stuck listening to this busker. I don't need his pain. This messed up drifter isn't going to crawl into my skull and start whining to me about his crash-and-burn. I don't want to hear how life fucked him over.

The train lurches out of the station. Drifter strums his Gibson and I get a shiver, but I can't grab onto what is causing it. The man plucks at the guitar. His voice is full and the words pop in my ear as I keep my eyes locked on a Burger King cup that rolls back and forth on the floor. The train lurches and shudders on the rails as he belts out a song.

What is this weathered dude singing and why do I care? What is this song? Then it hits me. This is "Fourth of July," a Dave Alvin tune from *Romeo's Escape* and also X's *See How We Are*. I cranked the X version on wax, my speakers propped out the window of the Hell's Kitchen pad on that 4th of July when Kasia helped me paint the apartment white. The air-conditioner was broken, and we made love and listened to the neighborhood kids shoot off fireworks.

What is this homeless busker doing playing this song for wine cash? I look up. With the subway rumbling, the dude is putting everything into it, slapping the side of his guitar, keeping time. People could give a damn. No one wants to look at him. No one wants to give him money. And he's good, his voice piercing, sad.

Ten years gone, but listening to this wino play his guitar and sing words makes me remember not just the color of the sheets on my futon, but the feel of the thin madras bedspread Kasia had bought me. I feel the crinkly white down comforter and can smell the wood frame I built for the futon. I am Scout Harris ten years ago. I hold Kasia and watch myself hold her from up on the ceiling, looking down on our naked bodies, sweaty in the summer heat. Firecrackers pop and crackle. The broken air-conditioner is on the floor. A fan is turning in vain over a bucket of ice from the freezer. Kasia rides on top of me, looking down, she leans over and her hands hold my hands back over my head. Kasia kisses me just the way Kasia kisses. Everything dissolves. The needle reaches the end of the record.

The train lurches into Penn Station and the momentum pushes me to the door, pulling one of my two five-spots out of my pocket. I drop it in the guitar case at the foot of the guy, not clocking him, just moving out with the crowd.

"Cool tune, huh?"

"Yeah," I can't avoid checking him. "Reminds me of a girl."

"The good ones all do, Scout."

What the fuck? I look at him, the subway doors starting to close.

"James." He holds the train door for me. "I played with the Blue Devils. You opened for us at CB's."

Shit. James Desoto. "James. Fuck yeah." His face is clearing up under the age and the dirt of sleeping wherever he was sleeping. "I remember. Fuck yeah. You were bad-ass. How are you doing?" The dude looks homeless.

"I heard about Billy." James pockets my fiver and grabs his case, takes his guitar and steps out onto the subway platform, guiding me ahead of him, his hand in the small of my back. "Too bad." He looks down at my guitar case. "You're still playing? Good deal."

"I'm at this coffee shop, an open mic gig, trying to raise some money. You know, donate something to the 9/11 relief."

"Good." James shakes his head. "Yeah, Scout, let's show those fuckers."

"So." I push. "How you doing, James?"

"I'm hanging in. Had a rough time with dope myself, but kicked it. I'm putting together some cash. Just have to keep playing. Even here." James Desoto spreads his arms at the crowded subway station. "I can do it, so I do it. You know what I'm talking about?"

"She's looking clean." I nod to his guitar.

"My old Gibson." He holds up the guitar and grins. "It's the one thing I never sold. They're going to have to rip this motherfucker from my cold dead fingers."

"You kicked it?" It's a dumb question, he said he did and either he's clean or he's lying. He doesn't look high, but it's something else, maybe the fact he doesn't go into a long story that never ends about his drug-free life, which means the total opposite in a junkie. The more they talk, the more they lie.

"Have to be," James says. "I want to get a band together, once I get a place to live." He squints at me, "We should keep in touch."

I pull out the ballpoint I used to scratch out the lyrics to "Severe Clear," write the Fat Mexican's number on a tag of cocktail napkin from my jacket and hand it to James. "I haven't played in years," I admit. "I'm not sure how it's going to go tonight, but call me at this dude's place. I'm crashing on his floor, broke as shit. Just lost my job, but I'd be down to jam."

A downtown local pulls up. James looks at it. "Guess I'll keep heading south today." His green eyes flash, "You okay? No one hurt with that World Trade Center shit?"

"No bad news."

James looks at me, "I'll give you a ring. We'll get together. Rock it hard tonight." James

142

strums his guitar. "We gotta stand tall."

I nod, "Right on." And slap him on the shoulder. James Desoto. I slap him one more time on his homeless-and-playing-on-the-subway shoulder. James taps my leather jacket with his fist, slips his guitar in its case and gets on the downtown train. The doors close. I watch James lean against a subway pole as the subway car rolls off into the black tunnel.

PERFORMANCE

Seeing James is cool. What the fuck am I whining about? I hoof it past three bars—each more tempting than the bar right before it—and finally enter an Irish dive called Patrick's and park my corduroy butt on a stool and order one shot of Cuervo. I look at it. I smell the dirt. I take a sip, the delicate sip of an aficionado, an artist appreciating true beauty. Tequila. The gold sails flutter. I place the shot glass on the table and slip a dollar underneath the glass of sweet fire and pick up my guitar. "C'mon," I say to my dead friend in the empty bar, "Let's rock it, Billy." I push out the doors into the fading sunset, just another person in Manhattan watching the red sky and missing a friend who won't be coming home.

The coffee shop has a multicolored sign that says, "Thundergrind." I notice the sign, but I only notice the sign right after I see the jammed doorway and the line of people spilling onto the street. I was walking to this gig only calling it a gig 'cause open mic was depressing, but this open mic has way too many people for whatever is about to go down.

Amy manages the door with Kasia. Kasia's turtleneck and jeans remind me of her look ten years ago. We all do a combo of air-kisses and half-hugs, and I give Kasia's ass a firm squeeze, making sure Amy clocks me. Amy goes off to talk with the sound guy and get the equipment set up. Kasia tells me I'm coming on fourth, after some spoken-word dude. Kasia glows, asking me if I want a chai latte or coffee. I go with a decaf. I'm shaking with adrenaline, about to bounce off the ceiling. The room is packed. My confidence was rocking on the dock, soothed by the river and the pleasure of being fired from a job I hated, but now that I'm here at Thundergrind to "Rock the Relief" it is faltering. I start recognizing all these faces from the Diamond. Saetha and her boyfriend Tommy are talking to Baron Jancet with that Viking chick I hooked up with way back—almost didn't recognize her with the red dye-job. Megan appears from the back room of sofas, holding a video camera. She points the black lens of the vid-rig at me, walking forward. "Are you excited?" she asks me. Are you pregnant, I want to ask, but keep my mouth shut. Jon Domogarow shakes my hand. "Yo, dog." Jon looks around as if the place is about to break out into group massage or interpretive dancing. Jon is uncomfortable outside the shadows and smoke and loud jukebox of the Diamond. "What is this place?"

"Hell," I say. "Jon, this is hell."

Jon doesn't laugh. "Yeah, I don't like the smell. Too much coffee."

"It is a coffee shop," I explain. Megan waves the video camera at my grid.

The Fat Mexican walks in with Rio.

He looks way too happy, dressed in a dark suit with a blue tie, overcoat folded over his arm. Rio wears a tight sweater and short black dress, tights and heels. The outfit makes it clear her hard body rocks. It wasn't the tequila playing tricks with me that first night I clocked her in the Black Clock.

"Don't you have something better to do, Senator?"

"Rio wants to hear you. She didn't know you were a musician."

Rio goes, "Ralph told me you used to be something special."

"Used to be," I say. "That's kind of the deal. Used to be."

"Still is in my book." Ralph slaps me on the back. "Hey, darling," he asks Rio. "Would you like a coffee?"

Kasia stands next to me. I nod toward the Fat Mexican with hot curvy Rio glued to his pricey wide suit. "That's the dude that lets me sleep on his floor."

Kasia puts her arm around me. "You're going through a rough patch. It'll turn around."

Her voice makes me shiver. I nod toward the amp and mic and boom stand. "I'm scared shitless."

"You?" she laughs. "Don't forget. You're still the kind of guy that tries to take a girl's shirt off on the street. Besides, you're helping. Remember that. Whatever happens tonight, we've got a crowd. People have paid. We can donate it."

"I didn't try to take your shirt off," I have to repeat. "I just unbuttoned your shirt and kissed your tits." I'm almost shaking from her touch and the pressing buzz of the crowd. I'm like Keith Richards, if he just got fired from a boatyard and was spooked to play guitar at a coffee shop. I'm probably more like Axl Rose, without the money or past success. But I haven't got hammered and I haven't smashed up and killed any of my friends in a car accident, so I'm doing better than some rock legends. Kenny Lee and Hardy walk in with a couple of the bored waitresses that for some not-good reason never try to fuck me. Everyone I know is dropping into this party.

Kasia excuses herself, and I make my way back through the crowd. I find Megan and whisper, "How are you, you know?"

Megan smiles very big, "Yes," she says loudly. "I'm fine, Scout." She looks past my shoulder. Kasia is standing behind me.

"Amy wants to know if you need to plug into the amp?"

I figured there were going to be about three people in the room. "I'll talk to her." Megan has the camera switched "ON," Kasia in frame. "Hi," Megan says from behind the camera and red "ON" light. "I'm Megan and you are…?"

Kasia smiles, "Hi, I'm Kasia, Kasia Crocetti."

"Kasia," says Megan, with a swift change of her expression, followed by a bright polite show of her teeth. "You must be the girl from the song?"

Kasia blushes. "Yes, Scout and I used to date a long time ago."

The video camera runs and for a few blissful seconds, the tension between the two girls takes my skull off my own tension. Megan asks, "Are you doing 'Kissing Kasia'?"

I shrug.

Megan shoves the video camera in my face. "How enigmatic. This is Scout Harris right before he performs for the first time since his best friend and bandmate Billy Cameron died from an overdose of heroin."

I give the camera lens the finger.

"It's for the D.O.T.," Megan explains, still with the black eye and red "ON" light pointed at my grid. "You're about to perform, Scout. You need to concentrate."

"I know what I need to do. Just keep that fucking thing away from me."

The Fat Mexican and Rio walk up. Megan turns the camera on the Senator. "Ralph Villalobos," says Megan to the camera microphone. "Thanks for the digital downloads on that CD. Can I get another one soon, with more of your notes?"

"Sure thing," Ralph says. "I'm sitting in the park on my lunch breaks and talking into the recorder. Sorry I lost those early files."

"Don't let it worry you," says Megan. "That's the nature of our digital world."

I swear Megan wrote a script for herself.

"Hey," I interrupt. "By the way, what is that shit about, Megan? This Fat—I mean," clocking Rio. "The Senator gets a tape recorder and I have to write everything in a big heavy fucking diary? It takes forever, and I usually forget half of what I want to get down." Kasia, confused, looks at me. I have no choice but to explain. "Megan has a project, collecting stories from all of us that used to hang out at the Diamond." It hits me, "Hey, did you know George was in town?"

Megan shakes her head. "Really? I tried to call him last week on his cell and out in L.A.

to see if he was working on his part of the project."

"What, did George get to do his D.O.T. gig?" I ask Megan.

"George told me he was going to type some thoughts down on his typewriter," Megan explains. "I wanted his side of the romance and break-up with Lilly. I know he's done preliminary notes, because he read them to me over the phone back in July. He said it was helping him come to terms—"

"With his grief?" I interrupt, a bit too edgy.

"Actually—" Megan starts talking to everyone else. "George said he might turn his notes into a longer story."

Actually?! Actually?! I want to slap Megan's ass. Why can't she just let me know she's not knocked up? How hard is it to slip me a simple word? She talks all the fucking time! Why not tell me what I need to know? Unless Megan still doesn't have proof. I start thinking about the moon and female cycles and days between periods and my skull is blank. I can't figure it out. If she starts bleeding, I'm cool. That's all I know.

"Are you talking to Lilly?" Ralph asks Megan.

"I haven't seen Lilly in a long time," Megan says. "I talked to her about the D.O.T. last New Year's at a party, but she didn't give me a yea or nay."

Megan goes to Kasia and Rio, "I had this idea for a while about creating a Document of Time, using different voices of people that were at the Diamond. The city was changing so fast, people come and go. I thought George and Scout and Ralph were an interesting mix."

Kasia nods, looking at Scout, "What are you doing, writing in a journal?"

"I think Megan's trying to torture me."

"Imagine a collage of voices," Megan says.

"Annie said something," I interrupt her. "Annie said Jon said George stopped into the Diamond, the week of all the shit." I watch the boom stand where I'm about to make a fool of myself. "You should go check with Jon. I think he knows more on this deal."

"Great week to visit New York," says Ralph.

Kasia runs her fingers up the small of my back under my white leather jacket. "Are you going to sing 'Puff the Magic Dragon'?"

"I have no clue what I'm going to do."

I squeeze Kasia's ass. Megan's got the video camera on us. Kasia has a great ass. It comforts me. I slap her ass and squeeze it: firm, round, ready to pound.

Kasia whispers, "Quit it. You look possessed."

REDEMPTION SONGS

I don't know what is worse, waiting to get up and play in front of a crowd or listening to bad poetry while I wait. The poet makes my ears hurt with some dumb poem about a tree that scared him as a boy. He really is lame, but the spoken-word dude that follows has the crowd busting up. He talks about waxing his butt hair and chasing guys around the city, trying to give them blow jobs. He can't remember any of the guys' names, just the names of their pets. He's fucking hilarious and there's nothing very fucking hilarious about what I'm going to do, but I think of James Desoto. I can't whine, Billy. Let's get this done.

Amy announces she is about to hand the microphone over to a guitar player that some people might remember from a band called "Johnson State" (a few people clap), but more people will know as the bartender who helped increase the number of alcoholics in the East Village (loud applause, hooting).

I start with "Pretty Smooth," going for the raunchy tune about women shaving their snatches. I am three lines into the chorus when I look up at the faces watching me. I stop. That song was from another Scout. That was the Scout that pushed Kasia away. That was the Scout that lived on strays and tequila. That was the Scout that mouthed off to his favorite regular in the Diamond and woke up with a sewer rat crawling near his face. That was the Scout that dreamed about fame while his best friend shot junk.

"Let's leave that one," I say in the microphone. "I bet every girl in this room is already pretty smooth." (A few laughs.)

I go to "Redemption Song," and even though I feel sort of stupid singing about pirates robbing "I" and selling "I" into slavery, I don't care. Bob Marley was the man. "All I ever had, redemption songs… these songs of freedom…" Kasia smiles at me and Megan watches me with the vid-rig pointed at the sweat dripping off my nose. A few people look bored, wondering how they got stuck back against the wall, listening to this white boozer sing reggae. I don't blame them and wouldn't blame them if they threw something. A fist-fight might kick this coffee shop into gear. The sweat runs down my arms and I fall deeper into the song, hitting the strings, remembering that Marley voice, fighting the cancer.

"All I ever had…" I think of James Desoto. I think of you, Billy, "redemption songs… these songs of freedom…"

(Some clapping.)

Then I butcher "Salad Days" for you, Billy.

I knock out Sublime's "Wrong Way."

Three down, one to go: "Kissing Kasia."

My eyes go to Kasia. I start in on "Puff the Magic Dragon." She smiles, a few people laugh. "Puff the Magic Dragon lives by the sea…"

My eyes tear up. I begin to cry. I don't look at anyone else, just close my eyes and sing the song.

It's lame, but I weep. Tears dribble down my face…

Someone coughs. I don't fucking care. I sleep on the Fat Mexican's floor. I just got fired. I'm crying like a bitch, but my eyes are open and I'm singing about Honah Lee and little Jackie Paper who loved that rascal Puff. You get the picture. I make it through the tune, tears streaming down my face. I wrap it up. "Okay," I say.

"Get him a beer!" someone yells from the back of the crowd.

"Let's do one more." I wipe the snot from my nose, smearing the back of my hand on my cords. "This is from Johnson State. I'm going to dedicate it to my friend Billy who left us a while back. This tune's called "Kissing Kasia." I look at Kasia. She smiles. Here we go, Billy.

Someone claps. Some other voice yells, "Rock it, Scout!"

I'm not done crying. I wipe my eyes with my shirt sleeve. "Jesus…" Start in on the song. I just play. It's not hard. I stumble a bit, but start working the frets, plucking the strings, surging adrenaline remembering the Kasia I left behind, the real Kasia standing in front of me in the crowd. The young Kasia time won't bring back. The older Kasia that turns me on and watches me with her pale blue eyes.

I finish the song and thank everyone for supporting Amy's benefit.

After two more performers—a stand-up comic and a rap poet—Kasia and I catch a taxi with Kenny and Hardy down to K.L.'s. Megan and the Diamond crowd have already cut out after Megan dragged me to the side and told me she was proud of me and I should write about this night in the journal. I was playing music again! Megan had a big smile. She was happy and I hadn't even cum on her tits or shot a load in her mouth.

I was wiped. How did I use to play those full-on gigs, leaping all over the place and picking fights? I wanted to just sit and watch people. Megan asked me if I was fucking Kasia. I said no. Megan said that was good. I asked her if she was pregnant, and she said no. Megan wasn't pregnant. She said it wasn't good for us to meet at night like we did and fool around. Megan told me that kind of behavior left her feeling bad about herself as a woman. I said I understood. Megan made me promise we would never do it again, no matter what. I said, "Promise." We hugged. Megan smelled nice. I shook hands with some of the other folk who hoofed it over from the East Village, thanking them for dropping in.

Jon Domogarow told me he was glad to hear me play again. Others said the same thing. I might have sounded like shit, but I gave it a shot, Billy.

Kasia takes a barstool next to me at K.L.'s. Kenny orders us all a round. "Scout," he goes. "Do you always cry when you play?"

"Sure. Don't you remember?"

Kenny shrugs. Hardy laughs. Kenny says, "It's been so long, I guess I forgot. Are you going to get in a new band?"

"I was thinking about it." I tell them about running into James Desoto on the subway.

"Crying," Kenny says. "It's a nice way to close a set."

"Thanks," I say. "Fuck you."

Hardy goes, "Puff the Magic Dragon was nice."

"Thanks," I say.

"But kind of stupid too," Hardy adds.

"Yes," I say. I feel calm, but pumped up. I'm glad the thing is over, but part of me is ready to go again. Mike works the bar. He slides the four of us shots of dirt.

"Here's to Scout," Ken says. "Crying like a baby." We all raise our glasses, tap them and drink the gold sails of the gods.

Kasia touches my leg. "You were great."

"You liked the crying?"

"It was honest." She gives me a half hug I can't figure out. "Amy thought you were brilliant," she adds. "She really used that word *brilliant*. She says you've changed."

"Yeah, I cried like a baby in front of everyone I know. That's a change."

"But it's not a bad change." She checks her watch. "I have to go in a few minutes."

"Why?" I'm surprised, figuring we were just going to get numb with liquor and I would figure out a way to play with her tits in public. It hadn't crossed my mind Kasia would skip out. "If you're not here, we can't get drunk and make out on the hood of a car."

"We're not going to get drunk and make out. I have plans uptown."

I want to tell Kasia I know she's going uptown to fuck the lawyer friend she doesn't like very much and doesn't respect, but I've already wept in front of everyone I know in town, it might be time to put the brakes on acting like a bitch. "Cool. We'll catch each other later."

"Right. I'm leaving tomorrow, going back to Montana."

"Cool." What a day. Great. Kasia is leaving for some big state in the middle of nowhere, the big middle of nowhere state where the lawyer works his evil work that Kasia doesn't respect, but spreads her legs for when he wants to hump her.

She can read my eyes and figure that I'm not down with this. "I have to get back to work," she explains. "I'm doing freelance jobs and if I don't get back to Livingstone, I'll lose the work."

"Got it." My eye twitches—the little bitch inside me crawling on all fours. And right after I've played live for the first time since Billy put on the blue suit! I flash my eyes on the curve of Kasia's tits, my heartbeat ramps up. "Did you like your tune?"

"I liked it." She smiles back. "It was something special to hear you sing it—and see it live tonight."

"C'mon," I reach for her jacket. "I'll walk you to a taxi." Kasia gives me a quick look. "No hanky-panky," I add. "Just a gentleman helping a lady to a cab."

At the corner of Downing and Varick, a yellow cab slips right up. What is it with these fuckers? Kasia's pale blue eyes watch me. "Maybe I'll see you in Montana?" she says. This is another thing I didn't remember about Kasia, her eyes look sad, but her eyes are hard to read. Do Kasia's pale blue eyes watch me out of sadness 'cause she's leaving me and wants to stay or do Kasia's pale blue eyes watch me out of sympathy, since I'm out of the deal, just a wild ex to flash your breasts at and kiss in the cold night after you roll into town and need a break from fucking a man you don't like or respect.

"Yeah," I say for no reason I can figure. I'm not going to Montana.

Kasia hugs me hard and tight and kisses me once on the lips. "You were great tonight, really great, Scout."

"Thanks," I say, and then the taxi is gone and I walk back to Kenny's to scam a few drinks before riding the slow uptown local back to 110th Street to sleep in a fresh puddle of cat piss, my two guitars safe in their cases by the moonlit window.

"Kissing Kasia." I did it, Billy, but I wish you'd been there to sing it.

I sing like shit.

SEVERE CLEAR

The anthrax scare is real news. People are picking up this weird death-dust and no one can figure if it's more Muslim terrorist shit or some kind of crack-pot redneck psycho shit. No one has died yet, but it's probably only a matter of time. For being a First-World civilized country, there are a lot of people out there that want to kill us Americans, and that's not even mentioning all the Americans that spend time killing other Americans. I haven't been trying to kill anyone, but I have been working on "Severe Clear," tooling on the guitar, trying to craft some lyrics and a melody, searching for something that doesn't sound lame. I used to figure I wrote about five lame songs before I got something I liked, but I've got the feeling that number might be cranked way up. I haven't done this in way too long, plus my expectations are high. If "Severe Clear" doesn't hold up, I'm tossing it in the bin. I'll write a hundred songs before I lie to myself and say it's good when it's shit.

Kasia is back in Montana. I phoned her last night and we talked for an hour. I asked her what the deal was with the lawyer. She admits she's been sleeping with him, but now it's over. He had money and he was crazy about Kasia, but it just wasn't right. She couldn't fake it anymore. I was about to ask her why she even let him get near her when I was standing under her balcony, but there were too many ways that question could bite me in the ass. I asked Kasia if she was flying back to the Tri-State area for Thanksgiving. Undecided. Her family wanted her to visit, but she wasn't sure it was going to happen. She has a small rental apartment in Livingstone and said she looks forward to spending time alone.

Okay, so the lawyer is out of the picture.

I tell her I want to see her again. Kasia laughs and I swear I can feel her blush on the other end of the phone. "You can fly out for a weekend, if you want."

"I would if I hadn't just lost my job, and wasn't flat-broke."

"You what?" I hadn't told Kasia that night at the benefit.

"The boatyard booted me for some kind of real security guy. I think he might even know what he's doing. It's okay. I'll figure something out."

"Like what?"

"I talked to the kid that owns the Diamond and he's giving me a few shifts next week, just to get some cash together."

"How do you feel about that?"

"I'll do what I've got to do. It's fucked, but whatever. I wrote a song."

"You did! That's great, Scout."

"It's not about you."

"That's okay. You already did that once."

I wish I could get a plane ticket to Montana.

"It's not finished, but I wouldn't have written this tune if you hadn't got me to that benefit."

"I'm really glad. What's it about? I mean, is it about something?"

"I guess. It's about a girl dying at the World Trade Center."

"Oh, that's sad. Someone you knew?"

"No, someone I didn't know. That's the point. She's gone and I might have known her.

But now I won't."

"We lost so many people and we'll never know them."

"Yeah, I guess that's it."

"If I don't make it back for Thanksgiving, I'll come back for Christmas, you can play it for me. You can even play it for me over the phone?"

"Maybe I'll wait until I see you."

"I'll buy the tequila."

"And I'll take off your shirt."

"No, you won't."

"You're tough when you're a thousand miles away."

"I'm always tough. You just never noticed because I was too nice to you."

"That was your first mistake," I say, as the Fat Mexican unlocks the apartment door. I look at the clock on the brick wall. Yes, it is the end of his Fat Mexican work day, slaving for business professors, the poor fuckhead. I should be hustling up a cold non-alcoholic Cutter's for him as he loosens his necktie and places his jacket on the back of a kitchen chair. "How's it going, Senator?"

"What?" asks Kasia.

"My roomie is back from the salt mines." I feel good for no real reason. I'm surprised, but the Fat Mexican has a bucket of Kentucky Fried Chicken and bottle of Cazadores reposado tequila. Ralph drops his wide body in the creaking kitchen chair and pulls out a chicken leg. "Hang on one sec," I say to Kasia. I go to the fridge and pull out a Cutter's pseudo-beer and pop it open for him. I find this part of my day humble and enjoyable. I think this is the service all those people in A.A. yap about. The Fat Mexican is my higher power. I place the frosty cold bottle of useless swill down in front of his bucket of fried chicken. Ralph looks at me and twists the top off the tequila bottle. I hold up my hands. "I'm cool for the moment, maybe later." The Fat Mexican takes the tequila bottle and burbles down a long swallow. "Sangre de Cristo," he mutters, takes another gargle of tequila, swallows it and shakes his head, exhaling with a good fire-water gasp.

"Whoa, big fella." I take the bottle from his hands.

"Drink or get out," goes Ralph, and that's when I figure something has happened with Rio. Ralph points at the phone. "You paying for the phone bill this month?"

I wait for the Fat Mexican to grin and give me some of that businessman spic charm, some sign that all is well, but he just stares at the phone as if looking through it. I say, "Kasia, I'll call you back. It looks like we got some kind of crisis here with the Senator."

"Is he okay?" Kasia is nestled in her small apartment in some big state I've never seen and don't have enough coin to visit, even for her pussy.

"I hope so," I say loud enough for the Senator to know I'm talking about him. "If he goes under, this whole hip world I've created living on his floor will fall apart."

"You sound good," Kasia says, "for a guy who, I don't know how to say this…"

"Doesn't have a pot to piss in?" I catch my grid in the mirror and toss some fast Clint Eastwood mirror. The Fat Mexican is on his third guzzle of tequila and third piece of fried chicken. When he goes off the wagon, the Hefty Hispanic goes large!

"I'm glad we got to hang, Kasia. I'll let you know if I get the song worked out, or find an airplane ticket to Montana."

"You do that. I'm glad we got to spend time together too. You know, Amy said you had turned into the guy everyone thought you could be, if you weren't—"

"—such an asshole?" I said.

"She didn't put it like that, but yes."

"Yeah, tell Amy thank you and I hope she raised money at her event. Also tell that Ice Cream Girl she's got nice legs and should call me if she gets lonely."

"Ice Cream Girl?" Kasia's laugh is muffled. "Scout, I don't even want to know…"

"I'd hold her by the ankles."

"Stop it!" says Kasia. "You're talking about my best friend."

"I'd hold her by the ankles and walk Amy around the room…"

"Scout," Kasia laughs. "That's just not right."

"And take a few licks."

"Stop it. Really."

"Okay, I better run or the Senator is going to choke to death on a bucket of chicken."

"Bye, you pervert." Kasia is gone and I am holding the bottle of Cazadores. "What's up, bro? I thought you were on the wagon and on a diet?" I look at the bottle of dirt and bucket of fried bird.

"Just taking a break."

"What happened?"

"Who said anything happened?" Ralph takes the tequila bottle from me and gurgles back a swallow that would rock most dudes. He wipes his lips with the back of his hand. "Get us some glasses. Over the sink."

"I know where you keep the glasses."

"I'm sure you do."

"This wouldn't have to do with that little filly who's been riding your uncircumcised brown Mexican cock, would it?"

Ralph pours two big tumblers of high-end dirt and pushes one glass my way.

I sip the dirt, the sweet burn moves up into my skull like velvet rose-petal fireworks. Ralph points at my glass. "Ready?"

I look at him. I have never heard a more stupid question.

Ralph pours more dirt in my glass. "We're celebrating," he says. "Drink your dirt."

I throw it back in one long burning song—fireworks spreading through my chest to my fingertips, gold sails fluttering against a red sky. Montana isn't that far away. I'll see Kasia again. I'll unbutton her shirt and pull down her pants. I'll play "Severe Clear" for her by the firelight while the coyotes howl.

The Fat Mexican picked the wrong dude to match tequila shots with tonight. I don't need some bitch to get me fired up for a dirt duel. I am in a good fucking mood. I can live on tequila. I pour us each a big motherfucker of a shot. "Celebrating what?"

"My new bachelorhood," goes the Senator.

"Can I have some chicken?"

Ralph pushes the bucket at me.

"I thought," I continue, "you already wrapped the paperwork on the divorce?"

"I mean—" Ralph nods in the direction of the Black Clock Lounge.

"Rio problems," I snap my fingers. "Knew it."

"No problem," says the Senator. "I just like her more than she likes me."

"That'll happen. Did you slap her ass and tie her up?"

"Didn't get around to it, but it sounds like a good idea now."

"It's always a good idea. Trust me."

Ralph stares at the tequila bottle. With my help, it's dented, but the Senator is a big man and has put back some greasy chicken. He pours more dirt in our glasses. I feel fucking righteous. I want that greasy fried chicken. I start gnawing on a thigh when the Fat Mexican stands up, adjusts his necktie, screams "Fuck!" and punches the brick wall.

PLAN N

I sit in the emergency room at St. Luke's, waiting for Ralph to get the cast on his hand. A guy sitting next to me has a rope of blood strung down his forearm wrapped in a red-stained white T-shirt. He looks calm. I don't have a cell phone, but if I did, I'd call Kasia. I watch the emergency room technician guide the dude with the bleeding arm backstage for a tune-up. I hope the Fat Mexican hasn't fucked his hand too bad. For all I know, that hand is important to whatever it is Ralph does in the office, paying for the apartment and food and liquor I need to make it through this motherfucker until whatever follows Plan M. I think back to that hot danger-zone Ralph married. I never met her, but have seen photos. Ralph and I had an unspoken agreement that revolved around the fact that he had dumped Kathleen, who was a sweetheart, for Caryn Hwan. Ralph didn't hold it against me that Kathy and I had hooked up for a short time. (He was married to Caryn by then anyway.) The Fat Mexican and I never talked about it, but I think he just figured he got what he deserved when love turned around and bit him in the hand. I thought of Kasia. I thought of George and Lilly running off to Los Angeles and going into the full-on crash-and-burn from what I heard through the grapevine and saw in Lilly's eyes when she showed up back at the Diamond. It was an endless circle and now Ralph and Rio have barely made it out the gate, and he's punching walls. I think of Megan. She deserves to find a nice guy… or a long chain of younger guys.

"Okay," I go as Ralph walks out into the harsh white light of the waiting area, his broken hand in a sling, his overcoat draped over his shoulders, his dress shirt wrapped around his waist. "Want to go kick the shit out of another building?"

"Let's get a drink," says the Senator, his brown eyes still blazing from tequila and probably some adrenaline/shock/pain/drugs combo. The Fat Mex was a bender waiting to happen. Except for one night back at the Diamond, when he jumped into a brawl and backed me up against a drunk skinhead from Boston, I never saw the Senator do anything crazier than sit with a cold beer and read a business book. I never saw the dark side, but then I never saw the Fat Mexican get dumped by a chick, unless you count his ex-wife… and back then he just drank and stared at the mirror behind the bar. When Kasia left me for Payback, I cried and cursed the dark, but I made sure to do it alone behind the locked doors of my Hell's Kitchen pad with a bottle of dirt and a photo of Kasia. I unplugged the phone and I didn't own a gun. I guess that makes it three times I've cried in the last ten years. First time, losing Kasia; then second time, losing Billy; and (most recently) losing my dignity at the Thundergrind coffee house. "We should get you laid," I suggest, and pat the Senator on his good arm. "You've got some serious excess energy, bro."

Ralph shoots me a look like he's going to kick my ass.

"Easy," I hold up my hands. "I'm on your side."

Ralph exits the electronic doors out of the E.R. onto Amsterdam Avenue.

"Didn't they give you any painkillers?" I ask hopefully. "Some pills to cut the edge?"

"I turned them down," says the Senator. "I'll just have a few drinks."

"That's manly, but very stupid. Didn't they even give you Tylenol with codeine for the hangovers you're going to make us get?"

Ralph pats his pocket. "I've got something, if we really need it."

I follow the Senator's wide steps as his polished black shoes stride down Amsterdam past St. John the Divine. We are heading in the direction of the apartment, which also means in the direction of the Black Clock Lounge gleaming on the corner of 106th Street.

"I want to keep my head clear," the Fat Mexican says, which sounds like a good idea since we're taking Ralph, his temper and his broken hand into a smoky bar where Rio slings beers and shots and strange men stare at her ass.

"I think this might not be smart," I suggest. I can already see the Senator going postal, breaking bottles, swinging his cast, kicking at people, his gelled hair across his eyes, sirens and flashing cop-lights in the Black Clock windows, tasers, choke-holds, gunfire, screaming.

The Senator could give a shit. "I'm buying," he says, motioning for me to enter the crosswalk first. Always a gentleman. As if anyone in New York cares about a Ped-Xing light? We're going to stack more pain onto the evening, poisoning our bodies with tequila. No worries. I've got this deal totally figured out. "Is Rio working?" I ask, like I don't know.

Ralph pulls open the door of the Black Clock Lounge. Rio washes glasses near a cigarette in the ashtray on the bar. She wears tight black pants that ride low and a tight gray long-sleeve cotton shirt. Her brown hair is loose and a leather cord is around her neck with some kind of shiny red amulet. She looks hot and not much interested in us, although I can tell she clocks us at the door.

Ralph slides up on a barstool. "We'll have two Patróns, Regina."

"Regina?" I whisper.

"That's her real name," says the Fat Mexican. "Rio is a nickname. She's Brazilian."

Rio watches the Senator. "I thought you didn't drink?"

"Sometimes," says Ralph, unfazed, "I'll have one or two."

Rio takes a hit on her smoke and squints, almost pulling her own chick version of Clint Eastwood mirror, with a thin stream of smoke leaving her pretty little tough mouth. "What happened to your hand, Ralph?"

"I broke it."

Rio pours two healthy tequilas and places the glasses in front of us. She opens two Coronas and places them on bar coasters beside our dirt.

"I didn't order those," says Ralph. "But thank you."

"No problem," says Rio. "How did you break it?"

"Punched a wall."

Rio nods, not surprised—men must do this kind of crazy shit over Rio every couple weeks. Rio takes another hit on her cigarette. Then I figure she might like the Fat Mexican 'cause she looks a bit jittery, not as cool as she wants to come across. "You going to keep coming here?" she asks the Senator.

Ralph takes the tequila glass, taps the glass against mine and tosses it all back in one swallow. "I don't know, I'm still thinking about what you said."

"And what was that?"

"That you didn't want to see me."

I slap him on the back. "I'm heading to the jukebox."

The Fat Mexican nods.

"I didn't really say that," goes Rio.

I hear Ralph say, "Anymore." I stand at the jukebox, watching some chick in a strange blouse covered with ribbons and this dude in a leather jacket with puffy leather sleeves pick tunes. I can't believe how long it takes them to decide between Fleetwood Mac versus Hootie and the Blowfish. I almost start clapping when the song read-out number clicks from 6 to 5. It looks like I'm going to get to listen to Classic Rock or bad fake-classic frat-boy blues-rock. It hurts me to watch, so I return to my barstool, sitting polite with my back to Ralph and Rio, staring out at Amsterdam Avenue.

"It's the same thing," I hear Ralph say. "We can't go back. It happened. I can't pretend I don't care about you."

He's going to crash-and-burn.

Rio pours us another shot, pours herself one. "Scout?" she slides the glass my way.

"Do you have a pen?" I ask. Rio flips one to me from a cup of pens beside the register. I take a bar napkin and write, "Crash-and-Burn." I look out at Amsterdam. A couple of chicks in biker jackets smoke cigarettes at a table by the door, playing chess.

Ralph and Rio tap their glasses and do their shots. "I am interested," Rio says to Ralph. "I just need to think. I was with a man for a long time."

Ralph nods. I scribble on "Crash-and-Burn," but my skull hops to Kasia. The tequila sails unfurled and full. I'm ready to steal a car or hop on a bus to Montana.

I listen to Ralph and Rio talk it over and wonder how often these conversations must get played out around the world: I want you, do you want me? I don't want you, stop wanting me. I want less. I want more. Somewhere on this fucked-up planet, two people looked at each other for the first time with true love on Tuesday, September 11th. That shit went down and two people kissed for the first time on some island in Indonesia or for the last time in one of those burning towers, held hands in the back of one of those airplanes, looked at each other across a crowded room.

"I understand," goes the Senator. "But I want to be able to see you, take in a movie or treat you to dinner. I'm not talking about sex. I'm talking about spending time with you."

Rio touches Ralph's arm, giving him this rare kind of wet-eye: sympathy and desire. The Fat Suave Mexican might pull it off.

"Okay?" Ralph goes.

"A movie again?" asks Rio. "And maybe dinner?"

"Definitely a movie and definitely dinner," says Ralph. "Nothing else."

Rio watches the Senator. I lean to Rio. "I still get the floor, bitch."

She slaps her bar towel at me. "Fuck you," she says lightly.

The Senator and I are at the door when Rio says, "Ralph?"

He turns with an overcoat wrapped around him like some Mexican godfather and his cast on a sling over his shoulder.

"Thanks," goes Rio and she smiles. She is one seriously hot stray. Anyway, let the Fat Mexican have her, right? He deserves something good. I have Kasia. Well, I don't have Kasia, but you know what I mean.

The Senator gives Rio a Fat Suave Mex half-wave.

We step out in the cold air. "I think I'm going to Montana."

Ralph nods. "Makes sense. But Fabio will miss you."

"I've got to get some money together, so you'll have me for a while, but then I'll hit the road. I think I could use the trip."

Ralph says, "The floor is yours for as long as you want."

"I appreciate that, but I don't know if I'm down for listening to Rio howl while I try to sleep in a puddle of cat piss."

"You heard her," says the Senator. "No sex."

"Yeah, I heard her. I might have been born yesterday, but I wasn't born last night. Once she believes you don't want her. She'll be begging to climb on your Mexican cock."

Ralph says, "She has an ex-husband. This is an emotional time for her."

"Whatever. You're in there, dude. It's done. Don't sweat it. You played it perfect. You don't think she has a hot friend, do you? We could get ourselves a four-way?"

"You're loco."

"I'm loco? I'm not the one punching brick walls."

The Fat Mexican keys open the door of the apartment. "You talk a lot of bullshit, but sometimes you make a point." Moonlight reveals the black shadow of Fabio waddling from my sleeping bag. Ralph clicks on the ceiling light.

The glittery star of cat-piss shines on the wood floor, and on my sleeping bag.

Ralph pours us each a closing shot of dirt. He's swaying a bit now, the adrenaline fading, his pussy hunt a big W. His broken hand is dulled from dirt and love. "What are you doing for money?"

"Not thinking about it," I say, but I am thinking about it.

"Can you type?"

It's amazing how the more you drink tequila, the better tequila tastes. My skull is singing. This is dangerous. Looking at my reflection in the tequila glass, I grin. Who cares that I'm going to wake up on the Fat Mexican's floor. Unless he ponies up some magic head medicine from the ER, this dirt will feel like a barbed-wire crown. The fire in my skull is like a movie house, Kasia standing in the falling snow on the Avenue of Kasia, showing me her white slender stomach. Her sweater is bunched up around her breasts. Can I type? What kind of fucking question is that?

"I can't do anything except play guitar and shake up cocktails, the easy cocktails," I add, to emphasize my limited employment opportunities.

"Maybe we can find you some temp work at Creative Action Planning?" The Senator is hammered. The adrenaline and any remaining smarts just skipped town if he's thinking of giving me an office job.

"I've got a few shifts at the Diamond. Hard to face, but I'll be a man. I've got a road trip to Kasia. After that, it's all Plan N."

Ralph looks at me. "Let me talk to the CAP team tomorrow, Scout. It would be good to keep you from working at the Diamond again." The Fat Mexican looks thoughtful.

"Yeah, that is cool, but like I said, I can't do anything." Ralph must be beyond hammered to think of getting me a job with business professors.

"They might be willing to give you some work updating our client lists, making phone calls, maybe an e-mail outreach, double-check if people are receiving our marketing material." It takes the Fat Mexican about five minutes to complete this sentence.

I dig myself in a tie and sports jacket, maybe a hipper version of the Fat Mexican's gear. My hair is trimmed back and I'm chatting on the speaker phone after a two-martini lunch with a hot stray in a black skirt, white blouse and those stockings with the black thread running down the back of each of her long legs. Maybe she has a satiny girdle deal under her high-collared blouse, writing on a note-pad, listening to me talk.

"Would I have a secretary?"

Ralph stares at me. "Yes," he says. "And she will have big hooters and she'll give you blow jobs under your desk." He goes into the bathroom to take a piss, his hand in the sling.

"Can you do that alone, or do you need help?" I finish my dirt and top both our glasses. Late night drinking is the best kind of drinking. Don't open the dirt bottle unless you are committed. "'Cause if you need help taking a leak, I think one of those male nurses at the ER was digging your wide ass."

Ralph unleashes one of his bullish pisses and yells over his drunk shoulder. "Do you want a redhead secretary or a blonde? I'm told the blondes fuck like rabbits." He laughs from deep inside his Hispanic belly.

Maybe I will look into this office work gig. It doesn't sound half bad.

"I want one that looks just like Rio," I answer. Fabio waddles close and I give him a sharp jab of the boot. "And I want to do her in the ass," I add as the Fat Mexican zips up and attempts to wash his hands, bending awkwardly over the sink. He bumps his head against the medicine-cabinet mirror.

"One more word," he says, "and I'll break my other hand on your face."

Okay, so I won't do Rio in the ass. I'd still like a secretary. Blonde, brunette, redhead, whatever.

RUNAWAY

I pull the barstools off the bar at the Diamond and wipe down the round cabaret tables. Each table will get one red ashtray melted in the guts from stubs of burning cigarettes. This is my first night back. I didn't escape. Here I am, in the Diamond Pub, the leather journal in a knapsack in the cupboard by the stand-up fridge. Jon Domogarow walks out of the back office, watches me prep, and lights himself a Marlboro Light, "How's it feel to be back home?"

"Shitty." But it feels okay. I might be going backward, but at least nothing in the bar smells like rotten fish and no dead bodies float past the windows. I move through the opening ritual like I worked a shift just last night. It all comes back to me and is cool in its own way. "Let's see if I can get you a good register," I say to Jon—half-sincere, half-full of shit. I want to get into it and serve a few drinks and find my groove, let the minutes on the clock dissolve into noise on the juke. I want to make sure I don't panic, quit or bail out the door.

I won't lie and say the shift is cake. This is a Sunday and the hours crawl while I try to balance the complex business of watching NFL highlights on the bar TV and clicking to "The Simpsons" reruns, standing as close to the TV as I can while still technically being behind the bar, chain-smoking Spirits and keeping the pouty, wounded drinkers staring into their beers and not staring at their ugly faces at the bottom of an empty glass. I comp a few rounds when Jon isn't clocking me with his I-own-the-crib grid. I scratch up some tips.

Saetha and Tommy show up. They both used to tend the bar at the Diamond. A nostalgia thing kicks in as a few other regulars walk into the cigarette coffin of red light, including the nice guy that punched me out. (I comp him.) Metallica's "Wherever I May Roam" is on the juke when I take my first shot of dirt. I play some tunes from System of a Down's "Toxicity." The clock tells me it is 1:00 a.m. on a Sunday night, and we have a crowd. Megan Bathe works one corner of the bar, flirting with some young rocker dude who I hear bagging on this band that's getting radio play. "I'm not a hater," he repeats, adjusting his trucker hat so it stays sideways. You know you're getting old when every young dude sounds like a complete fucking moron. Megan has her hand under the bar and I figure her fingernails are tickling Rocker Dude's thigh, if not tap dancing on his cock or flat-out jerking him off. Megan watches me watch her. Megan opens her pretty mouth, "This is fun," Megan says as I refill her Cosmo. "First I hear you play guitar and now I'm watching you work at the Diamond." Megan motions me to her small red mouth and whispers, "Same as it ever was, Scout." She runs a pretty finger from her free hand around the rim of her martini glass, acting like I don't know she's got her other hand planted on Rocker Dude's not-a-hater penis. "This will be great in the D.O.T. It's like nothing has changed."

These are not the good old days. "Things," I say to Megan, "have changed."

The Rocker Dude repeats his catchphrase, "I'm not a hater, but those guys had people help with their chord changes." He adjusts his trucker cap more sideways, bending down the bill, flexing his cheekbones in the bar mirror. He's definitely throwing some mirror, pouting and puckering. He kind of looks like Brad Pitt, if Brad Pitt was twenty-five, had a trucker hat on sideways and someone had completely filled his cheeks with sand.

Cut to three a.m. and Megan's stiff-dick-not-a-hater date is face down on the Diamond bar. Megan sips what I count as her fifth Cosmo. She's got the liquor glow, and it's not slipping into drunk and desperate. Megan's vibe is working for me, and I've only been sipping the dirt. I can't get hammered. It's been a while since I've run this gig at the Diamond, and I don't want to fuck up, pass out on the pool table and have Jon wake me up to show me an empty safe and register, with some junkie or drunk Moroccan or Moroccan junkie off to celebrate with my register. Megan and I talk over the rules we promised at Thundergrind. We promised to not get ripped and we promised to not bang each other and wake up feeling shitty. I'd like to give Megan a hard fuck in the Men's, maybe slap her tits, spread her legs and yank her hair in a gentle manner while doing her from behind— her mascaraed eyes watching me in the mirror over the sink—but we made a promise, and like the passed-out dude drooling under his trucker's hat, I'm not a hater. I want Megan to be happy. Real life is a sewer, and the good people are what save us from loneliness. Waking up against Megan the other morning after our drunken late-night session could have been more drama, more of what I don't need, but Megan didn't turn on me and Megan was pretty in her pink T-shirt and lazy pajama pants, hugging me in the cold hallway. I'm not a hater. I'm Megan's pal.

We used to fuck and that part is over.

"What's his name?" I point at the unshaven face planted next to a can of Tecate, empty shot glass and trucker hat advertising a bowling alley in Tennessee. "I bet he bought that hat at Urban Outfitters."

"Ross," goes Megan. "He's had a bad day. His girlfriend left."

"Good thing you're here to keep an eye on him."

"What do you care?"

"I don't, but you look hot."

Megan blushes. Jesus. That's all it takes? Too bad I can't break our coffee-shop promise. It'd be a hoot to take Megan in that cubicle while Ross slept off Mandi or Scarlett or Mariana or whatever chick woke up to her dim boyfriend and ran back down the road away from the horror of listening to him talk. But there are customers I don't know hanging in the Diamond and no bouncer. Jon didn't expect a crowd and figured I could handle the door too, which saves me from tipping some steroid bad-boy for staring at the cement on 6th street for ten or twelve hours, but it also means I don't have the safety net of the juiced dude leaping into the argument and stomping the shit out of an annoying customer.

"I don't believe you," Megan says. She's got a good buzz going, maybe I haven't counted her intake or she's drinking on an empty stomach, or, let's face it, five Cosmos is just a bucket of straight vodka for a small girl with all her weight in her tits and her ass. Who wouldn't be hammered at 3:00 a.m. after at least a pint of 80 proof? (Me, but that's a different story.) The more critical thing is that Megan's stiff-dick toy isn't going to rally and Megan swore off banging me and there's nothing else in the Diamond that will satisfy her lust. She could wander a few blocks to the other dives, but it's late enough and she's out solo. The Foo Fighter's "Monkey Wrench" on the juke, Megan was counting on Ross, but all that non-hating and too many Tijuana Specials has left Ross useless, with spit dripping from his mouth. No, there's nothing left for Megan in the Diamond. I am Megan's taste. Younger versions of me are even more Megan's taste. Megan goes for greasy haired punks that will unbutton her pricey designer tops and stare in awe at her tits then shoot a load of youthful spunk in her mouth or in the neighborhood of her mouth. That's how Megan gets to sleep at night.

"The jukebox ate my dollar," goes some chick I figure is a new regular who is picking the Diamond as her own and telling all of her friends about it. She is letting the boys watch her and getting to know the other regulars, so she can flirt and put on a buzz and not get in a bad situation. She places a pack of Dunhill Blues on the bar and hitches at the white belt and low-slung five-pocket jeans that show off her long legs and tiny ass. She's got a little-girl thermal with a pink-flower pattern on the white waffle-cotton pushed up to her elbows. Over the thermal is a T-shirt of the 1970s girl band, it reads, "The Runaways." The T looks like an original T cut-off that is sewn onto a newer T. "Did you hear me?" she slides up a barstool and perches her ass on it, looking down at the way her flared jeans cut across her narrow, pointy black boots. The ends of her brown Joan Jett hair have been dyed versions of the purple Megan likes in the pillows that stack her bed.

"I heard you," I said, tired of juke criticism from drunks, even hot strays. "It'll play in a minute. The songs don't always happen right away."

"What's that about? You should have a sign or something that says people can wait all night or until tomorrow and not hear the song they paid for, right?"

"It'll play," I explain to her, thinking there is a reason spanking has a permanent place in porn. "Just give it a moment."

Runaway goes, "Uh huh, except when? It's not playing anything at all."

This is what happens when some girl wakes up one day and finds out she's hot, it's open season on every dude that has to deal with her, while she proves her hotness day and night by demanding attention and getting it.

The juke problem could be this one album that has about four minutes of silence on the end of some tune, not that Korn album with the twelve non-songs that are all .04 seconds, but some other tune on a CD Jon put on 'cause some Cooper Union art stray asked him while puffing up her tits. What a pain in the ass. "Give me a second," I stub out my smoke and walk over to the juke, and sure enough, it's that same lame CD. I hit the skip button behind the juke. Nothing comes on. Silence. Runaway watches me with one of those "I-told-you-so" chick expressions, like she knows this place better than me. She's also tossing me wet-eye. I'm sure of it. Her eyes give an up-and-down flash and her pointy black boot taps against the floor. Maybe the jukebox overheated. I turn it off, lean against the paneling and watch Runaway watch me, sucking the dregs of her cocktail through a straw. I squat and reach behind the machine and click the juke back on. After it revs up, I punch the credit button. I pick one tune and motion for her to select some.

Runaway goes, "What'd you pick?"

"The Goops. Used to hang out here way back. Broke up, but a good band."

"Never heard of them."

So what? Who cares what you think? I flip the script on this stray and give her nothing. She's used to boys drooling. It's not going to happen with me.

Runaway leans into the jukebox glow, "Which song?"

"'One Kiss Left.'"

Runaway looks at me. "Do you have one?" she asks, "One kiss left?"

I point to the jukebox. "Pick some songs. Pick what you want." I grab the Tecate empties off a few tables and drop the red cans clacking on the bar. "What are you drinking?"

Runaway watches me with her three-in-the-morning wet-eye, like she's about two years out of high school and can't believe how hot she is and what men will do for a chance to fuck her. "Scotch. Something cheap, like the boys I've been dating."

"Tired of boys?"

"Men are fun. Not that I'd know so much."

"Here's something expensive." I pour her a couple ounces of Laphroaig, our one quality single-malt.

Runaway takes the glass to her lips, and I'm hit with the night at Spoon, Lilly with her dress at her neck, panties at her ankles, her girlfriend going down on her while I take sips of Oban single-malt and spill them into Lilly's parted mouth, my stinging tongue licking her shivering tongue, the single-malt whiskey dribbling down her chin—back before George fell for her and tried to take her to California.

The night doesn't go away. The night is always ready.

Runaway taps out a cigarette. I click my Zippo lit.

"Classy," she inhales, the red tip of the lit smoke trails as she turns to the jukebox.

Megan walks over. "Are you working on the D.O.T.?"

"You mean, right now?" I motion to Runaway, who sways to Soul Coughing's "Casiotone Nation." "Yeah, whatever happens, I'll write it down."

Megan gives me a serious, loaded look.

"You're the one," I point out, "that said we shouldn't fuck. And speaking of this D.O.T. gig, you better use some of my words, otherwise…"

"Otherwise what?" Megan shifts into her own heavy five-Cosmo wet-eye.

"Otherwise you're getting a spanking. A hard spanking on your big ass."

Megan arches her eyebrow, twists, peers down at her butt. "I've been doing yoga. My butt looks hot. You've been missing out." Megan's eyes sway. "I don't believe you."

"Just use some of my stuff. I can't take only hearing the other side."

"The side where you're a drunk slut?"

"That side," I admit, although I'm not sure how using anything I've been putting in the journal will change that deal.

"You look good behind the bar."

"I feel good." I pour myself a shot of dirt and toss it back.

"It was playing the music," says Megan. "You need to play music. Otherwise, you're not whole. Otherwise, you're not complete."

I pour myself a second shot, toss some quick Keith Richards mirror at Runaway as her hips turn from the juke, her slinky shoulders following, eyes flashing on herself in the bar mirror. Runaway slinks over to the bar, picks up her glass of single-malt. I can't clock if Runaway caught my Keith Richards. She might have caught it. Sometimes the strays just feel it, which is perfect 'cause then they don't know what's getting them all hot and itchy. I push the shot of dirt to the side. No reason to not wait a few minutes. "Whatever," I say to Megan. "Maybe you're right, but what do you mean you don't believe me?"

Runaway walks back to the juke, leans in the glow. "Hey, Bar Guy," she says over her shoulder. "Do you want another song?"

Megan watches me say, "Jane's Addiction, something from *Nothing's Shocking.*"

"Old man," Runaway whispers, but loud enough for me to hear. Runaway clicks the direction arrows thru the CD covers. "Which one?" She tosses me a sideways glance.

"Ocean Size."

Runaway punches in the number and saunters back to her barstool, sipping her single-malt. "This shit," she says, "tastes like the floor of a barn."

"I figured you were the kind of girl that liked the floor of a barn."

"Oooh," Runaway looks at me. "Tough guy."

"Scout?" It's Megan, still in front of me with her hazy eyes. I reach for the shot of dirt. The clock tells me there are fifteen minutes before closing.

Runaway takes a seat at the end of the bar and sips the pricey whisky. I'd bet my tips this isn't the first time she's been in the Diamond at last call.

"Scout?" Megan touches my arm.

"What's up?"

"Looks like you're right back at it. How old is that girl? Twenty?"

"She's twenty-one. Or she couldn't legally be drinking."

"Did you card her?"

"It's been a long night. Yeah, I carded her."

"You're a liar," says Megan. "And you better start carding 'cause things are different now with Giuliani. I know bartenders that have lost their jobs, because they didn't check IDs." Megan holds up a Parliament and her eyes do a serious drunk weave. "You might want to keep this job." I don't remember Megan ever smoking a cigarette.

"Since when do you smoke?"

"Fuck you."

I light her smoke, checking Megan's body. If I wasn't always so annoyed by her, I'd have to admit she's a cute stray, very fuckable. "You better stop giving me orders if you don't want to get fucked."

She motions to the passed-out dude in the trucker hat. "I've already got a date."

"Right. What was that about not believing me?"

"What are you talking about?" Megan sends a thin stream of cigarette smoke right to my face. This is the reason we keep ending up at her apartment after closing. Except now it's different. I've thrown back a few shots, but I'm the new Scout and Megan made me promise that we wouldn't do it anymore. Plus, she got sad after we fucked. I don't want to make Megan sad. Runaway checks me out and doesn't think I notice. I toss some Clint Eastwood at Megan, just for kicks and light myself a smoke. Why did I leave this bartending game? Oh, yeah, it was killing me and eating up my soul. Still…

"Megan." I talk to her like I'm talking to any drunk, ignoring her porn-star body and eyes. "You said you didn't believe me. I don't know what you mean, like what are you talking about?"

Megan drains her Cosmo, gives me her last-call, hammered wet-eye then licks the inside of the martini glass. "So?" she asks. "You didn't believe me?"

"No," I explain. "You said you didn't believe me." Jesus. I take her glass and fill it with ice and water to re-chill. I shake up a sixth Cosmo. Megan realizes what I'm doing.

Her Parliament waving in front of her, she says, "I can't… work."

"Hey, Bar Guy." It's Runaway. "One song still didn't come up. I picked a Beck."

I walk over and mess with the jukebox. Runaway's acting cool, wants attention.

She goes, "You're new here."

"I'm old here," I say. "I thought I escaped, but…" I wipe an empty cabaret table with a bar rag. "Here I am at closing, listening to some teenager gripe about the jukebox."

"Lucky for you," goes Runaway. "Do you wanna shoot pool?"

The only other people in the Diamond are two guys sitting under the blank TV screen. The two guys stab their smokes at the red ashtrays and talk, nodding their heads to the music.

"Sure," I tell Runaway. "But no more shit about the tunes. The bar's about to close and I'm done dealing with shit." I walk over to the two guys. "Gentlemen, last call?"

They wiggle the scum at the bottom of their bottles of beer. Tell me they're cool.

I walk over to Megan who is weaving on her barstool. I put my hands on her shoulders, rub them. "I'm going to shoot some pool."

Megan shrugs, "Okay."

I point at her passed-out boy, Ross. "He's not going to puke, right?"

Megan shrugs. "I said I didn't believe you about that girl."

"This girl?" I point at Runaway. "What about this girl?"

"No," Megan waves me off. "Not that child. That woman... Kasia."

It takes a moment. The Thundergrind gig. Megan met Kasia. "What about Kasia?"

"I don't believe you're not fucking her," Megan says.

"Believe it. I'm not fucking her. We fooled around a bit, but she's in Montana."

"C'mon, Bar Guy!" Runaway stamps her foot. "Rack 'em."

"You rack. I'll be there in one second."

"I'm not fucking Kasia," I tell Megan. "If you don't believe me, you can read it in your D.O.T."

Megan goes, "Oh, my," and I turn toward the front door of the bar expecting some late-night celebrity pack or a bloody victim from a fist-fight. Nothing.

"What?" I ask Megan's glazed eyes.

"I've got it, Scout." Megan nods at her pink cocktail.

"You've got what, Megan?"

Megan smiles. "You're in love with her."

"What?"

"You're in love with Kasia, aren't you?" Megan has me clocked with a whole different look. She shakes her head like a sleeping person opening her eyes to a burning tree. "You're in love with her."

"I'm not in love with her," I say. "Where do you get off with this shit?"

Megan points her cigarette at me. "Liar, liar, pants on fire." Megan is about to drop off the barstool, but she's still sitting like a lady, poised.

"Listen, I'm going to shoot a game of pool. Just hang out, don't fall off your chair."

Megan watches me, her mind working it out. "Scout," she grabs at my arm. I give her a serious *what?* with my eyes.

"Don't sleep with that girl."

"Megan, I told you, she's in Montana."

"Not that girl." Megan slowly points at Runaway, sitting on the pool table, tapping the heels of her pointy black boots, "That girl."

"Megan—"

"Fuck me instead."

"Chill out." This is my first shift and my tips are okay for a night I thought would be dead, but I'm already dealing with this scene? Righteous on one level, sure, as long as I got Megan's feelings out of my skull and don't lock on to the fact that she told me she didn't want to fuck me at the Thundergrind benefit. Now she is telling me to not fuck some stray I don't have any reason to think I'm fucking, but Megan wants me to fuck Megan instead, even though she made me promise not to fuck her. "I thought you said you didn't want to fuck? I thought we promised?"

Megan shrugs. "That was before."

"You've just had a lot to drink. Why don't I put you in a cab?"

159

Runaway walks over to the framed illustrations of the dogs playing poker. She leans close and looks at the dogs, knowing the two guys wrapping up their beers and the bartender are going to have a hard time not checking her out. Runaway lifts her glass of peat whiskey and takes a sip, watching the dogs play poker, their wooden frames screwed into the paneled walls of the Diamond. Runaway turns and the four Runaways watch me across Runaway's pert tits.

"Do you love her?" Megan asks. "Not this girl, but Kasia? Do you love Kasia?"

It's late. The honesty gig kicks in and I go, "Yeah, I love her."

"Are you going to see her?"

"I want to, but she's in Montana and I'm broke in the East Village. I'll work some shifts and try to pull it together."

Megan sips her Cosmo. "I'll give you the money."

"Megan, that's cool, but I'll figure it out."

"I'll lend you the money to go to Montana. If that's what you want, Scout. If that's what you need."

"Why would you do that?" I motion Runaway to hold for a second, her annoyed arms crossed, pointy black boots tapping. The two guys finish their beers and walk out, clocking Runaway. Runaway locks her eyes on the dead space where the front door of the Diamond closes behind them.

Runaway is a girl not cool with waiting.

The jukebox kicks into Linkin Park's *Hybrid Theory*.

"If you love Kasia," says Megan, "either win her or take the next step."

"C'mon." I watch Megan and know this is more than she should do for me. Didn't Megan tell me she was once in love with me? Didn't Megan have an abortion because of me? "Megan, you don't have to do that, but thanks."

"I know I don't have to do it. I want to do it."

Runaway slides up to the bar, puts both her hands on a barstool and presses up on her toes, crushing all four Runaways between her breasts. "Ah, Bar Guy?"

"Hang on," I say. "One second and we'll shoot." She slinks back to the table, making sure my eyes don't leave her ass.

"But," goes Megan. "Don't fuck that one." She points at Runaway. "If you want money to go see Kasia, I'll give it to you, but promise you won't fuck that girl."

The honesty gig? Once you start, you're in trouble.

"You're a trip, Megan. And you're drunk and you're not going to remember this in the morning."

"I'm a woman, Scout, and I will remember this." Megan takes a slug of her cold cocktail. "I'll lend you the money, pay me back when you can, visit Kasia, and don't fuck the child waving her ass at the pool table. Think you can keep that straight?"

"Yeah," I say, okay, sure, fine. "Great, thanks."

Megan holds out her hand. "We have a deal?"

I shake her hand.

"Now," says Megan, her eyes glazing. "Please escort me to a taxi."

OOPS

My first shift back at the Diamond and the front door of the bar has been locked for thirty minutes. Megan and her non-hater Ross stumbled toward Avenue A as I stood in the doorway and watched Megan put Ross in a cab and wave back at me as a second Yellow Cab pulled to a stop beside her. The clock reads four-forty in the morning. Wood panels are placed in the windows, blocking the inside from the street view so that any stragglers that might knock on the door and yell my name and think I'll let them inside

160

will just have to hustle on past the locked front door. The Beastie Boys' "Girls" is on the juke, while Runaway is stretched out on top of the pool table. I have a red votive candle in my hand. I lift up her designer rocker-T and Runaway arches her back so I can unhook her sheer red bra with one hand after scooching up her shirt. Runaway slips out of her T-shirt and her bra, tucking the wad of T-shirt behind her head. Her nipples are pink. I rub the glass base of the red cylindrical candle across each of her pink nipples. Her pink nipples get hard. I pinch each nipple once and rub the flat of my palm across each nipple. Her pink nipples get rosy.

"Wait a sec."

Runaway goes, "Okay."

I put down the votive candle and walk to the bar. I place a few ice cubes in a rocks glass and make sure Runaway can hear the ice clink and think about the ice and what I'm going to do with the ice. I pour a shot of tequila into a shot glass and down it. I pour a second shot and carry it to the pool table with the glass of ice. Runaway doesn't move. Hooded, her eyes gaze at the overhead pool light shining from the Budweiser pool table lamp.

"Let's get you ready."

Runaway whispers, "Okay."

I take an ice cube and run the ice cube in circles around Runaway's left nipple then reach over and let the melting ice trickle across her chest. I press the ice cube into the point of her right nipple. Leaning down, I give her nipple a hard bite then rub her nipple briskly in light scraping motions with the ice cube. I walk behind Runaway.

Runaway moans.

I lean over her from behind her head and lick her left nipple. After warming her nipple with my tongue, I rub it hard with the ice cube as I kiss her ear. I toss the melting ice-cube on the floor, grab each of her breasts and jiggle them under the ceiling lamp as if inspecting fruit. Runaway's hooded eyes open as she watches her tits jiggle, pressed under my hands. Alice in Chains' "Them Bones" kicks on the juke. I reach down the length of Runaway, cupping her pussy from outside the row of buttons on her jeans. I rotate my hand slow, pretending to try and slide my fingers inside her, pressing against the tight denim.

Runaway lifts her hips against my rotating hand. I stop circling my hand and lock it hard, letting Runaway work her pussy. Runaway grinds against my hand.

"Now, now," I say. "Don't get greedy."

I walk around the pool table and face Runaway. I take the votive candle and swirl it, red hot wax sways in the cylinder of glass.

Runaway goes, "No," but arches up her naked breasts.

A dollop of hot red wax splatters her left nipple.

Runaway makes a quiet moan, whispering, "Ouch."

A dollop of hot red wax splatters her right nipple.

"Fuck me," Runaway says to the harsh panel of light. "Fuck me." She flicks at the buttons of her jeans and shimmies her hips, crushing the tight jeans past her thighs toward her pointy black boots. Runaway wears white panties with tiny bows on each hip and two red cherries on the front. The red cherries rise and fall and rise as her hips thrust at the emptiness. "Fuck me," she says to the ceiling. "Fuck me now."

I put my hand on her clavicle and press her back to the pool table, placing her head back on the wad of her T-shirt. I take the candle and give each of her breasts another splash of hot wax, trailing a red string of wax to her belly button (outie). A red coin of hot wax splashes her navel and Runaway wiggles. "You better fuck me now."

RFN.

"No," I say. "I can't."

I kiss her on the lips and lift up my shirt. I stretch out over Runaway and lay my body down on her, my chest pressing against the warm, hardening splotches of red wax. She sticks her tongue out at me like a little girl. I suck on her tongue, pull up her thighs and grind on her pubic bone. Runaway kisses me, her tongue curling soft. She pulls the hips of my Levi's, tugging on my wallet chain, "Fuck me." Her arms loop around my neck. I duck my head, pulling out of the loop and tangle of her embrace. I swing my legs over the edge of the pool table and peel the dried wax off her nipples, her naked legs stretched across my legs. Wax dollops crumble. I hand Runaway her red brassiere. "C'mon." I motion for her to dress.

I give Runaway a tickle in her ribs with my finger. She squirms, leans up on her elbows. "Why not? Do you have a girlfriend?"

"Yes," I lie.

Runaway slings her legs over the pool table, stands on her pointy heeled boots and shimmies her jeans back to her flat stomach, buttoning her jeans as her breasts jiggle. "Who?" she asks, "That drunk slut at the bar?"

"No."

"Where is she then?" Runaway looks around the empty locked bar. "Call her on the phone and ask her to join us."

"She lives in Montana."

Runaway scrapes the remaining scabs of dry red wax from her perfect body.

Why did I make Megan this stupid promise?

The dried wax pills and breaks into crumbles that spill from Runaway's breasts and hips and flat stomach. "It's not fair," she says. "I'm horny." She tugs at my jeans. "I'll rock your shit. C'mon," she flashes a smile, "It'll be our secret."

I get the keys from the register and click off the light dome over the pool table. I squeeze Runaway's hand. The bar is pale purple in the juke glow. I kiss Runaway. She allows the kiss, body straight, hands at her hips. "You're beautiful," I say. I walk to the bar and pour us each a shot of Patrón.

Runaway goes, "You're a prick tease."

I tap my glass against hers, down it. She tosses hers back, wipes her lips. "You know what we do to prick teases, Bar Guy?" Runaway unbuttons her jeans, folds them down, slipping and wiggling to the white panties with the red cherries. I pour us each another shot, promise my cock to make itself quiet until Montana, until I do something because it's the right thing to do, not just bad girls, not just night, not just RFN. I drink my shot of dirt and follow it by drinking the shot of dirt I poured for Runaway. I pour her another, offer it to her. She shakes her head. "You better have it, Scout. You're going to need it."

Scout. Okay, so she knows my name. Probably asked someone at the bar and then played it cool with the Bar Guy thing. "What's your name?" I ask.

"It doesn't matter now," says Runaway. She rolls her panties down, tipping the elastic waist band as if she is about to reveal her pussy then pulling the panties back up with infinite care and concern about the package of her pussy lips. A full-on stripper move. She looks up. "I heard your band one night," says Runaway. "At UMass. I got in with my older sister."

I toss down the shot of dirt. My hard-on throbs. I was so close to being out the door, Megan. Billy, I almost made it. Kasia.

Wasn't Kasia fucking that lawyer friend she didn't even like?

But didn't I make Megan a promise?

And now I wasn't going to fuck this hot stray senseless because of Megan?

No, it was because of Kasia. And my word. What I stand for, Billy.

Runaway skims her white panties down, revealing her shaved pussy. Her finger runs, taps, traces her lips. Runaway looks back at me stripper-style, her finger slipping over the lips of her tiny cunt above the white X of her panties pulled down to her knees. She looks at me over her shoulder and sinks her finger inside the glossy lips of her cunt.

Runaway pulls the finger out and licks it. "Hmm," she says.

I can't fuck her. I can't fuck her. I won't fuck her. I won't fuck her.

I know why Billy got a habit.

Habits are easy.

Runaway faces me and shimmies her panties back up, tugging the red bow on each side high on her hip to exaggerate the white V. Her glistening finger is held out. She inspects it, gives her finger a sniff. "I changed my mind, Scout, pour me a shot."

I pour it, pouring myself another.

"Wait," says Runaway. She wiggles around the pool table in her pointy boots and her jeans. She taps glasses and we each kill our shots of dirt.

"Now," Runaway says. "Time for you to learn something, Scout." Runaway slips her slick, glistening pussy finger into my mouth, "Suck on this, guitar player."

I do.

Runaway tastes delicious.

She pulls her finger out, "Yummy, huh?"

I don't say a thing and Runaway goes, "Fuck yeah, I am yummy." She pulls her jeans back, buttoning up and latching shut her white leather belt. "How," and her eyebrow arches and her hip juts at me, "did you dare not fuck me?"

Runaway whistles in disbelief. Runaway strolls to the locked front door of the Diamond Pub. I click off the juke, grab the lock for the metal grate and follow her out into the cold black night.

I pull the metal grate down and bolt it shut. Runaway zips up her jacket and shivers. "Where do you live?" I ask. "I'll walk you home."

GOOD, I REMEMBER

My eyes open. My cock is hard and has slipped through the fly of my boxers, pressing a swollen crown against the silk-sheathed tailbone of the woman curled inside the curl of my body. I have one of her tits in each hand. The woman breathes in long quiet breaths. Oh, fuck. Runaway. I fucked sweet Runaway in a black out! I botched my promise.

The woman smells nice, familiar. I pull back. The purple pillows and sheets... Megan. She wears black silk pajama pants and no top.

I wasn't in a tequila black-out. Good. I remember.

I roll on my back and search out each moment from last night before the curtain closed. I've got it figured. Runaway lived on Avenue C. I walked her to her apartment telling myself I wouldn't hit on her. Runaway said thank you in a flat voice without turning around and walked into her apartment building, pulling the door shut. I shivered and thought about the long train ride up to the sleeping bag. Oh yeah, then I walked to Megan's and sat my thumb on her buzzer until she let me inside where we didn't have sex. I thought of Runaway slipping her finger into her tiny cunt and then into my mouth, her eyes clocking me as I tasted her. My first night back and I screwed up a gift from the gasoline sky. The city has been on fire with pain and sadness and I stand in the Diamond with the doors locked at last call, and I tell Runaway to slip up her pants and hustle home?! I could have tapped her on the pool table, flipped her over and sent her into shivers of Runaway bliss, but that wasn't the point of this whole falling for Kasia business. Was the Fat Mexican right? Was I going back to try and fix the past? It didn't feel like it. I felt like I was moving forward. That was why I wanted to go to Montana. I wanted to go into what was ahead. Going to Montana was the only way around hitting THE END way too fast. I wanted to get into what was down the road and not stick in the mud of the way things were back when doing Runaway on the Diamond pool table would have solved everything.

I crawled out of Megan's lavender and purple web and made my way to Megan's stand-up bathtub and shower in the kitchen, stepping up into the small tub, pulling the curtain around the tub so water didn't splash all over her kitchen floor. Megan had some nice hair product and I worked a mint shampoo into my hair. I slathered scented scrubs and lotions all over my cigarette-and-sweat-stained body. My head was okay from the late night and the drill of dirt shots I killed to stop from fucking Runaway. Megan's clock told me it was two hours into the afternoon. Not bad for working a late shift. When I stumbled in last night, I told Megan I had turned down the little stray in the bar. Megan told me not to use that term: *stray*. She said it was offensive. She told me I needed to grow up and face myself. She's right. My future needs to be different from my past. It's time to stop squinting in bar mirrors, acting tough. Last night, Megan offered to lend me the cash to get to Montana. It was time to hit the trail. I might as well get a bus ticket and figure out the Kasia thing. I told Megan I would stop being an offensive asshole. She laughed, stretched out on the purple pillows, "Give it a shot, Scout. It will help you with Kasia."

I was a fuck-up, but I could be different… a good kind of different. I laughed, felt loopy. I couldn't kill the good mood, no matter how my skull spun. Megan was giving me cash. I was going to work at not being a dickhead. I was going to find Kasia. Plan N wasn't so bad.

I towel off, smooth back my minty hair, pull on my Levi's, T-shirt, flannel and white leather jacket. I put coffee into the black coffee unit. I don't want to wake Megan. She's doing me a solid. I pull the journal from my knapsack, and there I am, working on her project, head dusty from dirt, but black coffee makes it work. I kept my promise last night. Megan will keep her promise. Megan asked me not to fuck Runaway and I didn't fuck Runaway. It was not fun, but I survived. I can be a slut, but these strays in New York don't own me. I'm a man of my word. I have honor. I just need to see Kasia. I'll play "Severe Clear" for her. I walked into my storage cell, looking for wax, and I found the Book Mouse.

It's been a strange stretch of weeks. Horrible if you were in the wrong place at the wrong time, lucky if you were somewhere else and not bad at all if you were me.

MONTANA

Port Authority Bus Terminal. Megan hands me a wad of bills and the bus ticket. The Fat Mexican watches me from the armor of his slick suit and leather overcoat. I scribbled in the diary until Megan woke up. We grabbed some eats at Life Café, and I told her over our huevos rancheros that I would take her up on her offer to visit Montana. Megan surprised me for the second time in about fourteen hours by sounding excited and smiling at me as if we were both about to get on a plane to Paris. I phoned Jon at his apartment on Avenue A near the Diamond and told him about my road trip. He was cool. Told me he'd work me back into the schedule if he could when I got back, but made it clear he couldn't promise anything. I said that was cool too. I asked him to keep an eye out for Runaway and comp her a Laphroaig on me. Jon's voice flattened on his okay, and I figured he had his eye on Runaway, so I didn't go into the wax-on-her-tits part of the night but made it clear I didn't hook up with her. I said I just owed her one 'cause she tipped me and I'd make it up to him if he covered for me. I also asked Jon to keep an eye out for George and get a phone number or something if George stopped back into the Diamond. I told Jon I didn't have a cell phone yet, but I'd call in from a pay phone and give him Kasia's phone number once she knew I was going to surprise her. I told Jon thank you, and I always knew he had my back.

The bus I had checked into from Megan's apartment was rolling out that day. I could take my time and catch one tomorrow, but I'm not about tomorrows. This is all about right fucking now. Megan and I finished our brunch and I called Ralph at his CAP office. He offered to put my things in the duffel and throw in a new packet of thermals and a boxer three-pack from a place on Broadway and meet me at the bus station with my Guild D-25. "Are you going to give that girl a heads-up?" asks the Senator, as we slap our arms in the cold terminal beside the puffing Greyhound.

164

Megan says, "Women don't like to be completely surprised. You know that, right, Scout? Just surprised enough to make it feel romantic, but not so surprised they get scared."

"I'll call her from some bus station on the way," I say. "Like in Idaho or something."

The Fat Mexican and Megan look at me. "I think Idaho is on the other side of Montana, Scout. Have you looked at a map?" asks the Senator.

"No, but I will." I stamp my boots, ready to get on the bus and take out Megan's journal and scribble a few more notes, maybe take another cut at the "Severe Clear" lyrics. "I asked the ticket agent and he said it only takes about a million hours."

The Senator whistles, "That's why they invented planes."

Megan asks, "Do you have the journal for my project?"

I tap my knapsack. "Right here. What is a D.O.T. anyway? Do we get paid for this shit? Do you get paid for this shit? Just tell me someone's making money off my pain."

Megan gives me a school-teacherly look and talks slow. "It's a Document in Time, Scout. It will be very important. I have more meetings lined up over the next few weeks and we will start transcribing the texts soon, so take care of that journal and keep filling it out."

Megan is living in a dream world, but the diary has helped me. I've got to admit. I look back through the pages and I'm not half as spooked as I was that first week of the attack on the World Trade Center. I'm still spooked, sure, but my eyes are open. I'm not just staring at the Hudson River with a fierce hangover, now I'm on a bus to Montana with a very mild hangover. I kissed Kasia. I played guitar in front of a cat. I even played guitar and sang in a coffee shop of real people. I'm moving into a new plan. Plan M... Plan O, whatever. I'm not facing THE END.

People file onto the bus, a sorry-looking crowd. Megan's eyes are teary. She hugs me.

"Thanks for the loan." I squeeze her ass. I pull back and look in her glistening eyes. "Have you been working out?"

"I told you." She wipes her eyes and smiles. "I'm doing yoga and pilates."

"Nice," I say. She smiles. I kiss her. The kiss is just a polite kiss on the lips.

I don't know how many times I banged this chick and she almost never said one kind thing to me, one word that wasn't bitchy. Then she lets it slip that she'd been in love with me? And had that abortion? And now she's giving me money to go visit some other chick, but she's crying in the exhaust garage of Port Authority like I'm her high school boyfriend going off to war?

Ralph crunches down a breath mint. Megan kisses each of my cheeks, kisses the tip of my nose. Megan wipes her eyes and loops her scarf around her collar, zipping up her jacket.

The Fat Mexican slides a wad of bills in my hand. I slip the roll in my pocket. "Remember," I tell him. "Tie Rio up and spank her, RFN."

"I'm way ahead of you." The Senator smiles. I see this greased up Latino in designer underwear, his hand in a cast paddling Rio as she wiggles and spits flames.

"Call me in two weeks," goes Megan. "I'm serious. I don't care where you are. I might need to talk to you about the project. We're on a timetable." Megan is crying.

I hug her. "I'll be back soon." I look into her pretty eyes, "Thanks again, Megan. Stay away from the young boys." I rub my finger along her neck, feeling like some dude in a movie. I kiss her one more time and hand my duffel to the bus driver who tosses it into the storage compartment with the rest of the passengers' luggage, pulling the door down and locking it. I pick up my knapsack and guitar case. I toss Ralph and Megan some serious Clint Eastwood mirror, but it breaks into a goofball smile on my grid and I shake my head at what I'm doing. Ralph and Megan wave and smile. I walk up the steps through the fumes and the comforting carbon monoxide stink of the terminal. I find myself a seat, kicking my boots out under the seat in front of me. Montana is a long haul, but I've got my guitar and I've got the journal. I've also got the Book Mouse in a white envelope in the zippered pocket of my white leather jacket. I slip the pad of tequila-blond pubic hair into my hand and rub it with my thumb and forefinger. I kissed Kasia and Kasia kissed me.

I look out the green bus window at my two friends as the bus kicks into reverse. This is my favorite part in all the old Westerns. If I had a cowboy hat, I'd wave it, but I just look out the green glass as the bus pulls from the terminal, leaving the canyons of New York City for the Lincoln Tunnel. I look up at the blue sky and silver buildings. I look at my reflection in the green glass. I think of Kasia and the big state of Montana.

I smile at the blue sky. Let's ride.

AT THE DIAMOND: LILLY LEJEUNE

Five nights after Megan and Ralph sent Scout on the road to Montana, Baron Jancet sits at the bar in the Diamond on a busman's holiday with a bottle of Heineken, a pack of smokes, and a copy of *NME* in front of him on the cherry-wood bar. Mercedes works her shift, but the bar is empty and she sits on a barstool, reading *Fear and Loathing in Las Vegas*. Baron has his eyes locked on Mercedes' stomach as she smokes a Winston Light and reads. Baron sips his beer, head haloed in blue smoke. It's eight o'clock on a Tuesday. The bar is empty. Mercedes is a new girl, started a few months back in the summer. She drove up to N.Y.C. from Tampa with her boyfriend. They broke up two weeks ago. Baron knows that for sure, which is fine with him. The TV over the pool table shows clips of Osama Bin Laden firing a Kalashnikov rifle into the sky.

"Where were you," Baron asks Mercedes, "when it happened?" Mercedes looks up from the book. Baron points at the TV, but Mercedes already knows he means Tuesday, September 11, 2001. Mercedes thinks Baron is kind of hot, but she just dated a musician, another guitar player, and it ended messy because he was a self-centered jerk-off. Mercedes figures Baron is a self-centered jerk-off too, but she hasn't seen him play guitar. Maybe he deserves to be arrogant? "I was in Brooklyn," Mercedes says. "I worked here the night before and slept through it. My roomie was at her boyfriend's, so I just didn't know what was going on. I had my phone ringer off and woke up with about two hundred messages."

"That shit was fucked up. Did you know anyone there, anyone that lost it?"

"No, the only person I heard about was that girl that used to come in here, I guess. It was before I started here, but Jon just found out. I can't think of her name."

Jon Domogarow walks out of the office at the back of the bar, with his Boston terrier, Bandit, waddling, spitting, tugging against the leash. "I'm going to walk her around the block then take her to the apartment," he says to Mercedes. "You won't have much of a crowd." He shakes hands with Baron.

Baron says, "You knew some girl that bit it at the Trade Center?"

Jon has been trying not to think about the bad news. Life is strange. Jon has been on the wagon for one week. He is still kind of shaky, but he feels better. He had been awake for two days straight and got some sleeping pills from his doctor. He had classes to attend and needed to think clearly about his investments and his plans to build up his new properties. He has promised himself that he won't slip into the kind of failure he has seen growing up in the East Village.

"Lilly," he says. "She used to come in here."

Mercedes shakes her head.

Baron says, "I knew her! What happened?"

Mercedes remembers something, "There was a guy in that night from L.A. I mean, he was in the night before and he mentioned a girl named Lilly. He named some regulars I didn't know. His name was George. I only remember, because George is my brother's name."

"George was the guy that dated Lilly a long time ago." Jon tugs the dog's leash.

Mercedes says, "He didn't know how to find anyone and asked me about that guy that used to work here." Mercedes points to the sign above the register: Tijuana Special $4.75. You know, that guy. The guy that created that drink with the Tecates and tequila. I think he just did a shift, didn't he?"

"Scout," says Jon. "I was doing him a favor."

Baron goes, "Fucking Christ. I knew that chick. She was smoking."

Mercedes and Jon look at Baron.

"Sorry, but she was hot."

"That guy George left a note," Mercedes says. "I told Annie about it, in case she saw, you know, Scout." Mercedes pops open the register and pulls out the change tray, flipping through receipts and scraps of paper. She pulls out a folded piece of an Amstel beer coaster, with a name and phone number on it. She looks at Jon, "With everything that happened, I forgot to tell you, and he said he was coming back, so it didn't seem like a big deal."

Jon shrugs, "It's not. I don't know the guy that well. Scout can call him when he gets back from his trip."

Jon sits down on a barstool. Bandit strains at his leash. Jon was nineteen when he found himself talking to Lilly late in the empty bar, angry and confused, growing up fast in the night scene of the East Village, running the bar after his father passed away. Lilly told Jon she had lost her real father, because he had run off. Jon needed to be strong and keep moving forward. It would all get better. Lilly listened like an older sister, not that Jon had ever had an older sister, but that's what it felt like to him. He would never forget the way she put her hand on his hand. "Move on," she said. "That's all you can do now."

"Was she in one of the towers?" asks Baron, draining his Heineken, wondering if he sounded sleazy to Mercedes by saying Lilly was hot.

"Mercedes, could you get me a Coke?" Jon pulls Bandit back. "Sit!"

Lilly told Jon California hadn't worked out for her. She just sat in a small apartment in Silver Lake and watched George type on his old typewriter, or she sat in the bedroom, while she tried to watch television and not hear his typewriter. Los Angeles reminded her of being a little girl again, stuck in her mother's house in Pennsylvania, except this small house had a noisy typewriter and her boyfriend had no money. "That's life," Lilly said. "You move to a new city because you think you're in love forever and you have found your prince, but the next thing you know, you're looking at red plastic signs in strip malls and parking lots, and walking down to a coffee shop to get out of the house. I was just a stupid bird in a cage."

Jon told Lilly managing the Diamond sometimes felt like a cage.

Lilly told Jon she understood. Lilly wouldn't let anyone put her in a cage ever again.

Since that night, Jon had walked past Lilly once or twice on Avenue A. She had waved, but if Lilly had come back into the Diamond Pub, Jon hadn't seen her.

"Some friend of Lilly's stopped in here on Annie's shift," Jon said, "Lilly'd been working at Windows on the World. Lilly went to work that morning. She never came back home. This friend tried her cell phone, went to her apartment, talked to her landlord. Nothing.

Lilly never came home. She was gone."

3. Long Minutes

THE WORLD CHANGED

As I speak into this voice recorder, sitting in front of St. John the Divine on Amsterdam Avenue, I am eating my second hot dog, after a chicken salad sandwich. It seems obvious that I need to make some changes in my life. The most-pressing issue is that I am still addicted to daydreams of having sex with my ex-wife, Caryn Hwan. The second, least-pressing issue is that the Rooster, Scout Harris, is still sleeping on my floor, getting ready to take his next step and holding it off as long as possible. No worries on that front. Scout gave me free therapy at the Diamond Pub, when I was going through my divorce. I owe him. The floor is his for as long as it takes. It's the least I can do for a friend. Before the world changed on September 11th, I was also making regular diary entries for Megan Bathe, using the Sony digital recorder and backing the files up on my Hewlett-Packard Jornada PDA as well as a 16 Meg USB thumb drive provided to me by Cliff, one of the consultant-professors at Creative Action Partners. In addition to the PDA and USB, I also had the year of my digital diary entries; in fact, I had all of my files, including critical tax and divorce information, stored on my laptop, my primary computer, until the data storage snafu occurred—then I had nothing. I had to start from scratch, but Megan understood.

I should have copied the files immediately and sent them to her, but I procrastinated and lost the data. You can lose things before you know it. My divorce taught me that lesson.

Megan's idea for a project on some of the Diamond regulars sounded like an opportunity for me to learn about myself. Megan entrusted me with the digital voice recorder. I used the device frequently, if not every day.

Because of my commitment to Megan's project, I was embarrassed to e-mail her that I lost the data, but I knew Megan would understand.

Megan first lent me the digital voice recorder at lunch at Café Tacci, across from Columbia Bagels, at 110th Street and Broadway. New York changes fast. Both of those restaurants are gone, and now the World Trade Center is gone, along with thousands of innocent people. I had just begun working for the Creative Action Planning (CAP) team as a research associate, when Megan asked me to join her documentary project. Creative Action Planning is a consulting company made up of three Columbia Business School professors who moonlight together on specific projects. Prior to this humble job, I had a rather impressive career as a complete failure as the CEO of an exciting first-mover in online retail called Wolf City Incorporated (WCI). We're an asterisk in any number of business books on the history of dot-coms.

The Columbia Business School runs a majority of their executive education programs an hour's drive up the Palisades Parkway, which is located in a former train-baron's mansion built in 1909 near Bear Mountain in Harriman, New York. The mansion is called Arden House. The train baron was Edward Harriman.

One week prior to September 11, 2001, the business professors at CAP were working on a special program on leadership for the consulting firm Deloitte. As a research associate, my job was to sit in the CAP office and research teaching material; however, I had been invited to "put on a new hat" and sit in the back of the auditorium at the conference center and assist the on-site coordinator in whatever needed to be done to make sure the three-day training segment went smoothly. I doubt this sounds exciting, but if it does, it isn't, except to me, Ralph Villalobos, failed student of the real world of business execution. I was responsible for handing out paper copies of Power Point presentations and reminding the overworked tech staff to put batteries in the Lavalier microphones. Once my tasks were completed, I had the chance to sit back and listen to interesting theories on leadership. A few of these theories had traction in my personal experience. I had screwed up as a leader and some of these speakers shed insight into why and how I had failed.

Megan told me not to worry about losing the diary entries. The world changed, she said. Keep logging in to the voice recorder, she told me, your new entries will matter to the Document of Time project.

At nine o'clock on the morning of Tuesday, September 11, 2001, I was running a slow jog in Riverside Park, oblivious to what was happening at the World Trade Center. I needed to shed some pounds, but it took a three-mile slog in my expensive shoes and nylon running gear, under the shaded cobblestones on the edge of the city, above the hum of the West Side Highway, to calm my nerves enough so I could face the walk into the Creative Action Partners office and not think too much about my failures as a business leader. I navigated around the few people out in Riverside Park with their dogs on leashes. I should have been curious about the lack of children in the jungle gyms and sandboxes, but I was concentrating on the stitch of pain in my gut. The homeless were sleeping in boxes or sitting next to shopping carts filled with their belongings. The sky was blue. The most-tragic morning in the history of our country was happening and I didn't hear about the collapse of the towers until I showered, walked up Broadway and entered the CAP office, where the grad-student intern, Jeff, pointed to his desktop PC that was showing CNN. I sat in one of the CAP swivel chairs and tried to get my breath, hyperventilating in shock as we watched the planes glide into the towers over and over, the buildings exploding, collapsing, again and again. Jeff and I monitored the news through the afternoon. Over the next two weeks, I would follow the lists of casualties from the attacks. My employer prior to the creation of my dot com start-up was Marsh & McLennan, and they had offices from ninety-third to the one hundredth floor of the North Tower. They lost two-hundred and ninety-five employees and sixty-three contractors, mainly younger sales and administrative hires, but even though I had left the firm five years before, I recognized names and could put names to faces. It was a terrible, sad process, but I also forced myself to monitor the Internet sites. I recognized five names from Cantor Fitzgerald.

That Tuesday on September 11th, sitting in the CAP offices, I had no way to manage my own fear so I forced myself to work. I attempted to complete notes on a Harvard Business School case on the operations concept of Six Sigma, but also made phone calls, locating friends and business acquaintances, confirming people were safe. I had a bad moment with shortness of breath and stretched out on the carpet. I could have walked home, but I knew I would just pace my apartment. It was more comforting to sit with Jeff and watch him work an Excel file. Eventually, I managed to finish notes on the HBS case and left Creative Action Partners before walking back to my apartment.

Megan was right. The world changed.

TOO BUSY TALKING

As a research associate at CAP, I am asked to read university-produced business cases as well as articles from all the usual players—*The Economist, Financial Times, Fortune,*

Forbes, Business Week—as well as the newer magazines that rose up from the dot.com bubble, such as *Fast Company,* and summarize them for the CAP team. I read the research resources and write up terse, economical bullet-point cribsheets. These cribsheets allow the three professors to digest the available material before meeting with prospective clients. In addition to locking myself away in a cubicle and taking notes, Cliff and Rachel and Ashwan might ask me to put an upcoming meeting on my calendar and join them with the Human Resource representatives from a particular company, serving both as an administrative assistant and informal colleague, should I think of anything helpful to add to the discussion. I dress professional, understated, but, I like to believe, with a style that fits me. I could never dress the way my ex-wife, Caryn, wanted me to dress, like some trust-fund stoner in a canoe wearing seven hundred dollar leather pants, a necklace of medallions and two scarves. I dress like an executive with good taste. However, most of what I wear these days at CAP are suits and ties and shoes I bought when I was flush and confident as the wunderkind CEO of the surging dot-com start-up Wolf City Inc. I should have spent less time at Paul Smith and Barney's, less time in the bar at the Tribeca Grand entertaining my direct reports by analyzing and explicating necktie choices of our hires and the correct break of the pants-cuff or the appropriate shirt collar to go with a specific lapel, less time discussing bespoke suits, and more time taking effective steps to be an effective leader.

These days I am not a leader. I am a very humble member of the support team that helps the CAP consultants do their work. If Cliff and Ashwan are not wearing neckties, I find a chance to remove the Brioni or Ferragamo or Hermès tie my ex-wife Caryn Hwan didn't manage to grab when we divvied up and she took everything, including our daughter.

The consultant business at CAP is lucrative. The CAP consultants each have a specific area of expertise—Cliff (Business Strategy), Rachel (Finance), and Ashwan (Marketing)— but this doesn't keep them from working on cross-functional issues or picking up projects that allow them to consult in areas of personal interest—Cliff (Innovation), Rachel (Behavioral Finance), and Ashwan (Globalization). I am the one research associate, but CAP also has Jeff, a work-study assistant from the university who is often in the office helping. Jeff is the kind of guy to construct action plans, develop flow charts, use Excel and Access as well as other assorted software to schedule each minute of the day four months in advance, not to mention tally each minute for evaluation. I could have used a few Jeffs at WolfCity.com.

With the exception of buying into the dot-com mania and forgetting every guiding business principle I ever learned in graduate school and the workplace, I've always considered myself to be a quantitatively driven individual, concerned with measurable data. This Jeff, though, makes me look like a hippie sitting down by Lake Travis in Austin, Texas, where I went to the University of Texas, playing the mandolin. Jeff would have been a good COO for WCI. Unfortunately, I hired big picture, innovator types, since I assumed I could handle the "left-brain," quantitative, analytic side of the shop.

I won't bore you with the history, but drunk on the limitless possibilities of the disruptive technology of the Internet, I wanted WCI to be a boundary-less organization with boundary-less possibilities. We raised money as an online retail store, focusing primarily on athletic clothes for young urban professionals too busy to leave their lucrative, demanding jobs to shop at sporting-goods stores. With me at the controls, Wolf City branched out into an octopus of unrelated ventures. I called it "innovation." And as my direct reports slapped me on the back and kissed my brown Mexican ass, WCI began to look like some Japanese trading company patched together by an LSD addict. We did a one-off magazine aimed at promoting the unlimited capacity of our company. We sunk a fair amount of cash into opening a restaurant in Tribeca. The concept was to run an economical but trendy idea diner, where people could barter ideas for food.

The Monday afternoon we opened the Wolf Diner, the press went crazy. It looked like we might have stumbled onto something so out-of-the-box, it would promote the ingenuity of our primary business. Unfortunately, the few ideas offered in exchange for expensive plates of Chilean sea bass in black-bean sauce or encrusted Monk fish with a Kiwi glaze didn't pan out into any operable action that could help Wolf City move toward positive cashflow. The barter system was a sexy concept, liberating our customers from the tired, restrictive concept of money, but then we were taken to court by a lawyer who felt his idea of an online legal counsel for accident victims was worth more than a double cheeseburger with fries and a chocolate shake. (Week by week, we scaled down the menu.) The idea diner was one of many failures dreamed up in the bar of the Tribeca Grand while I sat with my executive team and we got loaded on tequila and grapefruit juice. I should have known that running a concept restaurant might be a stretch, particularly for a struggling online retail company that had yet to make an actual sale in the retail business. I should have also noticed that all the staff that signed off on the idea and voted to move forward had no experience in running a restaurant. I should have noticed that my wife and the mother of my little daughter were about to leave me, but I was too busy talking to listen.

THE FATHER THAT DESERVES HER

When Caryn told me she was pregnant, I was surprised. I thought Caryn was on contraception, but my daughter Chloe is the miracle that makes the rest of my life possible.
Chloe. Chloe Villalobos. Chloe Hwan. Chloe Stokes.
Caryn liked the name Chloe when I suggested the name during the pregnancy. Caryn was born in Singapore to an East Indian father and a Singaporean mother of Chinese descent. I first met Caryn at a Fashion Institute party, when I escorted her, instead of my fiancée, Kathleen, whom I had dated since undergraduate school at the University of Texas. Even though Kathleen moved to New York City with me, at this point, our relationship was under stress. Kathleen was exploring the nightlife. Caryn was her friend. After too many cocktails that night, Caryn and I kissed on the sidewalk outside of F.I.T. A difficult time followed, where I stood by Kathleen while resenting her and Caryn waited on the side, speaking to me on pay phones as my confidant and ally. Kathleen stayed out later and later, bleary the following afternoons from liquor and coke and talking about her new public-relations company she was starting by herself. One dawn I woke up in our apartment, heading down to Marsh & McLennan, but Kathleen wasn't in the bed. That night after work, I met Caryn at the Tribeca Grand and after three of the longest cocktails I have ever watched a woman drink, we rented a room.
Caryn spoke with a very English accent. She said this was because of her childhood in the former British colony. I was surprised to find out later that Caryn had moved out of Singapore at the age of ten and had spent her childhood and adolescence on Long Island, including two years at Williams College before attending the Fashion Institute of Technology.
Caryn was her second attempt at finding a name that would fit her exotic background and support her goal of having an incredible life. Caryn Hwan's given name at birth was Wilma, which Caryn detested. I wouldn't be surprised if she becomes *Kie-Rynn* or some new mutation, attempting to find a name as frail as the sound of the wind rustling one of the expensive gowns she designs and sells to other wealthy women. I shouldn't say anything bad about the mother of my daughter, but Caryn is a bitch who pops up on the society pages of *W,* attending lavish parties with her very wealthy second husband. The man she walked out on me to fuck. The man she promised could be a new father for Chloe. John "Stoker" Stokes III is from old Hudson Valley money. "Stoker," as Caryn says his friends and business associates call him, avoided investing in the dot-com surge but continued to put his money in stable business ventures, including steel production that involved a new processing technology that reinvigorated the industry and allowed

"Stoker" to become a silent partner in two very successful restaurants with his extra capital. (FYI, neither restaurant attempted to trade food for ideas.) One restaurant was in Tribeca, and one restaurant was in the meat-packing district near the loft John "Stoker" Stokes offered to rent to Caryn when they met for the first time at the bar of the first restaurant. It was there she told Stoker about the husband who was wasting his chance at success, spending most of his evenings in the East Village and drinking away his sorrows, hatching half-baked plans to regain the financial security he had fumbled, despite initially having lavish VC investments and unprecedented support in the business press.

At first, Caryn told me ours was only a trial separation. She had a good deal on a loft to rent, a beautiful space that would give her time to think about how to save our relationship.

I doubt this was ever true. Once Stoker Stokes arranged the huge apartment with a beautiful view of the Hudson River, my marriage was over. The Hudson was the waterway to so much of the Stokes family history and wealth. Caryn's new apartment also had a grand view of the World Trade Center. I don't know too many of the details, but I know Caryn and I know she can use her manicured cunt to get what she wants. Honestly, I don't feel bitter, but the arrangement was transparent: A great apartment in exchange for sex was a perfect calculation on Stoker's part, and this first step preceded Caryn's commitment to divorce me and marry the Stoker. Caryn Hwan Villalobos and John Stokes celebrated their wedding vows in a grand ceremony in Connecticut. I might have gained custody of Chloe, but I had lost all my net worth when Wolf City went belly up after bungling our chance for an IPO.

I can blame Stoker Stokes and I can blame Caryn, but nonexistent strategic planning at the helm of Wolf City Incorporated was the reason I failed. By the time the IPO was shot down because of the bubble bursting, Wolf City Inc. had receivables we didn't receive. We managed to create a situation where we had inventory *and* most of the challenges and problems that faced bricks-and-mortar retail companies, without taking advantage of the fast and effective flow of information and competitive flexibility of the successful dot-coms.

One of the reasons Caryn was right to be angry at me was that I mismanaged my big chance. The second was that I couldn't face my mistakes. Once Caryn walked out, I spiraled down into a bad habit of drinking every night in a bar in the East Village, imagining Chloe trundled up in her outfits, tiny and beautiful in her high-tech stroller— every moment was a new miracle. And I became the guy with visitation rights on Saturdays, walking her to Battery Park.

At present, the situation is strained. I need to move forward and get past this. I recently met an incredible woman, but it's not easy. I still miss Caryn Hwan. It's hard to tell a woman you have just met and are involved with intimately that you still love and desire your ex-wife. It's hard to tell a woman you are dating that whenever you are alone, you fantasize about your ex-wife. There is one more thing. When I am with this new woman, Rio Cerchiari, and my eyes are closed, or half-open, she transforms into my ex-wife. This is hard to explain, which is why I haven't tried to explain it to Rio. The two women look nothing alike. This is just my obsession. The thing I'm stuck with after my failed marriage.

No chicken salad today. I ordered Greek salad again. I spent this lunch on the steps of the Cathedral of St. John the Divine, down the street from the CAP offices. I really need to lose some of this weight. It will be great if I don't order two hot dogs from the street vendor on my coffee break. Rio and I haven't talked much about my past. She knows I was married and have a young daughter. I have no idea how to address the fact that when I make love to Rio, she turns into my ex-wife—and I get off on fucking the woman that betrayed me.

As much as I desire Caryn, I know this is selfish, unbalanced, and unhealthy. My concern needs to go to Chloe. I must become the man who deserves to be Chloe's father.

Leadership is eighty percent communication and twenty percent strategy, and I look back at my days at Wolf City Inc. and realize that once I secured the role of CEO, I spent about ninety percent purchasing clothes for myself, as well as items that pleased Caryn and kept her in front of our bedroom mirror, trying on new outfits, shoes, lingerie. The other thing I did was sink cash in symbolic office junk—all wolf-related—acting the big-shot. For example, a large mural of wolves that was painted by some name and cost a bundle. Ten percent of my time was spent considering a way to build market share, but I had a chair in my office carved with the head of a wolf. I should have taken the venture capital and just bought a carwash in Jersey.

Carwashes in Jersey, that's the kind of innovative thinking John "Stoker" Stokes III would have made, laughing off the concept of an "Idea Café," not attempting to recreate capitalism in his own image. The Stoker made dull, intelligent decisions and woke up with everything, including my wife and my child.

THE OTHER KIND OF WOMAN

I'm actually talking into the recording device as I slip on a pair of charcoal slacks and a black cashmere sweater. I'm one of those guys that could use the razor in the morning and shave again at dusk if I wanted. I slip into my wing-tips, not forgetting to peel open a can of food for Fabio. Rio is walking up Broadway, I imagine, her heels clicking on the sidewalk. I imagine she has on her new dress, simple, black, a plunge to the neckline, drop-waisted, flared at her pretty knees. Rio showed me the dress she had found on sale on Madison Avenue. This was when we first made the plan to meet up tonight at Le Monde, next to the CAP offices. Regina was looking for an excuse to wear the dress and was also considerate about my work schedule and willing to stay in the neighborhood. Tonight the chef at Le Monde does an excellent coq au vin. The section of Broadway uptown near Columbia has a few passable restaurants, most of them casual, local-type places aimed at college students as well as one or two remaining Cuban-Chinese restaurants. If Rio was a high-maintenance lady, she might demand we take a taxi to the Meat-Packing District, SoHo or Tribeca. I'll make it up to her and take her downtown on the weekend. I'm thinking we could catch a movie one night. Rio told me she likes *Breakfast at Tiffany's* and suggested we see that on Sunday, down on the edge of Tribeca. This sounds good to me, but I'm late and better hustle. I cross Broadway and walk uptown.

The biting wind slices up the blocks from the Hudson River. I make my way along the grid of streets: 108th, 109th, 110th. It's a cold night, but we have our extremes in Texas and they revolve around heat that will fry an egg on the sidewalk and hailstorms with rocks of ice that will break your windshield. Rio might be miffed, I think, looking at my wristwatch. Hopefully she won't take my lateness as disrespect.

I'm wrong. Rio doesn't understand. Rio is not at Le Monde, patiently knifing a tab of butter on a slice of baguette. I am forty minutes late, caught up in my memories of a relationship that did nothing but wound me as I sat in my apartment and talked into Megan's digital voice recorder. When I get to the restaurant, I begin to order a glass of Bordeaux, but change it to a sparkling water. No need to drink alcohol. I convince myself Regina will show up, probably just strolled off on an errand to the Rite-Aid drugstore on the corner. I reprimand myself for not bringing along a copy of *Fast Company* or that book on value-investing I borrowed from Rachel at CAP. It is possible that Rio is late herself, but I wonder why she didn't call me on my cell. She has a cell phone, although it is a larger Ericsson and she often turns it off or leaves it at her apartment, claiming the phone doesn't fit well into her small purse or jacket pocket and she doesn't want to think about it. Ashwan did call me as I was leaving the apartment to confirm our lunch meeting tomorrow with the human resource people from the Asian Development Bank on a visit from the Philippines. I confirmed to Ashwan that I had followed through on my research obligations and had left a print-out on his desk.

I ring Regina's apartment. No answer. I leave a message. She could be in transit. The question is which direction? I leave a message on her cell.

When I say I borrowed the book on value-investing, I mean I pulled it off the shelf. The Goleman book *Emotional Intelligence* was one I purchased at the bookstore. I sip the mineral water and glance past the hostess to the frosted doors of the restaurant, waiting for Rio to push through the steamed panels, untangle herself from her scarf and show me her smile, but this will not happen.

The three CAP professors haven't shown any interest in the books I carry with me to the office. At first, I attributed their silence to professional courtesy. I assumed they were tacitly registering my own attempts to get up to speed with the current material available in the field. Now I believe they were—and are—just too busy to do much more than arrange development meetings with clients, catch plane flights and read the notes I generate on relevant teaching materials they are expected to present as leading-edge consultants affiliated with one of the world's premier graduate business schools.

From reading *Emotional Intelligence,* as well as some articles on team-building and leading horizontally and vertically in an organization, I now understand I got myself trapped in a comfort zone at Wolf City. Another way to say this, I bought my own bullshit.

I am more comfortable talking into this digital voice recorder than I was talking over any of the emotional or complex interpersonal issues that impacted the effectiveness of the different parts of our team at Wolf City.

The walls are falling. In this business of studying business, it's my business to notice what is easy to ignore. Supermarkets now have banks. Supermarkets now have Chinese restaurants. Bookstores sell CDs. Lingerie stores sell CDs. The technology that ignited the dot-com bubble has not burst. All that burst were the over-inflated egos and slow-thinking and self-centered behavior of people like me, the New Economy entrepreneurs who couldn't hack it in the competitive marketplace.

I still don't know why Rio is not walking into this restaurant, and I'm on my second bottle of sparkling water. It is an hour after our appointed time. I am well-hydrated and now sure Rio arrived and didn't wait for me. Instead of chasing her, I'm talking into this digital recorder, drinking expensive water and making the couple next to me nervous. I am a well-dressed man whispering in a French restaurant. I'm going to give Rio another phone call.

She is at her apartment. She is mad at me.

Rio and I meet at Cannon's Pub at the corner of 108th and Broadway. Regina in her stunning black dress stares at me with daggers in her eyes. I've known women that like to get mad a bit, just to show they care. Rio might be the other kind of woman: one who gets mad and tells you to get lost and means it.

Here's what happens.

Right now is tomorrow, the next day. I'm in the CAP office and Cliff reminds me I promised I would complete a short write-up on how to lead from the middle of an organization.

Let me tell you what happened last night with Regina Cerchiari.

I took a barstool at Cannon's and ordered an orange juice. Rio and I would work it out. It was just a simple mistake. She would understand. This was reminiscent of my efforts as a business leader. I had not made a simple mistake. I had made a mistake that looked simple on the surface, but was a complicated emotional issue. I had made a symbolic mistake.

Rio walks into the bar in the black dress. She tells me she has left an abusive relationship. Rio tells me we will not sleep together again. It is over. Rio walks out.

I turn to the empty barstool beside me. Caryn sits on the empty stool, her legs crossed. She runs a finger along her thigh, looks up at me, "You get what you deserve, Ralph." I tell Caryn to leave me alone. I tell myself not to order a glass of tequila. Caryn disappears, but I know she'll turn up again. She always does. It's my own fault.

Rio's eyes were dark and she was about to cry, holding herself together as she walked out of the bar onto Broadway.

I pull out my cell and call Rio's apartment, not wanting to reach her in tears on her cell. I say this to her answering machine: "Rio, I'm sorry. I didn't mean to upset you. I'll drop by the Black Clock tomorrow on your shift, in case you want to talk." I look at the tequila bottles behind the bar. I look at my glass of orange juice.

I finish my OJ and go back to the apartment. Caryn is right. You get what you deserve.

A GOOD KIND OF NERVOUS

Days later, I didn't get around to talking in this device. I was too nervous, knowing I would see Rio at her shift at the Black Clock. Greek salad again, forkfuls of it while talking into the voice recorder, all with the broken hand I gave myself when I went off the wagon, drank tequila, and punched a brick wall in front of the Rooster after Rio told me we were through because I was late to our dinner. I made it out of Cannon's without drinking, but a day later I lost it. The broken hand is my fault, but it cleared my head. I was trying to drink my way into giving Rio up. I was trying to convince myself Regina was like Caryn, a betrayer, a woman about to change her mind and leave me—but I knew I was wrong in the emergency room as they put the cast on my hand and took my medical insurance card to copy. I scrawled a few jagged marks for a signature on triplicate sheets with my left hand and walked down to Rio's bar, knowing that I needed to save what I was about to lose. Rio gave me a second chance. I am facing a challenge at CAP, since note-taking and typing are part of my current duties. Fresh off a trans-Atlantic flight, Cliff has me highlighting text with my good left hand, while scanning the Internet sources for future research articles and data. Cliff, Rachel, and Ashwan are being very generous; Jeff even offered to help if I needed working hands on the keyboard.

Last night, Rio invited me to her apartment for dinner. She wore a green, fitted sweater and tight low-slung jeans, a wide leather belt and brown shiny leather boots. Rio told me she left her husband because he hit her once when he was jealous. He had no reason to be jealous and part of Rio wanted to forgive him, but he hit her hard in the stomach with his fist. She believed he was a good man, but he lost her trust.

"I shouldn't think about everything so much," Regina adds, watching me.

Regina sits at her small kitchen table in her green sweater and sips a Rolling Rock, two bookshelves behind her shoulders filled with books, many in Portuguese.

I think of Scout, the Rooster. I need to find some of his drunken guitarist bravado when it comes to the ladies.

Rio watches me for a few moments. I want to say something, but more than talking, I want to take Rio in my arms. I stand up, put my arms around her and kiss her.

Rio says, "You're a good kisser."

"Thank you." I empty my wine glass of sparkling water.

Regina has a pleased look. "You seem like the kind of man that can handle me."

I haven't asked a question, but Rio is answering the one question in my mind. Why are we here together? She must get asked out fifteen times a day by men who aren't failures. "I am," I bluff, "the kind of man that can handle you."

This is good. The night at the Black Clock after breaking my hand, I pushed myself to be confident. I can't lose her. I was a fighter back before my ex-wife walked off with my balls in a velvet box. "I knew there was something between us the moment I walked into that bar." This is wishful thinking. "I thought maybe I scared you."

Rio laughs. "I don't think you scared me, maybe made me a good kind of nervous." Rio touches my leg with her finger, taps my gray wool slacks with her fingernail. "How do you feel about this? Our being involved? I'm not sure if we should continue."

I can't think of one reason to stop seeing Rio, except for when she morphs into Caryn.

My big secret.

When we were early in our marriage, Caryn would pose, flashing her naked body to me in different perfect positions. We had a big bedroom mirror on the wall and another mirror on the inside of the closet door that Caryn would always leave open. I'm surprised we didn't have a mirror on our ceiling. Caryn loved to watch herself when we made love, or when she made love to herself, and I helped her by being the man in the room. Don't get me wrong. There is nothing wrong with mirrors or anything Caryn did in bed or on the floor or in any room in our apartment or on the street, at the beach or in the mountains or in the car or once in an airport parking lot before the new security. The only problem was that I was a prop, and props get changed.

"We might end up hurting each other," Rio says, sitting next to me on her sofa, a black-and-white movie muted on her television. "I might end up hurting you, Ralph, and my husband is not in a good state. Is this just a rebound?"

I don't know if Rio is going to keep morphing into Caryn, but she is Rio right now.

"Let's not talk about it anymore."

"Ralph, you punched a wall and broke your hand when I said we couldn't have sex."

"I was angry at myself," I tell her. "I shouldn't have been late for our first date."

Rio looks at me.

"Don't make the last few days into a bigger thing than it is," I argue. "We both have histories and we reacted to them. You wanted to stop seeing me and I punched a wall and broke my hand. There it is. I'm fine. Men do these kinds of things."

"A very smart move," Rio tries not to laugh. "I was so excited to meet you at that restaurant. My feelings are bouncing all over these days. I don't want to hurt you."

"I told you not to worry about hurting me."

"And I don't want to be hurt."

I think of Rio transforming into Caryn.

I don't want Caryn to appear on the barstool, whispering in my ear or stealing the body of the girl I'm dating, watching me with Caryn's eyes and Caryn's parted mouth as I desire my ex-wife, the woman who left me. Fighting my own confusion, I say, "I want you." I don't tell Rio that I can't promise that each time we make love I won't also be making love to my ex-wife.

"I want you too," Rio says. "Let's be careful," Rio adds. "It's better for everyone that way."

I reach for my empty glass of sparkling water.

Rio walks to the kitchenette and returns with drinks, a cold Rolling Rock for herself and a bottle of Evian and a glass of ice for me. "You never say anything about your ex-wife."

And there she is: Caryn on the edge of the sofa. She finishes doing her nails and blows on them, shaking her fingers. She smiles, knowing I'm watching her.

"I'm still in love with her."

Rio begins to clear the plates from the table, taking them into the kitchenette, placing them in a stack in the sink. "She left you, right?"

"She left me, remarried, and has custody of my daughter."

Rio sits back down next to me, sipping her beer. "Was it friendly, this break up?"

"It was bitter. It was dishonest. It was mean. I only see my daughter one day a week, if I'm lucky, and that arrangement required an expensive lawyer. My ex-wife would be content if I never saw my daughter again and lived in a homeless shelter."

"And you still love this woman?" Rio crosses her legs. "That's interesting."

"It's hard to explain. I've been thinking about it, working it out." Regina watches me. "I guess I'm stuck on the time we had when Caryn and I were together and I could conquer the world."

"But you didn't conquer the world."

"No, I didn't." I lost the world is what I think, but that's too dramatic.

"You'll get another chance. You were good enough to get the first chance. You'll get a second chance."

I'm not sure.

"You're in love with memories, Ralph. The woman didn't treat you well, so you just remember what was good." Rio adjusts herself on the sofa, considers something, then says, "Your ex-wife could have just fallen out of love, which is fair, it happens, but it sounds like she had to make her break by hurting you."

It was a relief to hear someone tell me that Caryn treated me bad. Caryn wasn't a monster, but she had tried to hurt me, if only to make her departure easier for her. I wanted to cling to what had been good, because I didn't want it to end, but Caryn had wanted it to end, whatever the cost. She had fought to keep me from my own daughter and she had mocked my inability to lead Wolf City. I had to forgive her, but I had to face the truth. I had failed. I knew it and accepted it, but somehow I expected her to defend my failure. I expected Caryn to stay on my side and fight for me, but she didn't. She walked across the block and jumped in bed with John Stokes.

"Do you believe that rule, the rule about a break up?" Rio looks off at the bright windows on the apartment building across Amsterdam Avenue.

"Which rule?"

"That it takes half the time you were in the relationship to recover and get over the relationship?"

"I've never heard that rule, but if it's true, it means I should be getting over my marriage in a few months."

"That might not be a bad thing," says Rio. "I could suggest that carrying a torch for a woman that mistreated you and keeps you from seeing your child is unhealthy."

"How long until you get over the relationship with your husband?"

"I don't think the rule works in that direction. It only applies to the person who is left."

"Why is that?"

"The person who leaves will take longer to get over it. The person that leaves has the responsibility for the decision."

"Except that it didn't take Caryn more than about a week to get over leaving me."

"Maybe she can just move on, but maybe she still misses you?"

"You're generous. I would bet a fair amount of money that Caryn got over me two minutes after she decided our relationship was finished. But I think you were right that she treated me badly in order to break it off."

"I don't know Caryn," says Regina. "I just know myself. She might miss you and not know how to say it."

"You are two very different women."

"Maybe we're not so different. Maybe Caryn handled it badly, but maybe for her to stay and not handle it any other way would have been worse. For both of you."

Long pause. I think this one over. It never crossed my mind that Caryn just did the best she could do.

"How did you meet her?"

This was a night of small tests. "She was my ex-fiancée's friend."

"Uh huh."

"Kathy and I grew apart. We had moved here together from Austin after college. We had plans, and I think we both assumed we would get married and have children."

"Until you married her best friend?"

"Kathy got into the night life and was using drugs, staying out all night."

"Oh," Rio says. I could leave it with the unresolved implication that Kathleen had really caused the split. "I didn't have a big problem with her using drugs. We had done some of the same stuff at school, but I was changing. Kathy messed around behind my back one night. Caryn was the woman I turned to."

"And you slept with her?"

"And then Kathy started sleeping with this bartender."

"Bartenders are trouble." Rio pinches me.

"Scout," I say. "She started sleeping with Scout."

"The same Scout that sleeps on the floor of your apartment?"

I nodded, "But I didn't care. I was in love with Caryn. It made everything easier."

I didn't want to look across the room and see Caryn on six-inch black heels, naked, brushing her long black hair. That image was waiting, just like I used to wait swaddled under the covers like a boy about to get read the best story of his life while Caryn would comb her hair and look at herself in the mirror and pretend I wasn't in the room. It was a game. She would sing softly to herself, and I would wait. When I was married, I was addicted to having sex with my wife. Now I am addicted to sex with my ex-wife, and I can't have it.

"Was she good in bed? She must have been."

"At first Caryn wanted to have sex all the time, but that changed, so when she did want to have sex, I was ready."

"Was she loud or quiet?"

Rio is flirting.

"She made a *cooing* sound."

"Coo, coo." Rio goes, "Like that?"

"It turned me on."

"Yeah, and that's a challenge," Rio smiles. "Men are visual creatures. Did you like watching her?"

I try to decide how to answer.

"Be honest," she says. "I'm okay with it."

"More than anything."

Caryn was fascinating to watch as we made love, and she watched herself in the mirror. What happened more often, though, were long moments of silence from my wife or curt comments about the state of our finances and the potential downside to going into more debt, compounded by the future cost of our daughter and the need to sustain our unsustainable quality of living. Our apartment embarrassed Caryn. What had once been our romantic hideaway in Manhattan was now a closet in desperate need of remodeling right as Wolf City went belly-up and the IPO fell apart.

"Yeah, I loved watching her. She was beautiful."

Rio's fingers tickle my neck. "Okay, I think I know enough about your ex-wife. Let's talk about something new."

"Like what?"

"Like if I'm good in bed? Like if you enjoy watching me?"

"Do you have a mirror?"

Rio smiles, "Can I be Caryn? I know how to coo." Rio crawls toward me, *"Coo-coo..."*

"Sure." A shiver runs through me. This could be a good game.

"You be the old Ralph." She reaches for the buttons on my shirt. Her fingers tremble. "You can fuck Caryn, and Caryn can watch herself in the mirror." Rio takes my hand and leads me toward the door that leads to her bedroom. "But I have to warn you," she says. "My room is messy. I only cleaned it before because I was trying to impress you."

"It can't be that messy."

Rio's floor and bedroom furniture is littered with clothes, as if she works through each item in her drawer before finally deciding on a bra and a T-shirt.

Rio takes my hand, guiding me over a pile of jeans on the floor by the bedroom door. Rio pats me on the butt. "I'm messy, but I'll be a better Caryn than the real thing."

Rio's closet door is open. Clothes are half-draped on hangers and hooks or wadded on the floor. The inside of her closet door has a mirror. We stand, holding hands, facing the mirror. Rio says, "There's your mirror."

Rio lets go of my hand, crosses her hands at the bottom of her green sweater, and pulls the sweater over her head. She faces the mirror in her brown boots, low-waisted jeans and black bra. Rio unclasps the bra, crossing her naked arms against the swell of her breasts.

THIS IS CHANGE

A lot has happened since my last diary entry. First of all, the drunken Rooster is off my floor and on a bus. This morning I woke up at Rio's again. I kissed Rio's ear. I kissed Rio's neck. I pulled Rio on to my chest. She kissed me. I opened my sleepy eyes, and Rio had morphed into Caryn and I was slipping my cock inside Caryn. This wasn't the game Rio started a few nights ago. I was really kissing Caryn and looking at Caryn. The soft breath and tongue kissing me back were Caryn's tongue. I won't go into the details, but as we reached the final jolts of pleasure, it was extreme and satisfying and my heart pounded... guiltily.

Rio, glistening and blushed, looked at me and said, *"Coo, coo."*

"Sometimes," I told her, "when we're making love, you become my ex-wife."

Rio leaned back. "You mean our little game"

"No," I say. "It happened before. You start to look like her, and I can't shake it."

"That's fucked up."

"I know."

Rio sat up in the bed. "I don't look like her, do I?"

"Not at all."

"Why did I get involved with you?" Rio pinched my chest hard. "I'll let you know if you start changing into other men, okay?"

"Fine," I said.

"I'm going to sit on your face," she said. "Let's see if my pussy starts looking like her pussy."

I had an easy day at the office ahead of me, but I wanted to keep on point with the projects, still I'm not a fool.

Rio didn't morph into Caryn.

After a hot shower, I walked uptown to my apartment, changed clothes, walked to Columbia Bagels, bought a bagel and coffee, stopped at a kiosk on Broadway and paid for *The New York Times*. I wanted to be at the office at 9:00 a.m. sharp, although Cliff, Rachel, and Ashwan come and go according to their other obligations.

Unless I have a meeting scheduled, no one cares when I arrive. I am paid hourly and bill according to the hours I log; however, it is important to me to keep a schedule. I am more efficient if I operate during regular business hours. Finishing my coffee, I re-check my Outlook calendar and evaluate and update my to-do list.

Rio kissed me in her doorway, naked under her red flannel robe. "Did it?"

"Did it what?"

"Did my pussy look like your ex-wife's pussy? Did my pussy taste like your ex-wife's pussy?"

"No." I slipped my hands inside her robe, around her warm hips and pulled her to me.

"I had a dream you were sad."

"I'm not sad," I told her. "I was sad, but I met you." The robe slipped off her brown shoulders. I looked past her into the hallway and felt her press up naked against my belt buckle and the buttons of my shirt. Her naked feet stepped on the tops of my polished wing-tips; her naked breasts and pounding heart beat against my chest.

"That thing with your ex-wife, that thing about loving her and desiring her?"

"Yes?"

"Quit it, baby." Rio pulled my head down, guiding my mouth to her dark nipple. She balanced herself, standing on my feet, pulling me to her as if she was rappelling down a rock, her hands taut behind my neck. "Take it."

I did what I was told.

I kissed her breasts, moving back and forth, her nipples hard under my tongue. She touched her pretty mouth against my ear. "If you want, we can play the game where I am your ex-wife again."

"I want to fuck you instead," I told Rio, expecting neighbors to step into the hallway, children yelling behind closed doors, chairs scraping, dogs barking.

I lifted Rio up in my arms, leaned her against the open apartment door, her robe open, sash dangling to her naked feet. I gazed past the parted red flannel robe at her smooth brown body, her round breasts, the faintest trace of dark trimmed hair at her pubic bone, the scent of Rio, her black-brown eyes watching me.

Rio tugged me back into her apartment, closed the door and scrunched her shoulders and wiggled. Her robe fell to her ankles.

Rio undid my belt and reached her cold hands past my boxer shorts. "Lift," she whispered, and I did lift Rio and spread her legs around my hips as my belt jingled. Rio fit my cock inside of her, settling down on it with a deep sigh. Rio rocked and wiggled. Rio pressed against my shirt, trying to unbutton the shirt with her teeth, she whispered to my necktie. "And I fuck like Regina," she whispered as I held her ass cupped in my hands and fucked her against the closed apartment door. "Just remember," her voice a scratchy whisper, "I fuck the best."

At the office, I wrapped up my morning ritual on Outlook Express, tapping in reminders and key to-dos with the fingers of my left hand. I typed a few minutes with my broken right hand in the cast, but this hurt. I should be able to type with my right hand soon, but this hunt-and-peck is good discipline for my left hand, as well as calming to me. *Tap, tap, tap.*

Rio pressed against me after we made love. She didn't transform into Caryn.

The fax machine beeps. I walk over to check what paper is rolling through the line and if I should load a new meeting into my calendar and forward the news to the CAP team via e-mail. The cover sheet is from Ashwan, addressed to the intern, Jeff, with a scrawled note to file for later reference. Ashwan is attending a consortium on executive education in London. The attached two-page diagnostic is from a professor in Barcelona, a Fernando Bartolomé, who Ashwan is convinced could be a resource in the area of work-life balance. Cliff, Rachel, and Ashwan discussed in a recent CAP after-action review that the diagnostic could be the winning proposition for the consulting practice moving forward.

I review my recent notes on matrix management. The notes are dull. Organizational structure should interest me, but it doesn't and it shows in my notes. Even as a finance person and certainly as a person with ambitions in the direction of once again—and effectively—leading a company, I am interested in managing resources, reducing risk and achieving goals and objectives. That being said, a matrixed organization is something out of the realm of my interest. The mechanics of structuring org-charts and management systems is a job I would offload or hire the right person for and then listen to that person's thoughts on the matter, although I could have stuck by the rule that org-structure should follow your strategy. But what was our strategy back at WCI? I have no clue. Our strategy had something to do with patting ourselves on the back and getting drunk.

Scout Harris got up to play his guitar at that coffee shop—nervous and almost falling apart and actually weeping at the microphone—but I had to give him credit: He was engaged. Scout was invested. He wasn't bored.

Ashwan noted on the fax cover sheet that Bartolome's work predated and was synchronized with Goleman's material on emotional intelligence. Ashwan scribbled a postscript at the bottom of the page: "Jeff, give this one to Villalobos. He will be interested."

Ashwan had noticed that I was reading Goleman's book. I had three more research assignments color-coded teal for "High Priority" on my Outlook calendar. I slid the matrix management and the Six Sigma folders to the far edge of my desk. I decided to read the Bartolome piece.

I pick up a Hi-Liter and place the fax pages on my desk. There is a list of questions.

I highlight each sentence in yellow, reflecting on my current state of personal development. I try to ignore the current pain in my injured hand. I crimp a ballpoint, the pen hurts my wrist and fingers, but I proceed to fill in the answers.

Self-Management Worksheet
In the world of knowledge, each individual worker needs to learn to manage himself. This will require that individuals:

A. Assess their skills and strengths—
I work hard, but need new skills. What will they be?
I want to be a successful leader, driven by knowledge, not luck.

B. Assess accurately:
• How they learn—
I want to learn through success, not just failure, but learning is important, even if through failure. We all fail. I've done my share. Success is more fun.

• How they work best—
Driven by vision, like WCI, but vision with wisdom!
Need to learn balance and set goals with awareness.

• What are their values—
I need to get out of myself and look closer. I want to be a better man.
RESPONISIBILTY
KNOWLEDGE
CLARITY

• Where they belong—
With people I respect who respect me:
Ashwan who sees what I'm reading.
Rio who is secure and can talk to me.
Caryn never understood me in hard times. Was I responsible?
Where was I when Wolf City needed me???

• What they should contribute—
True leadership, even if I lead from the middle, has to happen.
Start with leading myself. Lead now. Lead today. Fix things w/Caryn.

C. Assume responsibility for relationships and manage them:
This goes with CAP team, but also with Rio and with Caryn.
I need a win-win. I want a relationship with Chloe, not a war with Caryn.

D. Plan for the second half of their life:
This is change. Change is necessary. Face it. Don't run.

I underline the words *RESPONSIBILITY, KNOWLEDGE,* and *CLARITY* then put down the ballpoint. My hand aches. I remove the voice recorder from my jacket pocket. I talk about this long day, my thoughts flipping from images of Rio in her open bathrobe in the hallway to the goal I have: affect some change in my personal and professional life.

Holding the two-page diagnostic from the professor in Barcelona, I think about my answer to question C: *Yes, I want a relationship with my daughter, not a war with her mother!*

I pick up the phone and call Caryn.

Stoker Stokes answers the phone with a friendly voice that changes when I inform the Stoker he is talking to Ralph Villalobos. One time I promised to kick the shit out of him and make him eat his teeth and shit them thru the bloody hole of his ass. Stoker is a big fellow, but I was angry and an angry big fellow can kick the shit out of an angry calm big fellow who is tired from fucking the first fellow's ex-wife. I ask Mr. Stoker to put Caryn on the phone.

Caryn and I talk for more than an hour. The details don't matter. She shared, I shared. I had scared her and filled her with doubts. There had been moments I had shown her a man she didn't understand. I apologized for what was true about what she said and let pass what was too late to discuss. I tell Caryn I had been hurt, but I want to move past that hurt and don't want our history to have a negative impact on Chloe. Caryn, who I expected to yawn or assume I was dying from a terminal disease, responded with a warmth and humor I forgot was part of her toolkit. This is the voice of the woman I had married, the voice of the woman I committed to honor, obey, and cherish in love. She isn't devious or aloof. She just changed her mind. Caryn chose a different path. Caryn tells me she respects my honesty and had been thinking of rewriting our divorce settlement to provide me with more time to spend with Chloe. She appreciates my phone call. "But you make John uneasy," she says. No shit. However, I tell Caryn not to worry about John Stokes. If I was going to fix up the Stoker for stealing Caryn away, I would have done it already. Caryn's voice is the soft muffled laugh of a woman appreciated and desired and a little embarrassed. I tell her I am going into the second half of my adult life and I don't have time for anger. Caryn tells me I am young to be going into my second half of adult life, and I say, "Maybe I'll have three or four halves before it's all done, but I want to be there for Chloe."

Caryn understands. We bid each other a polite good-bye with her promise to talk to her lawyer and get in touch with me soon. She will amend my visitation rights.

I pour myself my seventh or ninth cup of coffee. It has been a long and productive day. I think about my last answer on the diagnostic: *This is change. Change is necessary. Face it. Don't run.*

DINNER AND A MOVIE, TRY AGAIN

After the movie, Rio and I take a walk, with Rio's hand on my cast and my overcoat unbuttoned in the brisk air of an October evening in Manhattan. Why did I punch a brick wall? Rio wipes a tear from her cheek and tells me that movie gets her every time.

The city glitters, dark and cold.

Rio and I head east on Spring Street. The windows of the boutiques and galleries of SoHo glow as people walk in and out of lighted shops and crowded restaurants.

I kiss Rio. She asks me if she reminds me of Holly Golightly.

"Do I?" She tugs on my jacket lapel. "C'mon. Be honest."

"Maybe one thing."

"And what thing is that?"

There is nothing specific about Regina that reminds me of the actress Audrey

Hepburn… or Holly Golightly. Rio doesn't look as if she's about to fly away. Rio is not a wispy actress, but a Brazilian with booty and curves and a raspy, sexy voice.

"Make it two things."

She pinches my shoulder. "Let's have it."

"Your room is a mess."

Rio puts her hands on her hips. "That's the last time I'm pretending to be your ex-wife. And what's the other way I remind you of Holly Golightly?"

"You're the kind of girl that would look for the cat in the rain."

Rio gives my arm a squeeze. "I don't know if you'll ever be a very good businessman, but you're a very good romantic."

I ask Rio why she ended the relationship with her ex. Was it really because he hit her?

"Yes," she says. "But to be fair, he knew I didn't love him anymore. There was no other man. But still…"

"And why didn't you love him?"

We stroll toward Chrystie and Houston and the black-fenced basketball courts.

"I don't know if this makes me sound like a good person, but I was bored."

"You were bored?"

"It felt bad, but I was tired of him. Nothing he did gave me any excitement. And the bored feeling wouldn't stop. It became this dull thing that wouldn't go away."

We turn on Stanton Street. "I think my ex-wife would say the same thing."

Rio tickles my ear. Her fingers cold, "That's ridiculous. You're not boring." She taps the cast on my right hand. "Stupid, but not boring."

"I didn't give Caryn what she needed."

Rio is teaching me about Caryn. This is how I learn. I think of the two-pager from the professor in Spain. I have learned through failure, but I want to learn through success. I belong with people I respect and love, people that respect and love me in return. Of course Caryn was bored with me. I had mismanaged a gem of an opportunity and blamed my mistakes on the situation, chewing on what I couldn't control like an addict, blaming the marketplace, my employees, the customer, the rapid rate of change.

Rio shivers, wrapping her arms tight and pressing against me. I assume we will make our way up to Union Square and grab a train or jump in a taxi.

"You want a drink?" she asks. "I mean, not a drink, but a Coke or a coffee or something?"

I don't want a Coke or coffee or something, but I would like one nice sipping tequila. "Actually, I'd like a drink."

"You can handle it, right? You won't break any bones?"

"I just lost my temper that night."

"And you were drunk."

"You're the one that suggested having a drink."

"Okay," says Rio. "Let's give it a try. We will have a drink tonight when you're not mad at me, but don't get crazy."

"I'm not that type," I tell her. (I don't want to make a big deal about it, but sometimes I am that type.)

"Where should we go?"

"We can go to the Diamond."

"The Diamond?"

"It's a dive, not much different from the Black Clock, although it's got those pictures of dogs playing poker. The tequila selection is limited to Patrón, Cuervo Gold and some well-dirt I won't touch, but it's got a nice feel."

"Let's do it. Are we close?"

"Sixth and Avenue A." I turn my back toward Rio, my good hand and the hand in the cast like stirrups at the waist of my overcoat. "Jump on."

"A piggy-back ride? I'm an adult, Ralph. I can walk."

"I know you can walk, but can you ride?"

"You know I can ride." She flashes me her eyes. "What about your hand?"

Guess I'll know soon enough. "Hop in the stirrups."

"You're on!" Rio leaps up and I feel her lips press against my neck, her breath in my ear. My arms go under her thighs and I hold her against my wide back. I've always had heft on me, but the Rooster never dared call me the Fat Mexican in public. This padding covers muscle. I don't get mad often, but if I do, you don't want to be on the wrong side of it. Not unless you're a brick wall. My wing-tips carry us along Stanton toward Ludlow.

There are times when being a big guy is good. Rio is light as a feather. Heads turn as I carry her up Ludlow Street. I carry her all the way up Avenue A to 6th Street. The muscles in my arms and legs burn at 4th, sweat trickling under my clothes. I set Regina down on the corner of 6th Street and Avenue A. My arms are dead.

An attractive lady in a short leather jacket and a scarf, her cheeks rosy from the cold night, walks past and smiles as Rio stands next to me and I slap my numb good hand against the hand in the cast.

"My turn?" she asks us, smiling and shivering.

I shake my head. "Nothing left in the tank."

"Too bad." She pulls out a pack of cigarettes and a disposable lighter, offering us a smoke. We decline as she lights up. "I watched you carry her up Avenue A. That looked like a sweet ride."

I COULDN'T SAY THE WORD

Baron Jancet was working the bar in the Diamond. I know the guy, but not well. A few younger characters in trucker hats, knit caps, heavy sweaters, and thermals sit at the far end of the Diamond pub, drinking Tecates and shots of cheap tequila. Two women in their mid-twenties—one in corduroys and a fleece pull-over, the other in a long skirt over flared jeans and wearing a denim jacket—smoke cigarettes, with mugs of beer in front of them. The Jets game is on TV and some rock band I don't know is on the jukebox. Baron smokes a cigarette, reading a magazine called *Blender*.

Red lamps hang from the ceiling. It's been a while, but the place feels just like home.

"Baron." I park myself on a barstool, with my legs burning from carrying my Brazilian love up from Stanton. It was a long walk, but it went by like a song. Despite the pain, I would have carried Rio on my back to Van Cortland Park in the Bronx. "Keeping busy?"

Baron shrugs and puts down the magazine. "Haven't seen you in a while?" We shake hands, but I seem to miss a couple steps in his hipster handshake. We bump fists. Maybe it's the East Village nightlife, but Baron looks older and more worn out than his age. I introduce him to Rio. Baron's eyes skate her, not being subtle about it. I don't mind. Let him dream. "This is Regina Cerchiari."

Regina says, "Just call me Rio."

Baron pauses, looks at me. "I wanted to tell you something, but just forgot it."

"How's the bar been?"

"Cool," says Baron. "Same old, same old. What can I get you?"

"Do you have any wine?" Rio asks, unzipping her jacket. I help her with the jacket, folding it. Rio places the jacket on her lap and rubs her hands together.

Baron motions to the dust-covered screw tops of Cribari on the bottom of the liquor shelf. "We have wine, but…"

"How about a vodka tonic? Grey Goose?" Rio asks.

I order a Patrón neat.

"So this is the Diamond?" Rio looks around the bar. "I like it."

I place a twenty on the bar for the drinks. Baron puts Rio's V&T and my tequila on coasters and rings up the order. I raise my glass, "To Regina."

Rio taps her glass against mine, "To going back for the cat in the rain."

"To going back for the cat in the rain."

I sip the tequila.

"I'm having a nice night," she says.

"I am too." I can't take my eyes off her. Her eyes are bright. I remember a time Megan told me about the dopey gene. She said that's what women had, and why they had to be careful about sleeping with men. They could have sex with a man and get struck with the dopey gene and fall in love and never know if it was real love or just physiology. The dopey gene would make them fall in love. Rio looks like the dopey gene is taking over. I look in the bar mirror. The dopey gene is in my eyes too.

Rio smiles. "What are you thinking about?"

"I feel lucky."

"I do too," says Rio.

Then Baron remembers and comes over to tell us.

When he's finished, I stand up and walk to the jukebox and walk back to my stool and sit down, waiting for my body to react. I start breathing too fast, and my hands grip the edge of the bar. I pick up the tequila and sip, but I'm shaking. "How do you know?"

This can't be right?

"I scanned the lists of people that didn't make it out of the World Trade Center. I knew people from Marsh & McLennan and other companies. The lists were online, and I looked for anyone I knew. I would have recognized Lilly." I'm talking fast.

"Some girls came into the bar and told Jon. Lilly was working up at that restaurant at the top. She hadn't been in here for a while. She went to work that Tuesday and her roommate said she never came back."

Rio takes my hand from its grip on the bar.

"You knew her?" Rio asks.

Lilly up on the 107th Floor of the North Tower. "Did anyone tell George?" Scout said something about George visiting Manhattan. "Baron, did a guy come in here named George? Scout knew him. From California. The guy Lilly used to date?"

"Yeah, he was in here the night before it went down. That's what Mercedes said."

"Who?"

"This new chick that works here, short black hair. It's blonde now. She's got a great ass." Baron looks at Rio. "Oh, sorry. Mercedes said that guy George left a phone number somewhere. Jon knows about it. They were supposed to give it to Scout, but you know he just took off to Colorado or whatever." Baron opens the register and lifts the money tray, pulling out a scrap of ripped bar coaster. He hands the note to me with a number written to Scout, asking Scout to give George a call on his cell phone. I pull out my cell and ring George, trying to decide what I'm going to say. Maybe I should leave this alone and let someone else talk to him.

Baron adds, "He left that before 9/11."

George's recorded message asks the caller to leave a message, then follows with a service message, announcing his mailbox is full.

I click my cell shut. Then flick it back open and tap out the number for information in Los Angeles. George told me he lived in one of those neighborhoods in the San Fernando Valley. With a shard of pencil from Baron and a napkin ready, I wait as the operator searches and offers me three George Nichols and one G. Nichols. I try the first three numbers. One sounds like a married couple with a woman's voice on the answering machine. Could be a connection to George—parents, even a new wife? I leave a message with my cell number, maybe George is a George Jr.? The next call leaves me on the phone line with some angry guy that thinks I am a telemarketer, trying to pull a fast one. Baron pours more tequila in my glass. I try one more George Nichols in Santa Monica, but the phone just rings. I try the "G. Nichols," taking a long drink of the warm tequila.

My eyes burn and Rio rubs my shoulders as my cell phone rings.

I slam the plaster cast on my broken right hand against the bar.

The G. Nichols number clicks into a voice machine. The voice is George's voice. The machine asks me to leave a message. I tell George this is Ralph in New York and I'm sorry I missed him on his visit but never knew how to find him and Scout was looking for him too. I tell George to call me right away.

Megan. I click down my cell's contact list, locate Megan's landline and hit SEND. Four rings and Megan answers, "Hello?"

"It's Ralph, Megan. Ralph Villalobos. I'm in the Diamond. Can you come over? I need to talk to you."

"Is this about the project, Ralph? I'm taking a bath." I hear water splashing.

"This is important. Did you hear about Lilly?"

Long silence.

"That doesn't sound good."

"I'm at the Diamond. They're telling me Lilly was at Windows on the World, but I scanned the lists. Lilly's name wasn't on any of them."

"Oh, my God," Megan gasps.

"The bartender says some friends of Lilly's came in the other day. No one got out of that building above the ninety-first floor, but her name wasn't on the list."

"Lilly wasn't her real name, Ralph. Her name was Lee Ann Boxner." I hear more splashing. Megan must be standing and stepping out of the bathtub. "Hold on. Lilly must be okay, Ralph. She's okay, right?"

"I don't think so. I don't know, but I don't think so."

"Fuck!" I hear her drop the phone. She picks up the phone. "Where are you?"

"At the Diamond," I repeat. "A friend of Lilly's told Jon. We need to find George."

Megan walks into the bar, wrapped against the weather, eyes red. I introduce her to Rio. They remember each other from Scout's open-mic performance. Megan orders a drink. Baron pours with a heavy hand and tops ours. "Jon heard it," he repeats to Megan, "just the other day."

"George was in town. I tried him on his cell and in L.A., but I just got machines. He needs to know."

"He phoned me in early September and said he was coming for a visit. Something to do with a photographer he had worked for, but I don't know the guy's name. We were supposed to have dinner, but then everything happened with the attacks and I just forgot. Wait, no I did call him after Scout's gig and left a message. That reminded me to call him, but I assumed he was back in Los Angeles."

Scout was on a bus without a cell phone. Scout would want to know, but that would have to wait. George should be told soon, maybe he already knew? Lilly...

I couldn't say the words.

"George might have stayed with that musician that lives down on Stanton? Where George sublet that time."

"I know that building," Megan says. "Lilly lived there too."

We bundle up and walk down a different Avenue A. People in the restaurants and bars moved behind the glass like ghosts. I look southwest at the glow of light from Ground Zero.

Holly Golightly searches under the bed of her studio apartment, searching for her heels in the refrigerator, her phone in the record player. Holly steps from the bathroom, adjusts her hat and scarf, asking Paul Varjack, "How do I look?"

I hold tight to Rio's hand.

GEORGE NICHOLS

We tape a piece of paper on the door of the building at 101 Stanton, requesting any information about George Nichols. We include our phone numbers. The whole process reminds me of the copied photographs with names and numbers that still flutter on the sides of hospitals, the spontaneous shrines at fire stations and police stations, the random posting of people lost, their smiling faces taped on the chipped paint of street-light poles, U.S. Postal Service mailboxes, fences and walls.

I sit in the office the next day, but don't do much, drinking coffee. I wait for George to call me. Lilly was a wild thing, as Holly Golightly called herself in the movie.

George would need someone to talk to…

My cell rings. Megan. She received a call from a thirteen-year-old girl named Lupe Rodriquez who lived in the building on Stanton. This Lupe knew George from back when he had sublet that apartment. Lupe saw George the morning of Tuesday, September 11th. George was walking past the apartment building, holding a bouquet of flowers. He was in town with good news about his writing and had walked down to 101 Stanton just for old times. George told Lupe he was going to surprise Lilly at work. Lupe said George hadn't seen Lilly since they broke up back on the West Coast, but George was going to say hello to her before he had to fly back to Los Angeles.

She told George she hadn't seen Lilly for a long time. He said he would come back and take Lupe out for ice cream, if she wasn't too old for that sort of thing.

Lupe Rodriguez said George never knocked on her door that day after the towers collapsed. She never saw him again.

I leave the office and ride the train down to the East Village. Megan and I meet at the southwest corner of Tompkins Square Park. Megan and I find a bench. I take out the digital recorder and look at Megan. I click the recorder on and hold it up, capturing the sounds of the park, the flutter of pigeons, the barking of dogs and the voices of children on the playground. People wrapped against the weather play chess in fingerless gloves, with bodies padded in jackets and bundled in scarves and knitted hats. Squatter teenagers roll cigarettes and talk on cell phones, leaning against an iron fence, their dogs on leashes made of rope. Two guys toss a football, smacking their hands against their jeans in the cold.

George is gone.

Megan and I watch the tree branches and the gray sky. Lilly might have been a hostess or waitress, maybe she was working in the back office.

Was Lilly straightening a vase of flowers or speaking to the kitchen staff or helping the restaurant manager? George wants a cigarette, yet he feels okay. His nerves aren't too bad as the elevator doors close behind him. There she is in a simple gray dress, her hair tied back in a ponytail. Lilly turns and sees George standing still as people step around him, preparing for their day.

George holds up the flowers, "Hi, I was in town…"

Lilly takes the bouquet and thanks George, giving him a quick kiss on the cheek. George holds his breath as Lilly presses against him, Manhattan stretched out far below the windows.

There must have been screaming when American Airlines Flight 11 cut through seven floors. The building must have lurched and recoiled with the impact. We know e-mails were sent out and some cell phones worked. We also know there were no survivors above the ninety-first floor.

The fires followed the oxygen. The doors to the roof of the North Tower were locked from the roof. Helicopter pilots could see people throw fire extinguishers through windows to get air to breathe, but the shattered glass allowed more oxygen in, sucking the smoke and flame into the rooms. People began to jump.

Megan presses her fingers to her eyes. "We don't know anything."

Ralph listens to the voices in Tompkins Square Park.

"Do you think they had to jump?" Megan looks up at the silhouetted branches, a mourning dove flaps against the pale sky.

George and Lilly stand at the edge of a shattered window, wind slicing into the smoke and dim flares, flames ripping the air. George points at Manhattan fluttering between waves of heat and smoke and shuddering noise. The structure begins to hemorrhage inside the North Tower. Lilly takes his hand, "Don't be scared, sailor." Her other hand holds the bouquet George gave her.

In Quảng Trị, a wedge of shrapnel shears the lung of a military journalist. He sinks to his knees, thinking one final moment of the son he won't see grow into a man, the son he won't be able to teach and watch with pride. In New Orleans, an old woman remembers the days before the ambulance took her into this white room, the days back when she held the slice of peach on her silver fork and was once beautiful. The old woman won't allow herself to look in the mirror of the white room, only at the framed photograph of her granddaughter, a girl in New York City who has promised to visit. The girl's pretty face smiles from the photograph on the bedside in the nursing home as the old woman watches the fork fall from her fingers and her beautiful granddaughter, wearing the silver locket the grandmother gave her, asks her, "How do I look?"

"You look beautiful, honey. You look perfect," the grandmother says to the photograph. "Just like a movie star."

You were everything that made us not regret.

Megan squeezes my hand. A child cries out from the scary part at the top of the playground slide.

Lilly and George stand as clouds of poisonous air swell and break around them. They surface through waves of smoke that descend to their ankles and flatten out into sky. The floor is unstable.

"I'm sorry," George says. Lilly wipes her eyes with the back of her wrist, "Sorry doesn't feed the bulldog." She tosses her bouquet into the sky.

Lilly's hair whips at her eyes. She bites her lip, considering. George pulls her head close, shading her eyes from smoke. He kisses her lightly. She smiles. He can't breathe, but can't move from watching her. There is only one way.

Lilly smoothes her hair from her face as screams fade into the thin air and dissolve.

George, terrified, focuses on Lilly. A calm washes over him. He can't imagine standing anywhere else. There is nowhere else…

"We're right on top of the world." Lilly rubs her eyes. "I bet this is something you've never done before." Her eyes lock on George. He can't look away from her. He knows what they'll have to admit.

"C'mon, sailor, don't be afraid."

She squeezes his hand.

They step out.

ALSO BY BRUCE CRAVEN

Buena Suerte in Red Glitter

*Win or Die: Leadership
Secrets from Game of Thrones*

Fast Sofa

ACKNOWLEDGMENTS

Living in New York in the late Nineties, and hustling on various writing projects, I had caught a plane and joined my cousin, Don Craven Jr., for a Thanksgiving Day of fly-fishing outside of Austin, Texas. That night, after fishing, his sisters joined us and we watched one of my favorite films, *Breakfast at Tiffany's*. Inspired by the movie, Don offered to cover my bills for a number of months while I wrote a script that would revolve around a Holly Golightly character in the New York nightlife in the Nineties. I had spent two years tending bar in the East Village in the mid-Nineties and knew more than a few women that identified with the Audrey Hepburn character from the iconic 1961 film. I also knew a number of men, myself included, that had elements of the Paul Varjack character, the struggling writer played by George Peppard. I took Don up on his mega-generous offer. The finished script, titled *Dirty Martini*, was pushed towards production by the Los Angeles based film team of Chris and Roberta Hanley from Muse Productions. As with many film deals, after much hard work, creativity and enthusiasm on everyone's part, the project stalled. I flew to New York for one of my stints working in executive education for Columbia Business School. I arrived two days before the terrorist attacks on the World Trade Center and was staying in a small, dorm-style room at the Union Theological Seminary near the Columbia University campus. In the beautiful courtyard, the day before the attacks of 9/11, I decided to adapt the script to a novel. After the fall of the World Trade Center, I spent many years working on the project, finding the true shape of the novel. During the first couple of years, I lived in a rental house in Burbank, California. My landlord and friend, Alan Rodriguez, was generous and polite enough to ignore a solid year of rent that stacked up as I wrote. Novelists know how much support means during the long journey. *Sweet Ride* has benefitted from significant support. Single when I started the script and then the adaptation of the script to a novel, I now have two sons, and a wife. If it wasn't for Sherelle Craven, I wouldn't have experienced the serenity, optimism and transformation that her love offered me. My friend and ally, Mark Shaw, has brought continual faith and encouragement to *Sweet Ride*. He also gave his significant and unique design talents to the published book you hold in your hands. I was damn fired up to place the novel with Codhill Press. Susannah Appelbaum is the exact editor this New York City story requires. I also want to thank my friend and former boss, Robert Jeziorski, for hiring an unemployed writer to tend bar in 1995 at the Cherry Tavern. Some of the people from our scene in the East Village and the L.E.S. have been taken too early from the stage, but I remember them in their brilliance. This novel is my offering in thanks for them, and all the other cool people that contributed to the beautiful, wild intensity that was Manhattan in the Nineties.